Subjects in the Ancient and Modern World

Subjects in the Ancient and Modern World

On Hegel's Theory of Subjectivity

Allegra de Laurentiis

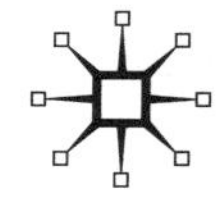

First published 2005 by
PALGRAVE MACMILLAN
Houndmills, Basingstoke, Hampshire RG21 6XS and
175 Fifth Avenue, New York, N.Y. 10010
Companies and representatives throughout the world

PALGRAVE MACMILLAN is the global academic imprint of the Palgrave Macmillan division of St. Martin's Press, LLC and of Palgrave Macmillan Ltd. Macmillan® is a registered trademark in the United States, United Kingdom and other countries. Palgrave is a registered trademark in the European Union and other countries.

ISBN–13: 978–1–4039–3824–4 hardback
ISBN–10: 1–4039–3824–5 hardback

This book is printed on paper suitable for recycling and made from fully managed and sustained forest sources.

A catalogue record for this book is available from the British Library.

Library of Congress Cataloging-in-Publication Data
De Laurentiis, Allegra.
Subjects in the ancient and modern world : on Hegel's theory of subjectivity / Allegra de Laurentiis.
p. cm.
Includes bibliographical references and index.
ISBN 1–4039–3824–5
1. Hegel, Georg Wilhelm Friedrich, 1770–1831. 2. Subjectivity—History—19th century. I. Title.

B2948.D37 2005
126′.092—dc22

2005042520

10 9 8 7 6 5 4 3 2 1
14 13 12 11 10 09 08 07 06 05

Printed and bound in Great Britain by
Antony Rowe Ltd, Chippenham and Eastbourne

Questo libro è dedicato a mio padre,
Giovanni de Laurentiis:

ita enim senectus honesta est,
si se ipsa defendit,
si ius suum retinet,
si nemini mancipata est
(Cicero, De Senectute, *xi)*

Contents

Acknowledgements

I am grateful to editors and publishers for their permission to use materials that I have previously contributed to their journals and collective volumes.

Chapter 1 is an expanded version of an article on Hegel's 'Metaphysical Foundations of the History of Philosophy' forthcoming in the *Journal for the History of Philosophy* (The Catholic University of America). It also contains passages from a chapter (entitled 'On Hegel's Concept of Thinking') published in *Societas Rationis* (Festschrift for Burkhard Tuschling, Duncker & Humblot, 2002). In Chapter 2 I have integrated excerpts from an earlier contribution ('The Difference between Understanding and Reason') to the volume *System and Context: Early Romantic and Early Idealistic Constellations* edited by Rolf Ahlers (Mellen Press, 2004). The last part of Chapter 3 contains in revised form the last three sections of 'The Place of Rousseau in Hegel's System' from *Hegel's History of Philosophy: New Interpretations*, edited by D. Duquette (SUNY Press, 2003). Chapter 4 is a slightly revised and expanded version of 'The One and the Concept', forthcoming in the *Cardozo Public Law, Policy and Ethics Journal*. In the third section of Chapter 5 I have integrated passages from 'Silenced Subjectivity' that appeared some time ago in the journal *Studies in Practical Philosophy* vol. 2, no. 1, 2000 (Humanities Press). Finally, Chapter 6 is a revised version of 'The Tenacity of Contradiction', my contribution to the volume *Aufklaerung durch Kritik* (Festschrift for Manfred Baum, Duncker & Humblot, 2004).

My acquaintance with Greek and Latin antiquity did not begin as a case of love at first sight. It was rather a peremptory requirement of the Italian public school system in the sixties and seventies. Some of my teachers persisted stoically in their appointed task, which was to disclose the philosophy, poetry, syntax, declinations and conjugations of the canon to an increasingly recalcitrant generation of young revolutionaries, for whom the present was insufferable, the future was everything, and the past was nothing. Among these teachers I owe particular gratitude to Olga Bonjean and Maria Pia Miraglia, under whose guidance the forced acquaintance with Homer or with Cicero eventually morphed into a personal intellectual interest.

I was introduced to Hegel by German philosophers at the universities of Tuebingen and Frankfurt. The most enduring impression was made on me by the last seminars that Ernst Bloch (1885–1977) held at the beginning of the seventies in the Tuebingen Stift. His immense knowledge about conceptions of truth and justice from Heraclitus to Lukàcs disclosed to my generation precisely that unity of past, present and future that, left to ourselves, we were incapable of seeing. In the second half of the same decade I attended at the Goethe Universitaet of Frankfurt several semesters' worth of lectures and seminars by Alfred Schmidt and Norbert Altwicker on the history of materialism, on modern idealism, and on the history of philosophy. Their teachings have been essential to form what understanding I have of Hegel's system, its predecessors and its legacy.

At the university of Rome, Mauro Nasti De Vincentis taught me nothing about Hegel, but everything I have ever been able to grasp about logic and the philosophy of science. In a perhaps not unforeseeable turn of events, he eventually added to his Leonardesque list of scholarly qualifications that of the single-handed discovery of Hegel's worm in Newton's apple. Thus, I have after all learnt from him aspects of Hegel's thinking that I knew nothing about.

In more recent years, I have been fortunate enough to be able to discuss Hegel's work with a number of scholars and friends from Europe and the United States. The Kant scholar most knowledgeable and trenchantly critical of Hegel, Manfred Baum of the University of Wuppertal, is probably responsible for the fact that despite the enormous appeal of Hegel's philosophy I still consider myself only a student of Hegel, not a Hegel believer.

My deepest gratitude, however, goes to another Kant scholar, Jeffrey Edwards of SUNY at Stony Brook. His at once skeptical and sympathetic approach to Hegelian argumentation has spurred many a discussion between us that proved immensely helpful for my writing. And this is not all I owe him. I cannot praise in him the proverbial patience of male authors' wives, silently but cheerfully enduring years of neglect for the greater good of humanity's enlightenment through their husbands' groundbreaking work. But I will say truthfully that this book would not have been written without Jeff's taking care of all life events that will not be put on hold for book-writing. As for our children, I don't know whether without them this book would have been written long ago or not at all. Either way, I thank them, too, for their graceful endurance of this highly impractical fact of their lives: having philosophers for parents.

List of Abbreviations

Hegel

GW	*Gesammelte Werke*	
	GW 4	Jena Writings: Faith and Knowledge
	GW 9	Phenomenology of Spirit
	GW 11	Science of Logic: Doctrine of Essence
	GW 12	Science of Logic: Doctrine of the Concept
	GW 18	Introduction to the History of Philosophy (1820)
	GW 21	Science of Logic: Doctrine of Being (1832)
W	*Werke in zwanzig Baenden*	
	W 7	Philosophy of Right
	W 12	Philosophy of History
	W 18	Lectures on the History of Philosophy I
	W 19	Lectures on the History of Philosophy II
E	(= *GW* 20 and *W* 8–10)	Encyclopaedia of Philosophical Sciences

Kant

CPR B	Critique of Pure Reason, second edition
MAN	Metaphysical Foundations of Natural Science
Logik	Logic

Introduction

The essays presented here explore Hegel's conception of subjectivity against the background of his interpretation of ancient Greek notions of persons, subjects and individuals.

The contemporary thinker attempting to define and circumscribe the uses of the elusive notion of subjectivity in classical texts of the philosophic tradition runs into several difficulties. As so often, the principal hurdles are found in the conflicts of philosophic conceptions of philosophy itself, that is, in opposing interpretations of what the proper topics and methods of philosophy are, or should be.

On the one hand, historically informed philosophic inquiry focuses on identifying the meaning and place of subjectivity in past and present theories as well as in human history itself. But in the present cultural context that fancies itself free of metaphysical prejudices and is unwilling to separate epistemology from psychology or ethics from sociology, contemporary readings of the tradition tend to diffuse such distinctions, making the task of defining and delimiting one's topic all the more arduous. The result is often that the ancient, medieval and modern canon appears as having spoken all along with our own voice—which frees us from the burden of having to assume a radically different perspective from the contemporary one, not to mention the burden of learning something new. In this view, the intelligibility of classic texts of Western philosophy is predicated upon the belief that they must be meant and must be arguing in what are essentially our own terms. If it weren't possible, for example, to translate their terms into our technical terminology or to strip their philosophy from its metaphysics, then they may reveal themselves to be utterly irrelevant to our condition. Thus, for example, it has been argued that Plato's dialogue *Crito* must have been intended as an articulation of the conflict between individual and state rights; that Aristotle's concern must have been to found empiricism; or that Hegel's aim must have been to address the modern European condition.

On the other hand stands a contemporary philosophic movement that is historically un-informed by choice and bases its stance and methods precisely on the assumption of the irrelevance of what it ignores. In truly pioneer-like spirit, this philosophy inquires into mind, truth, even ethics as if it were inscribing these topics for the first time in rational characters on the *tabula rasa* of philosophers' collective mind. Century-old arguments and debates that identified, refined and sharpened the topics at issue (mind, truth, justice, for example) are set aside in favor of philosophizing *ex nihilo*. In successful cases, the results reached are interesting reformulations of the insights and wisdom of historically well-identifiable schools.

The following essays have been written under the assumption that it is not necessary to side with one or the other of these attitudes of thought towards subjectivity (to modify an Hegelian expression). They also do not aim at a radically novel definition of what it has meant or what it means to be a subject, but are more simply aimed at a better grasp of a major modern conception and its explicit relation to relevant documented conceptions from antiquity. It is hoped that by way of this comparison some new light might also be shed on what subjects are and what they are not in the contemporary world.

This book insists on the necessity to distinguish in order to identify. For example, it follows Hegel (and the German idealistic tradition in general) in holding that the metaphysical category of being-subject, the logical notion of individuality, and the psychological concept of the ego must be kept separate in the course of a philosophic argument aimed at explaining their confluence in the notion of really existing individual subjects.

The contemporary frame of mind leads us easily into taking for granted the semantic identity of 'subjectivity' and 'individual subjectivity.' However, by recognizing that the two notions are not identical *per se*, it becomes possible to better understand past conceptions in which they appear indeed as being separate. Thus, impersonal references to the subject of thinking, as in Aristotle's expression 'it thinks, it imagines' or Descartes' use of thinking 'thing' to categorize what he feels otherwise compelled to name in the first person ('I' think), begin to lose some of their awkwardness. By stressing logical difference, semantic correlations, and historical continuity and change, we come to appreciate the meaningfulness of ideas that strike us otherwise as alien and paradoxical.

In surveying the fate of 'subjectivity' in the history of modern philosophy and literature, some may see in the early modern and Romantic exaltation of 'the subject' a signal of the impending triumph of 'individualism' understood as a historical and psychological phenomenon paradoxically (or perhaps dialectically) arising in emergent mass societies. To others, however, the same philosophic and literary manifestations may well appear as an elaborate ideology concealing by compensation a massively anti-individualistic trend typical of industrializing society. More recent appeals to a qualified return to pre-modern conceptions of morality or the social good are based in part, whether intentionally or not, on the idea of a congeniality of sorts between the post-industrial, post-modern neglect or denial of 'the subject' on the one hand, and, on the other, the apparent absence of discernible forms of individual subjectivity in the life and consciousness of ancient peoples and cultures.

'Subjectivity' has been and is being used with widely different connotations also depending upon the disciplinary context in which it arises as a problem. As a generically anthropological category, it may simply indicate human self-centeredness (or anthropocentrism). Psychologically, it may be used to denote egocentrism, egotism, even individualism *tout court*. In epistemological contexts, 'subjectivity' may signify lack of objectivity or outright anti-objectivism and is then being associated with skepticism, relativism or solipsism. In social psychology, it often figures as an explanatory term of social interactions among individuals, now indicating the necessary condition, and now the result, of these interactions.

The philosophic tradition today known as German idealism takes the term to signify primarily a metaphysical category on which to base or from which to deduce its theoretical and practical accounts of human freedom. Two of Hegel's formulations from the 1821 *Philosophy of Right* stand for the conviction of many of his fellow philosophers: 'Only in the will as subjective can freedom, or the will as it is *in itself*, be actual' (§ 106) and: 'Subjectivity constitutes the ground of existence for the concept of freedom' (Remark to § 152).

Though sharing a common emphasis on subjectivity as the foundation of human emancipation, German idealists often define the originality of their respective theories by focusing on widely different, sometimes mutually antagonistic assumptions regarding their common concern. The road that leads from acknowledging the pivotal role of subjectivity in thought and action to acknowledging individual subjectivity, and from here to the moral and juridical recognition of a right to it, is not a straightforward road. 'Subjectivity' and its derivatives may carry a negative as well as a positive connotation in German idealism, depending upon the context. Kant, for example, confines teleology to the realm of problematic ideas because of what he alleges to be its merely subjective meaning and validity. On the other hand, post-Kantian idealism's standard criticism of transcendental philosophy is often carried out by the systematic disclosure of its allegedly merely subjective (and that means subjectivistic) character. Schelling's 'absolute spirit' is meant as antidote to Fichte's 'absolute ego' that Schelling perceives as extravagantly subjectivistic—and yet each of these principles stands for the idea of subjectivity in their respective systems. While some see in Fichte's 'deed-act' (*die Tathandlung*) of an ego that posits its own existence the conceptual epitome of subject's creativity and sovereignty, the Romantics diagnose neglect or suppression of subjectivity in virtually every contemporaneous philosophic theory. Finally, Hoelderlin's notion of a consciousness that travels on an 'eccentric path' (*eine exzentrische Bahn*) from non-reflected being back to its reflected unity with being is perhaps the most paradoxically a-subjective notion of the subject voiced by the *Zeitgeist* of German idealism.

Even in the body of one and the same work, the uses of 'subjective' or 'subjectivity' may take on different, indeed opposing connotations. Hegel is as likely to accuse Kantian or Fichtean idealism of being 'merely subjective,' as he is to hail Christian theology and early modern philosophy for having paved the way to the discovery of subjectivity. And while he insists on calling his idealism non-subjective, he structures the metaphysical foundation of the entire system, the *Science of Logic*, in such a way as to make it culminate in a 'subjective logic' or doctrine of the Concept: *der Begriff*. On the other hand, whether for expository or substantial reasons, Hegel also uses 'subjective spirit' to denote the systemic antecedent to 'objective spirit.' From the *Phenomenology of Spirit* of 1807 to the Philosophy of Spirit of 1830, the subjective dimension of spirit is only one of two equally one-sided, necessary moments whose unity alone constitutes true or absolute (that is, subjective–objective) spirit.

This study attempts to unravel some of this complexity by beginning to answer questions like the following: Since the senses in which Hegel uses 'subjectivity' span a wide arc—from negative limit of knowledge and agency to affirmative ground of truth and freedom—how do these connotations of the same concept relate to one another? What is the continuity in their difference? How are we supposed to understand the notion (already announced in 1807) of a knowing substance that develops into a knowing subject? How can subjectivity, like an Aristotelian immanent *telos*, mark both the beginning and the end of spirit's movement? What exactly is the inward 'master builder' (*der Werkmeister*) that Hegel describes as being at work throughout human history, surviving neglect and always rising anew from its ashes, enlarging its domain while allegedly thrusting ever-deeper roots in human institutions, moral systems, and the self-understanding of individuals?

In what follows, these and similar questions are being addressed in three steps. Chapter 1 outlines Hegel's conception of the history of philosophy as a self-differentiating process, or self-development, of human thinking. Chapters 2 and 3 offer an explication of the logical account of the subject of thinking in Hegel's system. Chapters 4 through 6 emphasize the historical dimension of this logical concept under the aspect of Hegel's critical reading of Greek philosophy. These chapters do not consist only of a reconstruction of Hegel's reading. They also test his claims regarding the absence of a rational notion of subjectivity in ancient philosophy against selected Greek texts themselves.

This approach, though by no means the only viable one, has several advantages. First, it makes use of the venerable principle of Spinoza according to which 'all determination is negation.' The Hegelian version of this principle is that the determination of a concept (here, the concept of a subject) must contain both the negation of that which is excluded from it as well as the negation of the concept itself. Accordingly, if we aim at obtaining a positive concept of subjectivity we must include the notion of its absence, a-subjectivity, and then grasp the ways in which subjectivity relates to its negation and makes itself objective. By reconstructing the opposition and interplay between absence and presence of 'the subject' in pertinent texts of the classical tradition, the contours of what being-subject means acquire sharpness. In proceeding in this way, one simply abides by accepted rules of logic as well as of psychology: something is thought or felt as missing only from the perspective of its presence and, *vice versa*, something's presence becomes remarkable or problematic only from the perspective of its absence.

The second benefit of this approach is that it requires comparison between distinct parts of Hegel's body of work (for instance, the Logic, the Phenomenology and the Philosophy of Spirit) as opposed to limiting one's frame of reference to a single, relatively self-contained work that was explicitly conceived by its author as organic part of a larger whole. This means taking Hegel's claim to systematicity seriously, at least to the extent that making the system into the proper frame of reference for concepts' meanings and arguments' completeness allows one to provide as rich an account as possible of the matter at issue. By allowing the concept of the subject and its cognates to be treated in the light of different works in- and outside the system, one can hopefully circumvent the partiality of analyzing subjectivity only as a moment of phenomenal consciousness, a metaphysical category, a natural event or a product of social interaction.

The procedure followed acknowledges of course the necessity of respecting the letter of the works published by Hegel. A partial contribution towards this goal is represented by the new translations of numerous passages offered here. But in making use of Hegel's lectures and of the notes compiled from students' manuscripts published as 'Additions' to the main texts this study acknowledges as well the legitimacy of addressing the spirit of Hegel's arguments.

Last but not least, this interpretive strategy allows for comparisons of the historical dimension of Hegel's claims with the extant testimony of ancient *Geist*, namely with Greek literary and philosophic works that he himself calls upon as illustrations of his theses. This feature of these essays may be seen then as an instantiation of Hegel's own explicit requirement that there be an 'external touchstone of the truth of a philosophy', as he urges in the introduction to the *Encyclopaedia* (§ 6). In other words, the readings being offered here of selected Platonic dialogues and of passages of Aristotle's work aim at putting to the test the adequacy of Hegel's interpretation with regard to the role played in them by ideas of subjectivity and personality.

There is a diffuse opinion in contemporary Hegel receptions according to which the meaning of his philosophy can and must be assessed independently of his Logic. In the influential words of Allen W. Wood: 'Hegel's system of dialectical logic has never won acceptance outside an isolated and dwindling tradition of incorrigible enthusiasts.' Moreover, since according to this same view the history of philosophy is one of 'spectacular failures', it is no surprise that a major philosopher like Hegel is expected to have contributed a major debacle of his own. This, it is indeed determined, is precisely the case of the *Science of Logic*, the embodiment of a failure even 'more final and irredeemable' than those of Descartes and Kant (*Hegel's Ethical Thought*, 1990, p. 5).

The programmatic rejection of the metaphysical foundations of Hegel's thought in contemporary reconstructions of it is often accompanied by a summary assessment of the Logic as a sort of cabalistic shroud threatening to envelop an otherwise almost intelligible system, rather than providing the key to its disclosure. In this perspective, the role of Hegel's logical and metaphysical categories as foundations of pivotal notions of the system (substance, nature, spirit, consciousness, mind, reflection, and so on) is ignored, the principles of each part of the system are taken as presupposition-less (ultimately, dogmatic) beginnings, and Hegel's philosophic contribution is reduced to that of an unduly elaborate social theory or of a prolix epistemology. According to other readings, Hegel's main and only merit would consist of having anticipated (though in clumsy nineteenth-century German terminology) contemporary logical and epistemological 'solutions' to traditional problems of philosophy—the latter being identified mostly as 'Cartesian dualism,' the 'application' of concepts to objects, and the possibility of 'selves,' topics that it would be actually difficult to identify among Hegel's concerns. (Paradigmatic of this approach is the work of Robert B. Brandom, according to whom Hegel's absolute idealism is at bottom an original form of pragmatism.) Still other interpretations tend to privilege one stage in Hegel's reconstruction of spirit's movement (what Hegel himself would call one moment of the Idea) as clue to all others. For example, the dialectic of lordship and servitude from the fourth chapter of the *Phenomenology* is being occasionally elevated to the role of centerpiece of Hegel's general theory of consciousness, or even of history; or the stages of 'natural consciousness' from the first few chapters of the same early work are being understood as comprising Hegel's theory of knowledge *tout court*. H.S. Harris's comment on this latter trend sums up the problem as follows: 'it can be said that hardly any of the critics who have discussed Hegel's theory of "Consciousness" in English (and there has been more Anglophone discussion of his first two chapters than of any other part of the book) have been in a position to embark upon Hegel's quest for absolute knowledge at all. They already have the only "absolute knowledge" they can conceive of' (*Hegel's Ladder I: The Pilgrimage of Reason*, 1997, p. 211).

An invaluable contribution to understanding subjectivity as the foundational principle of Hegel's absolute idealism was made in 1976 by Klaus Duesing in the seminal study *Das Problem der Subjektivitaet in Hegels Logik*. More recent in-depth studies of the role of single, pivotal concepts of Hegel's work have provided crucial insights into his philosophy of the subject, its influence on nineteenth- and twentieth-century thought, even its usefulness for the analysis of contemporary concerns. One such contribution is Robert R. Williams' 1997 *Hegel's Ethics of Recognition*, a comprehensive study that includes in its analysis the historical as well as systemic antecedents of the role of *Anerkennung* in Hegel's *Philosophy of Right*.

All too often, however, a systemically subordinate concept is moved to center stage for the purpose of explaining much broader categories. This results inevitably in a reductionist account of the latter. 'Intersubjectivity,' for example, is sometimes chosen as a Hegelian key notion for the explanation of the phenomenon of 'the subject'. In this kind of approach, Hegel is made to deduce the origins of subjectivity from the interactions among subjects—just like, as Marx put it in the *German Ideology*, a theologian explains the origin of evil by introducing the original sin. The circularity can only be avoided by placing Hegel's notion of the interaction among a plurality of subjects (including their reciprocal recognition) in the context of his conception of absolute subjectivity.

In the *Philosophy of Right*, for example, the concept of a 'subject of right' is not assumed as a dogmatic beginning to be analyzed in terms of three dialectical moments: right as abstract, as morality, as ethicality. The concept is rather derived from that of mind as will from the Philosophy of Spirit (see §§ 440–82 of the 1830 edition of the *Encyclopaedia*; in particular, 'free will' is defined in § 481); mind, in turn, is a form of spirit, and spirit is the end result of the self-externalization of the Logical Idea. In the introduction to the 1821 *Philosophy of Right*, Hegel warns explicitly that the notions of a juridical, moral and ethical subject are derived from that of a cognizing and willing subjectivity he has developed previously. The birthplace of 'right' or 'freedom' is the will, and the meaning of 'will' is presupposed but not justified in the philosophic exposition of the Idea of right:

> The soil of right is, in general, the *spiritual* [das *Geistige*], and its more specific place and source is the *will* that is *free*. . . . The basic features of this premise—namely that *spirit* is at first *intelligence* and that the determinations through which intelligence advances, from *feeling* through *representation* to *thinking* proper, are the path by which it begets itself as *will*, which as practical spirit in general is the proximate truth of intelligence—these premises have been presented in my *Encyclopaedia of the Philosophical Sciences* (*Philosophy of Right*, § 4 and Remark).

The reading of Hegel that is being offered here is based on the conviction that one cannot do justice to his conception of being-subject without recourse both to the 'philosophy of reality' (*Realphilosophie*) and to the Logic that gives that reality, in its natural and social dimensions, structure and thus intelligibility. One need not be an 'incorrigible enthusiast' of the *Science of Logic* in order to advocate its necessary place in grasping Hegel's philosophy of reality or, as he more precisely puts it, of what is rational in actuality.

As the following passage makes clear, the meaning of 'subjectivity' in Hegel's philosophy is crucially dependent upon his concept of thinking, that is, upon the Concept of the Logic, and the latter is in turn inseparable from the 'objectivity' that is thought's content—the totality of all actualizations of spirit:

> Both subjectivity and objectivity are thoughts . . . and indeed they are determinate thoughts, which have to prove themselves to be grounded in the thinking that is universal and self-determining. . . . Furthermore, however, this subjectivity . . . is not to be regarded as an empty framework that can only be filled up from the outside, by objects that are present on their own account; on the contrary, it is subjectivity itself which, being dialectical, breaks through its own barrier, and opens itself up into objectivity by means of syllogism (*Encyclopaedia* of 1830, § 192).

Viewed as determinate thoughts, subjectivity and objectivity show themselves to be two sides of the same coin. Because subjectivity exists as thinking, it is neither a form superimposed on thoughts as if these were its contents, nor is it an empty receptacle for impressions, intuitions, or their (*an sich* thought-less) objective sources. Rather, subjectivity consists of a thinking subject's dialectical activity of permanently trespassing into objectivity and relating it to itself, an unremitting going beyond itself and coming back again, finding oneself, as Hegel likes to put it, 'at home in the other.' Thus, neither subjectivity as such, nor Hegel's 'absolute' subjectivity is the antipode of objectivity. As he remarks in an introduction to the lectures on modern philosophy, the consciousness of the opposition between thinking (or subjectivity) and being (or objectivity) is a feature of thinking, and the opposition is permanently overcome and can only be overcome by thought itself. Even more crucial, however, is the recognition that this opposition is first produced by thinking in an act of internal diremption that literally defines subjectivity. According to Hegel, not this fact, but the explicit grasp of this fact is a revolutionary event of historical proportions. Ancient philosophy and literature (as well as much of medieval theology) show an intuitive awareness but no conceptual grasp of the productive self-differentiation of subjectivity. Rather, the archetype of such a conception is to be sought in the foundational principle of modern philosophy: I think, (and thus) I am.

The last of the major categories of the Logic, 'the concept of the Idea' or the Concept *tout court* (*der Begriff*) (see § 236 of the *Encyclopaedia*) is the culmination of the Subjective Logic, that is, the end result of Hegel's analysis of the dynamic structure of thinking. The logical Idea contains the notion of a complete (though still abstract, because only logical) determination of subjectivity. Hegel conceives the parts of the system that follow the Logic (that is, the Philosophy of Nature and the Philosophy of Spirit) as accounts of two forms of externalization of the logical Idea: nature and spirit. In the transition from the system's Logic to the Philosophy of Nature, Hegel explains the intelligibility of nature in terms of its being the spatial and temporal 'externalization' of the Idea:

> The absolute *freedom* of the Idea, however, is that . . . it *resolves to* freely *release* itself as *nature out of itself* (*Encyclopaedia* § 244).

> Nature has yielded itself as the Idea in the form of *otherness* . . . [Thus] nature is not merely external relative to this Idea (and to the subjective existence of the same, spirit), but the *externality* constitutes the determination in which the Idea exists as nature (*Encyclopaedia* § 247).

Far from being simply the 'outside' of what thinks, nature (and this includes of course the individual body) is rather the first form of objectification of the Concept itself. This implies that the first (we might add: primitive) realization of the logical concept of subjectivity expounded in the Logic is found in nature (paradoxically, the realm of blind causality and iron necessity), namely in the natural form of organic life. For Hegel, nature is ultimately not the completely other of thinking because thinking, as the Logic has shown, has otherness as one of its constitutive moments—just like soul has the living body or freedom has necessity as an integral part of itself.

At the other end of the Philosophy of Nature, in the transitional sections leading out of it and into the Philosophy of Spirit, after discussing the rational necessity of individual death, reproduction and species preservation in organic nature, Hegel characterizes spirit as arising precisely out of the subjectivity intrinsic to the Idea as 'life':

> The last *self-externality* of nature is sublated and the Concept, which has in nature merely being *in itself*, has now become *for itself*.—With

> this, nature has passed over into its truth, into the subjectivity of the Concept, ... so that that Concept is posited which has its corresponding reality, that is, the Concept [itself], as its *being* [*Daseyn*],—*spirit* (*Encyclopaedia* § 376).

In its first externalization as nature, the Concept exists merely in an 'immediate' manner, in-itself. In acquiring a new form of externality, spirit, the Concept begins to exist also in 'mediation' or for-itself. It has now become the Concept whose adequate reality is its own objectification—the Concept, we might say, in its objective subjectivity: *Geist*. This spiritual externalization differs from the natural in that it results from the Concept's relating to itself. This is a new mode of determinate existence of the Concept, a new *Daseyn*, in the course of which its object ('its corresponding reality') becomes increasingly determined by the Concept itself. The just-quoted claim that spirit as 'subjectivity of the Concept' is the dormant truth of nature implies that, once it releases itself from nature, spirit's activity consists of an ever-expanding inclusion of itself in its realizations. In phenomenological perspective, Hegel described this process in 1807 as a self-transformation of substance into subject:

> This substance ... that is spirit is its own *becoming* what it is *in itself* ... Spirit is in itself the movement that knowing is,—the transformation of that *in-itself* into *for-itself*, of *substance* into *subject*, of the object of *consciousness* into the object of *self-consciousness* ... or into the *Concept* (*Phenomenology of Spirit*, Chapter VIII).

In other words: the systematic relation of spirit to nature parallels the phenomenological relation of self-consciousness to natural consciousness, a relation described at the beginning of the chapter on self-consciousness in the following terms:

> But now there has arisen what did not emerge in these previous relationships [that is, in sense-certainty, perception and understanding], namely a certainty which is the same as its truth, for the certainty is to itself the object, and consciousness is to itself the true. In this there is also an otherness [ein Andersseyn], insofar as consciousness does make a distinction, but one which at the same time is for it not a distinction (*Phenomenology*, Chapter IV).

The thesis of a radical difference between ancient and modern conceptions and experiences of subjectivity is a crucial theme in the philosophy of the history of philosophy that Hegel outlines in the introductions to the *Lectures on the History of Philosophy* and is operative in the body of the Lectures themselves. Accordingly, the first chapter of this book is dedicated to a critical discussion of these texts. The selection of Greek sources against which Hegel's reading is being tested in later chapters is guided—and I hope justified—by the focus of the book and by Hegel's explicit interest in them. Plato's *Apology, Crito, Parmenides* and parts of the *Politeia* figure prominently, but many other equally relevant works had to be sacrificed. As for Hegel's debt and critical relation to Aristotle, I do not presume to be doing justice to it to any reasonable degree. Given the rich and detailed literature on the subject, Hegel's (nineteenth-century) Aristotelianism is simply presupposed in the discussion of those parts of the Aristotelian *corpus* that are directly relevant to the topics at issue, in particular, arguments found in the *De Anima, Physics* and *Metaphysics*.

In exploring Hegel's thesis of the absence of key features of individual subjectivity in Greek thought (mainly, self-reflexivity and self-determination) I have learnt much from contemporary philological and historical works on Greek society, rhetoric and jurisprudence that are entirely innocent of Hegelian philosophy. Principal among these are K.J. Dover's *Greek Popular Morality in the Time of Plato and Aristotle* (1974) and G.E.M. de Ste Croix's *The Class Struggle in the Ancient Greek World* (1981). Though my understanding of these sources is perhaps inevitably influenced by the fact that, before becoming acquainted with them, I already took Hegel's reading of Greek antiquity to be convincing, still I consider it a testimony to the power of his thought that what I learnt from these works, including most of the authors' commentary on the historical and anecdotal material, is entirely consistent with Hegel's interpretation of the ancient mind.

1
A Philosophy of the History of Philosophy

Philosophic concepts are incomprehensible unless the history of their formation is included in the investigation of their meaning. This thesis can be generalized to include the whole of the philosophical enterprise: rational philosophizing is only possible on the basis of a rational reconstruction of the history of philosophy.

Hegel explicates these theses in several introductions to the various series of *Lectures on the History of Philosophy* held one time in Jena in 1805–6, two times in Heidelberg from 1816 to 1818, and almost seven times in Berlin, starting in 1819 and ending the day of his death in November 1831. The introduction to the second cycle of Berlin lectures (1820) survives in Hegel's own hand and in form of a completed text.[1] Other introductions that are either shorter or fragmentary in nature (1816 and 1823) appear to be integral parts of the 1820 text. Accordingly, an analysis of the latter will provide a reasonably reliable account of Hegel's theory of the history of philosophy.[2]

Hegel lectures on the history of philosophy mainly as a philosopher, not as a historian. 'The history of philosophy must itself be philosophical,' he declares in a brief address premised to the 1820 lectures.[3] Thus, he is not interested primarily in delivering a chronicle of philosophic ideas, propositions, claims, arguments and counter-arguments in the historical order of their formulation. He presupposes his audience's general acquaintance with historical facts and events pertaining to philosophic theories, as well as with major thinkers' most basic tenets. Hegel is rather concerned that his lectures attain three goals. He wants to show, first, why philosophers' principles were relevant to their times; second, how and why these principles underwent transformation; third, how a core meaning may be discerned in them that persists throughout their historical and ideological transformations.

A paradigmatic illustration of Hegel's procedure in interpreting fundamental principles of the philosophic tradition is provided by the following comment on 'being person' in a Remark to the property-section of the 1821 *Philosophy of Right*:

> The notion that what spirit is according to its concept or *in itself*, it should be also in its existence and for-itself (thereby that it be person capable of property, having ethicality, religion)—this idea is itself spirit's concept (as *causa sui*, i.e. as free cause, spirit is such *cuius natura non potest concipi nisi existens*; Spinoza, *Ethics* I, Def. 1.) Precisely in this concept . . . there lies the possibility of the opposition between what spirit is merely *in itself* and not [yet] also *for itself* . . . and thus the *possibility of the alienation of personhood* (*W* 7, § 66 Remark).[4]

In other words: the comparatively late, modern conception and political existence of persons as subjects with rights (to property, to moral convictions, beliefs, and so forth) is explained by Hegel as realization of the pivotal feature of Spinoza's god (or, as in other passages, of Descartes' *res cogitans*, a substance that is equally inconceivable unless as existent). Ever since its ancient inception as *nous* on the philosophical stage, the core meaning of 'spirit' as complement and opposite of 'nature' has been the idea of a being capable of determining itself into what it is. Modern political philosophy's idea of an 'autonomous' or self-determining subject is the latest and richest (Hegel: most 'concrete') expression of this meaning.

The first of the goals outlined in the address and introduction to the *Lectures*, namely the reconstruction of the epochal intelligibility of philosophic notions, implies a serious attempt to grasp and convey the sense in which philosophic concepts and arguments are meant and understood at their inception, independently of further developments. This is where the philological and historiographic skill of the *historian* of philosophy has its rightful and necessary place. The second and third goals (regarding the transformation and permanence of philosophic principles) presuppose a theory of philosophy as a particular kind of thinking with specific logical and epistemological features. Here is where the *philosopher* must deliver an interpretation of historically documented theories and their principles that includes but also goes beyond the meaning ostensibly intended by each of them.

The philosopher lecturing on the history of philosophy has, then, two sets of criteria guiding the exposition. The first pertains to the chronological order of philosophic concepts as they appear in the history of philosophy. The second consists of concepts' theoretical order as unveiled by their logical and metaphysical analysis. While it is plausible to assume in general terms that these two orders cannot exist in utter independence from one another (after all, philosophy's principles are concepts, and thus they must be rooted in human logic as much as in human history) Hegel's explicit claim about their relation is much stronger than this. The two orders in which philosophic thought has developed are, in principle, one and the same:

> According to this idea I now maintain that the succession of the systems of philosophy in *history* is *the same* as the *succession in the* logical *derivation* of the conceptual determinations of the Idea (*GW* 18, 49).[5]

Far from considering this thesis a mere rhetorical flourish, Hegel recurs to it even in the Logic to justify its beginning with the Parmenidean category of 'being': 'thinking . . . must be referred back to the beginning of science as Parmenides made it, who purified and elevated his representations to *pure thought,* being as such . . . What is the *first* in the *science* must have shown itself *historically* as the first. And we must regard the Eleatic *one* or *being* as the first knowing of thought.'[6]

As the logical sequence of philosophic principles cannot be thought of as random, so their historical sequence cannot be considered accidental. Just as little can the reconstruction of these sequences in a history of philosophy as a discipline be arbitrary. Indeed, only the most superficial observer would think of philosophers' choices of themes and methods as of a random series. To the contrary, as if engaging in epoch-transcending conversations, philosophers invariably (though often only tacitly) relate to, criticize or make use of preceding theoretical and practical notions and concerns. Where no full-fledged philosophic precedents are given, as in the case of the pre-Socratics, philosophers refer to concepts implicit in the representations (*vorstellendes Denken*), language, mythology, religion, poetry and popular wisdom that have preceded and still surround them. Even the most skeptical eye perceives philosophic theories in their historical succession as engaged in some sort of sense making. Hegel's *Lectures* follow the logic of this sense making as a thread of Ariadne running through the history of philosophy.

A thorough justification of the strong version of Hegel's claim, according to which the logical sequence and historical succession of philosophic principles are 'the same,' would require a book-length treatment of its own. This chapter attempts to make plausible a weaker version of the claim, one that by itself helps support Hegel's views on ancient thought—in particular, his claims regarding the fragile understanding and stunted development of individual subjectivity in the Greek world. The weaker version, it bears repeating, purports that the logical succession and historical emergence of fundamental notions in philosophy are not independent from one another. This chapter elucidates two theories from the body of Hegel's system that help support the claim. In so doing, it also addresses some pertinacious views about Hegel's understanding of the nature of the philosophic enterprise, views that the chapter attempts to correct.

According to Hegel, the primary—that is, both first and fundamental—subject matter of philosophic thinking is human thinking itself. The history of philosophy is thus spirit's gradual fulfillment of the Socratic command: know thyself. Thought's simultaneous double role as philosophic subject and subject matter lends philosophy the character of a peculiarly 'speculative' enterprise, much in the sense adumbrated in Aristotle's investigation of the highest function of the soul: 'Thought itself [*autos de noetos*] is included among the objects which can be thought. For where the objects are immaterial that which thinks and that which is thought are identical. Speculative knowledge [*he episteme he theoretike*] and its object are identical.'[7] In this Aristotelian spirit, Hegel explains the dynamics of thinking as a progressive actualization, a becoming *fuer sich*, of what thinking is potentially, namely *an sich* or according to its concept alone (*nur dem Begriffe nach*). It may not be superfluous to point out that this notion of thinking is deeply influenced by eighteenth- and nineteenth-century conceptions of living matter: organic nature is defined by the fact that the succession of the stages traversed in the overall development of every organism is not a mere function of elapsing time but rather, more fundamentally, of the genetic laws—that is, the laws of the *genus*—that are internal to each exemplar of the kind. In this sense, every organism is a progressive actualization of what it already is potentially. Time flow and surrounding material conditions alone are not sufficient explanations of the peculiar 'motion' of teleological entities.

If there is not only chronological but also logical continuity among philosophic principles in the course of their history, it is possible for Hegel to identify a common, evolving meaning in notions that apparently refer to vastly different objects of reflection. The introductory chapter to the Doctrine of Being in the Greater Logic is dedicated to justifying precisely this claim: 'Thus the beginning of philosophy is the foundation that is present and self-preserving in all subsequent developments, that which remains immanent in all its further determinations.'[8] This self-preserving foundation of philosophic science is thought itself. Philosophy's history begins with the most abstract, non-mediated shape of thought, namely pure being, and Hegel's Logic begins correspondingly. The culmination of philosophy's development is still a shape of thought, albeit in the mediately immediate, or absolute, form in which thought is both object and subject of itself, and Hegel's Logic culminates in the concept of the Concept, or absolute Idea.

In the preliminary essay of the Greater Logic entitled 'With What Must the Science Begin?' Hegel defends the thesis that the history of philosophy instantiates a necessary process of human thinking toward self-knowledge and self-determination. In the course of the Logic, he illustrates this thesis by interpreting major historical changes of philosophic method and conceptuality in view of its corroboration. No such justification, at least no explicit one, is given in the *Lectures on the History of Philosophy*. Here, Hegel defends his claim mainly by pointing out that, given the nature of philosophy's subject matter, philosophizing is impossible without including the history of its fundamental concepts. This contention is being elucidated below in section 1.1.

One must still reckon, however, with the fact that in the 1820 introduction Hegel takes the radical thesis of the in-principle sameness of thought's logic and history very seriously indeed. Even without embracing it, one can still appreciate the strength of Hegel's thesis as offering powerful answers to eminently a-historical notions of philosophy that enjoy popularity in our own day. These conceptions view the history of philosophy as an ancillary discipline having at best instrumental value for proper philosophizing—as if philosophy were in itself a non-historical discipline. In their most narcissistic form (possibly, the form most representative of the contemporary state of mind in Western culture) past philosophic theories are glanced at and occasionally cited as exotic or downright clumsy introductory material for the alleged sophistication of contemporary thought.

Section 1.2 below discusses the idea of the unity of logic and history in philosophic thinking from the perspective of its consistency with other arguments within Hegel's system. The chapter concludes (section 1.3) with a critical reflection on the relation of philosophies to their *Zeitgeist* in the light of the theory of philosophy presented by Hegel in the 1820 introduction.

1.1 Movement and moments of truth

The 1820 introduction begins by highlighting the continuity of, and marking the distinction between, nature and spirit as grounds of human life and thinking. While nature remains fastened throughout its metamorphoses to unchanging laws, spirit, though necessarily anchored in habit-forming tradition, is capable of transforming the 'principles, prejudices and . . . riches' constituting that tradition. The productions of each generation are both form and matter of the next: they are the latter's 'soul, spiritual substance, . . . [and] the *material* present to it.'[9] Thus, in the history of what Rousseau calls our 'second nature' the matter being transformed and the activity producing the transformation do not differ in substance. One epoch's spirit is made up of that of all previous epochs and transforms the latter by assimilating it into something new, namely itself. This is why to read history is for us not to read a story of extraneous events, but our own story. As for the history of philosophy, it does not tell a tale of alien and disconnected ideas. It rather recapitulates the story of human thinking in self-reflective mode. The development of this mode of thinking takes place in a variety of historical forms: the philosophic systems.

Accordingly, the history of philosophy is not a history of opinions—not even of opinions about topics of the most general interest such as god, justice, or human nature. In the history of philosophy we are confronted with arguments leading to notions that are not only the particular, subjective convictions of groups or individuals. They are rather (as the systematic principles of material nature in the natural sciences) objective notions upon which depend the meaning and consistency of the entire theory being propounded. What marks a concept out as a mere opinion is for Hegel the fact of its intrinsic particularity, or perhaps even singularity. There are, of course, in the body of every philosophic work innumerable concepts that represent merely particular, on occasion even singular, convictions of the respective philosopher. These may well represent philosophers' social standing, existential interests, or personal idiosyncrasies. Most certainly, they reflect their historical horizons. However, not just every concept featured in a philosophic theory is for this reason alone a philosophic concept. The latter is rather a representation vested with the systematic function of a theoretical *principle*: the theory is logically dependent upon its meaning and consistency. These principles shall be called in the following 'system-identifying' concepts. Hegel refers to them as *Grundbegriffe* to mark them off from particular conceptual representations.

The particularity of concepts embodying mere opinion affects both their form and their content. For example, insofar as my community's ideas about divinity or rightfulness are merely our opinions, their contents are our local gods, customs or positive laws. As such, they are of little philosophic import. At best, these representations are important as psychological precedents or cultural frameworks of possible, full-fledged notions of divinity and right. On the other hand, some particular concepts do eventually develop into philosophic principles. What enables this transformation is the fact of the concepts' intrinsic universality. Local gods and positive laws are a case in point. No matter what their mythological, aesthetic, religious or theological guises, particular representations of divinity or rightfulness imply the universality of their referents: the idea of the divine or the idea of law. Indeed, as particular representations they harbor contradictions that press for resolution, because their objective meaning is inextricable from the connotation of universality, while their representational form is particular. A goddess is not *the* divine if she presides over Athens alone, or the juridical institution of slavery, despite its legal validity, is not according to right. In the *Philosophy of Right* Hegel argues for example that the very idea of law (*Recht*) contains that of freedom (namely, in form of free will). Thus, laws instituting or regulating slavery 'depend on regarding man [den Menschen] . . . as an existent not in conformity with its concept.'[10] Contrary to positive or statutory right, the concept of right (or the idea of law) is objectively universal. In the same way in which the *Dasein* of a newborn animal does not yet coincide with the proper concept of its species (which will be expressed in the actualization of that concept at the stage of the animal's maturity), so legal validity (the reality of right) and rightfulness (the concept of right) do not yet coincide in ancient stages of the concept's development. Thus, we read in the Addition to this section, slavery 'occurs in a world where a wrong is still a right.'[11] From the historical moment of their inception, some representations are implicitly universal, but it is only in the course of the material and intellectual history of humankind that they are grasped (*begriffen*) as such, or become concepts (*Begriffe*).

As for the truth-content of universal concepts, Hegel reminds the audience of these lectures that philosophic theories' mutual differences and contradictions do not prove that philosophic truth is relative or, what is the same, that there is no truth in philosophy (as little, we may add, as difference and contradiction among scientific theories prove that there is no truth in science). Skeptic or relativistic truth abstinence, Hegel comments, only stimulates thought's hunger for truth.[12] At first sight, the fact that philosophic theories differ or even oppose one another, while each upholding that philosophy provides true insight into the nature of world and thought, seems to thwart rational expectations. But reason itself can make it clear that difference and contradiction among theories can only be perceived and understood against a common ground. Hegel refers to this ground repeatedly as the 'instinct of reason' that orients thinking towards finding truth: '*The truth however is one,*—the instinct of reason possesses this invincible feeling or belief. . . . Already the instinct of thinking pursues [the idea] . . . that the truth is one.'[13] To engage in thinking without an instinctive belief in the possibility of truth would be akin to engaging in eating without belief in the possibility of satiety.

The subject matter ubiquitous in philosophy is then neither individual witticisms nor particular cultural beliefs, but rather the concept of what is true. The history of philosophy consists of a rational series of formulations of this concept. Akin to the phenomenological description of the path traveled by consciousness through manifold shapes towards its true self, the *Lectures on the History of Philosophy* describe the continuous process of self-differentiations of thought towards its true content. And as the *Phenomenology* presents self-conscious spirit's reconstruction of its own development out of the urge of knowing itself (the 'absolute knowing' that concludes the phenomenological journey), so the *Lectures* present conceptual thought's incessant retracing of its own history as having the goal of grasping itself.

Hegel stresses that his identifying conceptual thinking as philosophy's medium and subject matter is not equivalent to defining philosophy as a science of abstractions. Philosophy does not consist only of formal determinations of concepts and their relations—put in contemporary terms, philosophy cannot be reduced to formal logic, linguistics or mathematics. Philosophy consists rather of identifying, analyzing and making explicit the content of system-identifying concepts. The meaning of a concept that serves as principle in a system is not exhausted by its relations to sub- or super-ordinate concepts. As already mentioned, not just any notion that arises in a philosophic theory ought to be taken as a philosophic concept in the technical sense. *Grundbegriffe* are concepts whose meaning, internal consistency and mutual compatibility provide the grounds of justification of the theory in which they are embedded. A system-identifying concept, for example Plato's idea or Leibniz's monad, is a unity of other concepts each of which differs both from this unity and from one another. A (necessarily conceptual) unity of different concepts does not erase their difference, or it would not be their unity but their replacement with an unrelated concept. Thus, the concept that functions as unity is internally differentiated. It is a 'concrete concept' that contains not just the common but also the mutually differentiating features of the notions it encompasses. In other places of Hegel's system we find the logical and philological justification of the use of 'concrete' and 'abstract' in connection with conceptuality.[14] In the text we are considering at present, he merely illustrates the distinction between an abstract and a concrete concept through that between an abstract and a concrete sensible representation (*sinnliche Vorstellung*). The first is a sensation proper, the second, a perception. The sensible representation of 'red' is abstract because it is merely an abstraction from similar sensations. The sensible representation of 'rose,' on the other hand, is properly speaking a perception. It is concrete in that, besides being an abstraction from many sensations, it is also the unity of different kinds of sensations (life, shape, color, smell)—it is, Hegel says, 'One subject, One idea.'[15]

Contrary to the familiar rule holding for concepts as classes, according to which a concept's increasing extension always implies its decreasing intension, the more general a system-identifying principle is, the more determinations it contains: 'Here the most extensive is also the most intensive.'[16] Accordingly, philosophy is the most concrete of all forms of knowing. Neither common sense nor enlightened ratiocination are sufficient by themselves to generate genuinely philosophic principles or to account for the consequences deriving from them: 'It is in this that knowledge of reason [Vernunfterkenntnis] distinguishes itself from knowledge of the understanding [Verstandeserkenntnis], and it is the business of philosophizing to show against the understanding that the true, the Idea does not consist of empty generalities, but of a universal that in itself is the particular, the determinate.'[17]

This 'universal' is concrete, then, in the sense that it is a unity containing differentiation ('the particular, the determinate'). It is precisely that whose formulation has been the perennial concern of philosophic theories since their inception. The just-quoted characterization of the Idea is an abbreviated form of the abstract definition of 'the Concept as such' (*der Begriff*) found in the *Encyclopaedia* Logic:[18] 'The *Concept* as such contains the moment of *universality*, . . . of *particularity*, . . . and of *singularity*, as the inward reflection of the determinacies of universality and particularity. This negative unity with itself is the *in and for itself determined* and at the same time the self-identical or universal.'[19]

This definition will be discussed in detail in Chapter 3 below. In the 1820 introduction to the *Lectures* Hegel limits himself to commenting that the Idea cannot be grasped by the understanding alone but requires reason.

In its epistemic sense as cognitive faculty, reason grasps concepts that can be characterized, in a first and general way, by the fact that they are self-reflexive. Hegel refers to them as 'concepts of reason', and to their referents as 'objects of reason.'[20] On account of their self-reflexive nature, concepts and objects of reason, as well as reason itself (the mode of thinking in the light of which these objects become intelligible), are referred to as 'speculative'. One such speculative concept is for example self-consciousness. Self-consciousness is the concept that consciousness has of itself. Thus in this case concept and referent coincide. As Hegel explains in the chapter of the 1807 *Phenomenology*[21] bearing this name, 'self-consciousness' refers to mind's taking on the self-contradictory (and thus also self-negating) role of being subject and object of one and the same act of cognition—simultaneously and in the same respect:

> If we call the movement of knowing, *concept*, but knowing as motionless unity, or the ego, the *object*, then we see that not only for us, but for knowing itself, the object corresponds to the concept.—Or alternatively, by calling what the object is *in itself*, the *concept*, while [calling] the object what it is as *object* or *for an* other, it becomes clear that the being-in-itself and the being-for-another is the same (*GW* 9, 103/Miller 104).[22]

Self-consciousness is thus an object of thought that the understanding cannot analyze because it involves the sublation, and thus the inclusion, of contradiction. It is a speculative concept arrived at and grasped only by speculative reason.[23]

The speculative character of concepts of reason is the common trait of all system-identifying concepts in the history of philosophy. Thus, Hegel's characterization of this discipline as description of the development of the Idea can be usefully summarized in the following terms. According to this theory, the subject matter of the history of philosophy is thinking as articulated in time through a series of theories (*Systeme*) centered upon concepts (*Grundbegriffe*) that are intrinsically speculative and thus properly intelligible only to reason.

In the course of the 1820 introduction, Hegel highlights different but connected features of philosophy's quest for an adequate grasp of the 'developing Idea': (i) its organic structure (philosophy is an evolving system of systems); (ii) its speculative nature (philosophy is self-knowing knowledge); and (iii) its characteristic movement, consisting of a simultaneously outward and inward unfolding. As these are the features that justify Hegel's claim of the intrinsically historical character of philosophic concepts, we shall turn to them first. Incursions into the Greater Logic are made necessary by Hegel's present use of notions deduced and explicated in that work. The logical development of the Idea, one must bear in mind, only exists as historical movement of spirit. Spirit, in turn, consists of the real occurrences of human history: 'The history of spirit is its *deed*', Hegel writes in the closing of the 1821 *Philosophy of Right*, 'because spirit is only what it does.'[24] Accordingly, the systematic principles displayed in the history of philosophy represent, in speculative form, the fundamental phases of spirit's theoretical self-knowledge and practical self-determination.

(i) Organicism

In its historical unfolding, philosophy can be likened to a living organism. Philosophic thinking is one, but it exists only as a dynamic whole of vitally interrelated parts, the philosophic theories. It maintains its specific identity throughout its transformations. It develops through time due to an internal 'drive':

> [T]he liveliness of spirit . . . is an urge, passes over into the hunger and thirst for truth, presses for knowledge of it, for the satisfaction of this urge . . . (*GW* 18, 43).
>
> [T]he true has the urge . . . to *develop* itself. Only the living, the spiritual moves, stirs itself inside itself, self-develops. In this way the Idea, concrete in itself and self-developing, is an organic system, a totality that *contains in itself* a *wealth of stages and moments* (*GW* 18, 47).[25]

Urge (or drive) in general is Hegel's term for the essential characteristic of life, be this the life of nature or, as here, of spirit. The urge of anything that is self-moved is its thoroughgoing concept. The latter is the form of (or informs) living objectivity. An urge is two-directional: it is aimed outwardly, towards a means of satisfaction, and it is self-directed, namely towards preserving the source of the urge. In this sense, the urge's aim is as much its satisfaction as it is its reproduction.[26] If the aim of philosophy is finding the true, each system satisfies truth-seeking all the while it reproduces the seeking itself.

Like the description of an organism's ontogenesis, the description of philosophic knowing requires a concept of change that does not imply the connotation of 'transition to another.' Hegel's technical term for organic or self-movement—and the term he uses in this introduction to characterize the history of philosophy—is *Entwicklung* (development).

Rather than using the term indiscriminately to denote any kind of process, Hegel reserves the use of this term in the *Realphilosophie* (that is, in the Philosophy of Nature and the Philosophy of Spirit) to denote self-determining movement. In the Logic, he uses 'development' to denote the movement of self-reflexive thinking. It is precisely self-relation that sets development apart from other kinds of change. In the opening of the Doctrine of the Concept (in the *Encyclopaedia* Logic) we read:

> The progression of the Concept is no longer either passing-over [Uebergehen] or shining into an other [Scheinen in Anderes], but *development* [*Entwicklung*]; for the [moments] distinguished are . . . at the same time . . . identical with one another and with the whole, and the determinacy is as a free being of the whole Concept.[27]

This passage summarizes the three structural features of thinking whose distinction Hegel considers so fundamental as to constitute the organizational principle of the entire Logic. The differences in thinking Being, Essence, and the Concept are functions of the difference in the relation of each to thinking itself.

When thinking has categories of Being for its generic objects (for example, indeterminate being, nothing, becoming; determinate being, quality, quantity or intrinsic measure, and so forth) its dynamics is described by Hegel as a passing-over from one to another category. In this context, the denotation or signified of each category is supposed to be independent of thinking itself and thus is related to another category by a reflection extrinsic to both.

When thinking has categories of Essence (and this means, the Essence of Being) for its generic objects, Hegel prefers to describe its movement as a shining-into-another. This indicates that here the relation between meanings of different categories is a reciprocal reflection among them. Each of the categories involved in this logical sphere constitutes part of the meaning of the preceding as well as of the following one, though only logical analysis can detect their mutual reflection. For example, the category of identity (*Identitaet*) already implies (upon reflection, as it were) that of distinction (*Unterschied*)[28] and *vice versa*. Both imply a common ground (*Grund*), which in turn contains them both: the ground of something's identity is necessarily distinguishable from, though also identical with, what is grounded by it. Equally, the notion of the world as appearance (*Erscheinung*) implies a notion of the world in-itself (*Ding an sich*) and *vice versa*. Through both, in turn, is reflected (shines through) a notion of the world's actuality (*Wirklichkeit*) that includes both its essence and its appearance. Each of the categories of essence is meant as referring simultaneously to a determinacy of being (essence is, after all, the essence of being) and a determinacy of thought (essence is also the concept—or truth—of being): the ground of 'x' provides the objective reason for the existence of 'x' while providing also the concept of what 'x' is essentially (or truly).

It is only when thinking has itself as its object—as in the system-identifying concepts of philosophic theories: idea, *nous*, god, *res cogitans*, substance, monad, reason, mind—that Hegel refers to its movement as development. In the 1820 introduction, in particular, he makes it explicit that self-referentiality is the *differentia specifica* of genuinely speculative thinking over against all other modes of thought. Thus, the movement of philosophy is correctly identified as self-development:

> [T]hat philosophically known truth exists in the element of thought, in the form of universality, . . . this is familiar to our common way of thinking. But [to say] that the universal itself contains its own determination, . . . here begins a properly philosophic proposition—here it is, therefore, that a consciousness that does not yet cognize philosophically withdraws and says that it doesn't *understand* this (*GW* 18, 45–6).[29]

Philosophy is neither a thinking of being *per se* nor of essence *per se*, but rather of being and essence as already mediated by thinking itself: philosophy is the thinking of the Concept. Herein lies its organic aspect, its nature as system of systems or, in Hegel's metaphor, as circle of circles. Accordingly, the organic or systematic character of philosophy is a consequence of its speculative character.

(ii) Speculation

In a move that parallels that from natural consciousness to self-consciousness in the *Phenomenology*, where the ego is said to have become both 'the content of the relation [of knowing to object] and the relating itself,'[30] Hegel argues in the *Lectures on the History of Philosophy* that philosophic inquiry always includes the investigation of both the inquirer (that is, thinking itself or 'the universal') and of the medium of investigation (the concepts or 'universals'). In other words: whenever the task is to determine the nature of thinking—how thought affects its objects, whether it distorts their truth or belongs in their innermost constitution, whether it is adequate to or incongruous with them—there is no other criterion, instrument or tribunal to appeal to but thinking itself. With regard to philosophy as a whole, this implies that the recognition of thought's role in the identification and analysis of the objects of philosophizing is always and necessarily intrinsic to the latter. Thought's role in determining itself is made explicit in the passage from the Lesser Logic quoted above: 'The *Concept* . . . contains the moment of *universality*, . . . of *particularity*, . . . of *singularity* . . . This [latter] . . . negative unity with itself is what is *in and for itself determined*.'[31]

A further way in which Hegel's notion of 'speculation' is able to exploit the metaphor of the mirror (*speculum*) is by highlighting that self-reflexivity also implies the becoming objective of what is otherwise understood as merely subjective. By reflecting about the history of philosophy, philosophic thinking objectifies itself.

As has been mentioned, these introductory reflections premised to the *Lectures on the History of Philosophy* echo Hegel's opening remarks in the phenomenological history of consciousness. Philosophic science, we read in the introduction to the *Phenomenology* of 1807, is apt to convey truth because thinking is neither merely an instrument nor a medium that modifies or distorts a subject matter alien to it, but is rather this subject matter itself. Since any object of philosophic investigation must be conceptual, philosophic thinking always investigates itself in the investigation of truth:

> If the Absolute is supposed to be simply brought nearer to us by the instrument [of knowing] . . . like the bird by the lime-twig, it would certainly, if it wasn't in and for itself already with us, laugh at this stratagem. . . . Or if the testing of cognition, conceived as a *medium*, teaches us the law of its refraction, it is again useless to subtract the latter from the result; for not the refraction of the ray is cognition, but the ray itself is that whereby truth touches us (*GW* 9, 53–4/Miller 47).[32]

In this view, the historical beginning of philosophic thinking coincides with the appearance of a self-reflexive stage of consciousness, namely self-consciousness. As long as consciousness has for its objects contents that it does not consider to be moments of itself—such as beings that it senses, things that it perceives, or forces that it understands to exist beyond the things perceived—its history belongs to the *natural* history of knowing. Hegel is explicit about the fact that, whether individually or collectively, the stages of natural consciousness (sense-certainty, perception and understanding) do not yet constitute knowing proper—let alone philosophic cognition. He reminds his readers that this pattern is already found in a phase of spirit's development that precedes that of consciousness, namely the spirit's phase as soul. Despite being moments of spirit, the stages of the natural soul (described in the so-called Anthropology) do not yet constitute spirit proper:

> [S]ince this exposition has for its object merely appearing knowledge ... it can be taken as the path of natural consciousness making its way to true knowledge; or as the path of the soul that journeys through a series of its own configurations as stages set for it by its own nature, that it may purify itself into spirit.... Natural consciousness will prove itself to be only concept of knowing, or non-real knowing (*GW* 9, 55–6/Miller 49).[33]

The phenomenological presentation of knowing as it 'merely appears', namely as related to what seems to be the wholly other from thinking, is the negative prelude to what the introduction to the *Phenomenology* calls 'free science moving in the form proper to it.'[34] The latter, then, is the proper subject matter of a philosophical history of philosophy: self-investigating and thereby self-determining or free thought. 'Real' or philosophic knowing begins with the realization[35] that thought's objects are being determined by thought itself. Knowing the object and self-knowing, then, join together in one activity: 'ego is the content of the relation, and the relating itself; ego is itself over against an other, and simultaneously grasps beyond this other which for the ego is likewise only the ego itself.'[36]

(iii) Externality and inwardness

In the 1820 introduction, Hegel argues further that the actualization of philosophic thinking in the historical sequence of its systems is at the same time an inwardization (*Insichgehen*) or recollection (*Erinnerung*) of philosophic consciousness—a deepening of its self-reflexive character.

> Further, this development is not directed [only] outwards as in externality, but the developmental unfolding is also a going inwards;.... As the outward going of the philosophical Idea in its development is not ... a becoming other but likewise a going-into-itself, a deepening of itself in itself, so does the progression render the Idea, previously general and rather undeterminate, more *determinate* in itself (*GW* 18, 47).[37]

If self-reference, or the inclusion of thought in the thinking of the object, is characteristic of philosophy, then the advance of philosophy through time and at different places will also follow, in conformity with the Socratic command issued at the onset of its history, an inward trajectory: advancing philosophic knowledge will imply increased cognition of the knowing self.

It is true of course not only of philosophy but of all other forms of spirit as well that their movement is always more than objectification in an 'other,' be this the spiritual or the material products of our species' second nature. Their development is as well a recollection (*Erinnerung*), whereby spirit enhances its grasp and determination of itself precisely through self-externalization.[38] Through change, spirit attains an ever more concrete shape of itself. As in the *Phenomenology* self-experience is said to lead the soul to self-knowledge (the soul 'achieves cognition of what it is in itself through the complete experience of itself'),[39] so in the Philosophy of Spirit, spirit's experience of its own externalizations leads to increasing self-knowledge. And since spirit essentially consists of the deeds of human thought, then increased self-knowledge means also increased inner determination (concretion) of spirit itself. This, again, may be illustrated by recourse to the Anthropology.[40] In the development of spirit from natural soul to consciousness proper (that is, the movement traced from the Anthropology to the Phenomenology) every stage in the externalization of soul—its taking possession of corporeality, its positing and taking possession of the external world, and so on—also represents a phase of spirit's inwardization, namely a progressive transformation of its in-itself into for-itself, or of its substantiality into subjectivity. Both sides of the soul's development, externalization and inwardization, are teleologically directed towards the full sublation of soul into conscious selfness or egoity:

> *In itself*, matter has no truth within the soul; as being-for-itself, the soul separates itself from its immediate being, and sets the latter over against itself as corporeity. . . . The soul that has posited[41] its being over against itself, that has sublated and determined it as its own, has lost the meaning of *soul* as *immediacy* of the spirit. The actual soul . . . is in-itself the *ideality* for-itself of its determinacies; in its externality [it is] *recollected* in and infinitely related to itself.[42]

Only a philosophical history of philosophy can capture the inwardizing or recollective dimension of spirit's external development, namely by reconstructing the successive sublations of philosophic principles in the history of the systems. The logical concretization, that is, increasing intension and extension,[43] of philosophic concepts is then the all but contingent complement to their chronological succession. The principles of ancient philosophies are comparatively more abstract and their signified are more 'external' than later principles, but they are included or recollected in these:

> Philosophy is, now, for itself the knowing of this development and, as conceptual thinking, is itself this thinking development. The further this development has thriven, the more complete philosophy is (*GW* 18, 47).[44]

The history of philosophy is not *Historie*, a story told from a perspective external to philosophy or a report on real occurrences as opposed to a fable about unreal ones. Hegel's specific use of *Historie* is not original. He simply relies upon a tradition, going back to at least the seventeenth century, that uses 'history' to refer to any ordered exposition of facts of nature, psychology or even epistemology.[45] The history of philosophy is rather *Geschichte*, a developmental history without which what has developed cannot be made intelligible and, *vice versa*, a history that cannot be made intelligible without knowledge of its results.[46] For example, a philosophic investigation of mind ignoring all that 'mind' has meant since Anaxagoras would resemble the procedure of a psychologist attempting to grasp her patients' personalities without including their personal history.[47] 'Mind' *per se* does not name a thing but a concept. In theorizing 'mind' one cannot indicate any signified to which the term corresponds other than the concept of mind itself. 'Mind' signifies 'the concept of mind' and this, as all concepts, has a history. The contemporary meaning of 'mind' cannot but be codetermined by the meanings it has carried through the history of philosophy. An adequate contemporary concept of mind would have to overcome and include (sublate) all previous ones. In announcing that 'the STUDY *of the history of philosophy is study of philosophy* itself,—as cannot be otherwise,'[48] Hegel prepares his audience for the radical idea that a philosophical history of philosophy is a chronological recapitulation of the intrinsic logic of philosophic thinking.

1.2 Logic and chronology

It may be no overstatement to say that Hegel's thesis (quoted in the opening section but to be repeated here) lies at the foundation of the encyclopedic system as a whole: 'According to this idea, I now maintain that the succession of the systems of philosophy in *history* is *the same* as the *succession in the* logical *derivation* of the conceptual determinations of the Idea.'

The claim can be paraphrased in two formulations that have been characterized above as strong and weak versions of the thesis. The strong version states that the historical sequence of systems in the history of philosophy coincides with the logical succession of phases in spirit's logical and theoretical activity. The latter, in turn, is specified by Hegel as consisting of spirit's process of self-cognition: 'It has been mentioned . . . regarding the essence of spirit, that its being is its deed.'[49] The weak version states that the relations among philosophy's principles parallel, or perhaps reflect and are reflected by, their historical order of appearance. A common denominator between these two formulations can be given as follows: Hegel's thesis states at a minimum that the sequential whole of theories (*die Aufeinanderfolge der Systeme*) displays phases that correspond to internal principles of human thinking and acting (*Begriffsbestimmungen der Idee*), and that the sequence of the phases is dictated by the necessity intrinsic to the logic of those principles.

If the systems in the history of philosophy are different expressions of one thinking process, then their principles, though necessarily *known* (*erkannt*) only through historically documented theories, can only be adequately *grasped* (*begriffen*) as determinations of one Idea, determinations whose logical connection is expounded in the Logic:

> I maintain that if one strips the *fundamental concepts* [*Grundbegriffe*] of the systems that have appeared in the history of philosophy of what concerns their exterior shape, their application to the particular, and similar features, then one obtains the various stages of determination of the Idea itself in its logical concept.[50]

Put somewhat differently: the philosopher reconstructing the history of philosophy understands the theories succeeding each other in time to be expressions (or real appearances: *Erscheinungen*) of principles of the theoretical and practical activity of self-knowing called the Idea.[51]

As has been already mentioned, in the text under discussion Hegel does not offer an argument to prove that the history and logic of philosophic thinking correspond to one another—let alone to prove that they 'are the same.' In support of his thesis, however, he does refer us here to the metaphysics of time whose exposition is found in the Philosophy of Nature.[52]

After a brief (by no means exhaustive) treatment of the philosophy of time invoked by Hegel to justify the logical and historical character of philosophic conceptuality (i), we shall turn to a related doctrine that provides additional, inner-systematic support for the thesis (ii). This is the theory of the parallel and contrary directions of the ontological and logical developments of 'knowing substance' (*wissende Substanz*) into its conceptual form (*Begriffsgestalt*) or subjectivity proper. This theory will be elucidated with reference to the section on Absolute Knowing of the 1807 *Phenomenology*.[53]

(i) A space and time for thinking

When he refers to the theory of time from the Philosophy of Nature, Hegel intends to remind his audience first of all of the theory that nature and spirit are both forms of the self-external being (*Aussersichsein*) of the Idea. The spatiality and temporality of natural as well as spiritual existence are the two dimensions in which the one Idea externalizes itself. This is argued in the section on natural mechanism ('Mechanics': the first subdivision of the Philosophy of Nature), where space and time are derived from a more fundamental determination, or concept, of nature, namely pure externality (*Aeusserlichkeit*). Space is nature's in-itself externality, and thus it is called immediate externality;[54] time is nature's for-itself externality, and thus it is called mediated externality.[55]

The same conception underlies the exposition of the spatial and temporal dimensions of the natural soul in the Philosophy of Subjective Spirit.[56] Spirit as natural soul is described at first in its spatial existence, that is, as a multiplicity of geographic, ethnic, familial and individual traits and temperaments characterized by the inertia and reciprocal indifference typical of all natural things regarded merely in their spatial existence. These are the 'places' of spirit's first self-externalization, or the soul's natural qualities as they coexist on earth.[57] The other dimension of the natural soul is temporal: it consists of the stages of organic life, its reproductive cycles, and the oscillations of the individual soul between sleeping and waking states. These are the 'epochs' of spirit's first shape as soul. Each of these is a way in which the soul undergoes natural changes. Taken together, these stages lend to human and other animal life its character as a *continuum* of differentiations.[58]

The distinction of spatial (or immediate) and temporal (or mediated) forms of the natural soul is, of course, purely analytical. What there is, in all places and at all times, is their unity, that is, the mediated immediacy of the living body.[59] It is precisely the dynamical and dialectical unity of qualities and changes in and of the soul that explains how this phenomenon of nature can eventually distinguish itself from its own corporeality and acquire inwardness. Soul is the stage at which nature has exhausted all its potential as absolute extrinsicality. Soul is the point at which nature may only continue to exist by turning inwards. It is the extreme actualization of the very concept of corporeal nature, the first phenomenon to realize the logical transition condensed in Hegel's laconic statement: 'Spirit is the existent truth of matter, that matter itself has no truth.'[60]

Soul, the first concrete unit of spirit, is the natural as much as spiritual unity of diverse impressions of qualities (sensations) with the experience (*Erlebnis*) of their continuity. The soul that senses or finds in itself (*empfindet*) a totality of sensations is the feeling soul (*die fuehlende Seele*).[61] Merely feeling soul turns eventually, through the repetition of sensations or sentient habituation,[62] into actual soul, the natural ego that is the precursor of the conscious 'I': 'The ego is the *lightning* that strikes through the natural soul and consumes its naturalness.'[63] These original features of the existence of spirit in its most natural mode will be found in sublated form in each of its subsequent shapes. Spirit exists, that is, it acts always and exclusively in the external world of space and time.

The 1820 introduction to the *Lectures*, while stressing the role of space and time as particular representations (*Vorstellungen*) of self-reflective thinking, presupposes this metaphysics of space and time as expounded in the *Encyclopaedia*. As activity, thinking exists only in its externalization. Only that is actual (*wirklich*) that has effects (*wirkend*). Philosophic thinking is no exception: it only exists through its actualizations.

> It has been mentioned before, regarding the essence of spirit, that its being is its deed. . . . Specifically, its deed is *self-knowing*. I am immediately, but as such I am only as a living organism; as spirit I am only insofar as I know myself. *Gnothy seauton, know thyself* . . . is the absolute command that expresses the nature of spirit (*GW* 18, 52).[64]

If time and space are dimensions of extrinsicality in general and if thinking itself exists only in extrinsic form, then time and space are constitutive of thinking as much as of nature, of the natural soul, and of all other determinations of the Idea. This, Hegel clarifies, applies to individual consciousness as much as to spirit in general and its absolute expressions. The time-space of individual consciousness is its life; the time-space of spirit is human history; and the time-space of philosophy, the history of philosophy:

> This being-there and thereby being-in-time is a moment, not only of single consciousness in general . . . but also of the development of the philosophical Idea in the element of thinking. Indeed, conceived in its stillness, the Idea is non-temporal. . . . But as concrete, as unity of

> differences . . . the Idea is essentially not stillness . . . rather, as internal differentiation . . . she becomes . . . extrinsicality in the element of thinking, so that in thinking pure philosophy appears as an existent proceeding in time (*GW* 18, 52–3).[65]

In sum: Hegel determines space and time as, respectively, the immediate and mediated dimensions of the Idea's externality. In the element of thought, the speculative mode of which is philosophy, the Idea displays its immediacy in thought's logic and its mediation in thought's history. The fact that nature as a whole is one mode of actualization of the Idea explains why every natural event must always be codetermined by space and time. The fact that spirit as a whole is the other mode of actualization of the Idea makes it intelligible why both logic (spirit's 'space') and history (its 'time') are quintessential determinations of thinking in general—and of philosophic thinking in particular. Only ratiocination, an artificial operation that abstracts from actual existence, separates thought's logic from thought's history and explains their coincidences as matters of contingency. Reason, instead, finds them always together, co-determining the progressive actualization of spirit that is the history of philosophy.

(ii) From knowing substance to knowing subject

The thesis of the coincidence of logical and historical phases in the development of philosophic thinking finds intra-systematic support in Hegel's conception of the movement of spirit (as consciousness) from substance to subjectivity, a movement that he conceives as equally necessary on logical and real (*realphilosophisch*) grounds. In the chapter on Absolute Knowing of the *Phenomenology of Spirit* (1807), Hegel recapitulates briefly the phases of consciousness described in the book. Consciousness started out as 'substance,' that is, as simple identity of form and content or thought and object. It then developed through progressive internal diremptions by which the originally immediate identity revealed itself to be (and thus became for itself) a mediated one: a unity of opposite determinations. In the end, absolute knowing represents a phase in which consciousness has sublated its own diremptions so that it now recognizes its initial substantiality as having been all along, though in a qualified sense, also subjectivity. Hegel then remarks that, taken as a whole, the movement of consciousness described in the *Phenomenology* appears to be proceeding in two parallel but seemingly contrary directions. *Realiter,* consciousness as substance, must be thought of as preceding self-knowing consciousness (in the same way that nature must be thought of as preceding spirit, or the natural soul as preceding consciousness and mind): 'Now, knowing substance is there in actuality earlier than its form or conceptual shape.'[66] However, for substance to self-develop at all it must contain from the beginning the internal principle of its movement. From a logical perspective, then, substance's capacity for knowing and then self-knowing, its subjective *dynamis* or 'conceptual shape' is a principle that must be contained in consciousness in the substantial mode. This *arche* is, in Hegel's terminology, the concept or truth of consciousness, namely self-consciousness. Spirit is the dynamic unity of the principle or concept of consciousness with that of which it is the principle or concept, namely knowing substance: spirit 'is in itself the movement that knowing is,—the transformation of that *in-itself* into the *for-itself*, of *substance* into *subject*, of the object of *consciousness* into object of *self-consciousness*, that is, into the equally sublated object, or the *Concept*.'[67]

Being a form of spirit, self-consciousness is a process, not a state (it is *metabole* and not *hexis*). It consists of the permanent recapitulation, that is, acknowledgment and preservation of all stages of knowing that have led up to it. In absolute knowing, past forms of consciousness are not present only in their in-itself mode (as archeological curiosities, as it were) but always also in their for-itself mode, that is, as stages and components of consciousness's own grasp of itself. In this way, while Hegel must realistically deny definitiveness to every single shape of self-consciousness (precisely on account of its being only a stage) he can restore validity to all thanks to the logical nature of the transitions by which each is overcome and preserved in the next.

This entire movement from substantial and abstract to increasingly subjective and concrete forms of spirit could never take place if the possibility of the latter was not included in the former logically, namely as their intrinsic *telos*:

> Thus, in the *Concept* that knows itself as Concept the *moments* emerge earlier than the *fulfilled whole* whose becoming is the movement of those moments. Contrarywise, in *consciousness* the whole, though un-conceptualized, is earlier than the moments (*GW* 9, 429/Miller 487).[68]

The phenomenological thesis that the logical and real developments of consciousness appear as parallel but contrary movements re-emerges in the introduction to the *Lectures on the History of Philosophy* in order to explain the definition of philosophy as unfolding of absolute spirit.

The notion of the true, as we have seen above, is for Hegel the most basic 'impulse of thinking.' Logically, this notion implies that truth (that is, cognition of the true) can only be one: 'the truth is the whole' because the true itself is the whole. The notion of the true is both principle and end of knowledge. All insights of science and *Realphilosophie* into the laws and phenomena of nature and of spirit are attained in the light of that unifying notion. Though it may appear that those truths are found independently of the notion of the true, in reality they are only found because that notion is presupposed. Accordingly, when the phenomenon being investigated is thinking itself, philosophic inquiry appears to proceed in a direction opposite to its historical unfolding. The seeming inversion arises from the circumstance that the philosopher studying the real progression of philosophy has to 'already bring along *the knowledge of the Idea* in order to recognize the process as development of the Idea.'[69] On the latest stage of the Idea's unfolding, a philosophic system is enabled to grasp the Idea thanks to its historical position: it can look back at the Idea's unfolding. This unfolding is what makes up the content (the 'fulfilled whole') of the concept of philosophy. Since philosophy is thought that thinks itself, it fulfills two roles at once. As object of itself, its past phases or moments appear to it as precedents to present thought, the latter being the subject of philosophic knowing. As subject, however, philosophic thought grasps its present state (the unity resulting from the sublation of those moments) because it lends intelligibility to its own past in the first place. In their embodiments as principles of systems, the moments of this process are the logical elements of the present concrete concept of philosophy. In this sense, the series of systems in the history of philosophic thinking can be interpreted as being 'the same' as the logical series of self-determinations contained in the Idea.

1.3 Completions and transitions in philosophy

Taking seriously the central claim from the 1820 introduction has far-reaching consequences in one's grasp, interpretation, and evaluation of Hegel's conception of philosophy as a systematic science of what is true. Only one such consequence, bearing upon Hegel's understanding of philosophic theories' role *vis-à-vis* their respective epochs will be discussed in concluding this chapter.

A widespread contemporary view attributes to Hegel the thesis that philosophy's function in relation to the cultural and political reality to which it gives voice or against which it reacts is purely past-oriented, or recollective. On this interpretation, Hegel views any sufficiently articulated philosophic theory as a posthumous theoretical reflection upon (and thereby also a reflection of) social arrangements, beliefs and institutions whose historical vitality and validity have been exhausted for good. Once each real system of beliefs and institutions finds itself teetering at the brink of a fundamental change, it is crowned with the merely intellectual self-recognition embodied by philosophy—the owl of Minerva beginning its flight when night is falling.

This interpretation does not distort entirely Hegel's intention but is one-sided. Due in part to the paraphrasing character of English translations of a famous passage from the preface to the *Philosophy of Right*, and in part to the isolation of the 'owl of Minerva' allegory from its polemic context, only one-half of Hegel's conception of philosophy's relation to its time is given its due. The passage in question is the following:

> As the *thought* of the world, [philosophy] appears only at a time after actuality has completed its formative process and made itself ready. This, which is a lesson taught by the Concept, is also demonstrated necessarily by history [itself], namely that it is only in actuality's fullness that the ideal appears to be confronting the real, thereby constructing for itself the same world, [albeit] grasped in its substance, in form of an intellectual realm (*W* 7, p. 28).[70]

The lesson concerning how being and its essence become disjointed in appearance, only to be re-united in the full comprehension provided by the Concept, is a complex lesson taught by the Logic. This needs only to be mentioned here, for our present concern is with interpretations of Hegel's characterization of philosophy as making its appearance 'after actuality has completed its formative process and made itself ready.' Available English translations tend to disregard the reflexive form of *sich fertig machen*, a common expression that means to 'make oneself ready,' and interpret the phrase as indicating that actuality is, in some sense, 'finished' (*fertig*).[71] But the reflexive form implies simultaneously completion and preparedness for a new phase. Since completion is expressed in the first part of the sentence ('actuality has completed [vollendet] its formative process'), and since Hegel's prose is seldom redundant, the connotation of 'preparedness' should be stressed in translating the second part. Actuality, then, is said to have completed one of its phases thereby making itself ready for the next. More importantly, since the subject of the phrase is *Wirklichkeit*, the available translations are also at odds with Hegel's consistently dynamic, Aristotelian use of 'actuality' as an activity that by definition does not attain any ultimate or definitive state. Thus, the translations neglect to convey Hegel's idea of a recollecting and simultaneously anticipatory function of philosophic theory.

Indeed, if the history of philosophic thinking follows the logic of the Idea, then philosophic principles must be as much determined by those they have sublated as by the ones they contain as yet only implicitly. As in the dialectic intrinsic to causal chains, where effects must be implicit in the causes they in turn sublate, or in that of syllogistic chains (the image Hegel invokes at the end of the *Encyclopaedia*[72] to illustrate the whole of philosophic systems as 'Idea *thinking itself*'),[73] the sublation of earlier into later principles implies equally the immanence of the latter in the former. Thus, while it is accurate to state that for Hegel the principles of a system, in sublating all previous ones, do express an epoch whose *raison d'être* is exhausted, it is equally correct that these same principles inaugurate an epoch whose cycle is about to begin.

As for the allegory of the owl of Minerva that concludes the same paragraph, *prima facie* it may appear to contradict the above. But the allegory—which, having almost attained the status of a slogan, is often quoted out of context—intends to highlight only one of the functions Hegel attributes to philosophy. It is embedded in a passage vigorously directed against the idea of a moralistic, ideological or generically normative vocation of philosophy and philosophers. Hegel's main concern here is to criticize the assumption that philosophers' role is to set the world aright by positing normative criteria taken, as it were, from another world: 'By way of adding one more word about *giving instruction* as to how the world ought to be: philosophy at any rate always arrives too late to do so.'[74] If the history of philosophy is the outward expression of spirit's process of self-knowing, the owl allegory cannot be taken to capture the whole of philosophy's functions. By expressing the final wisdom of one decaying epoch, philosophy provides the first full grasp of it. But to grasp is always to go beyond the limitations of what is being grasped (*Begreifen* is *Uebergreifen*).[75] Thus, if philosophy is 'the *thought* of the world', then by achieving systematic form at the closing of an epoch, it already thinks beyond it. The conception of philosophy underlying the preface to the *Philosophy of Right* is indeed the same as the conception of spirit we find in its conclusion, where the coincidence of completion and transition is spelled out more explicitly:

> The history of spirit is its *deed* because spirit is only what it does, and its deed consists of making itself, precisely as spirit, into the object of its consciousness, to comprehend itself by exposing itself to itself. This comprehending is its being and principle, and the *completion* of one comprehending is at once its externalization and transition (*W* 7 § 343).[76]

Thus, Hegel's theory of the history of philosophy understands each of its systems as articulating and grounding both an epochal closure of human spirit and a new beginning for which spirit has 'made itself ready.'

2
The Experience of Thought

The theory of philosophic thinking that underlies the *Lectures on the History of Philosophy* (discussed in Chapter 1) is embedded in Hegel's broader theory of experience (*Erfahrung*), of thinking as such (*Denken ueberhaupt*), and of the particular form that thinking takes in conceptual cognition (*begreifendes Erkennen*).[1] Concise expositions of these notions can be found in the introduction to the 1830 *Encyclopaedia*[2] as well as in the Preface to the Greater Logic published in 1832.

Thinking without qualification (*ueberhaupt*) is said to pervade every activity that is specifically human. Our species' distinction from other animal species lies as much in our philosophizing or composing of music as in the institution and violation of laws, the regulation of sexual behavior, or the invention of the gastronomical arts. Thinking as such is present in all of these. In the introduction to the *Encyclopaedia*, Hegel chooses religion as an example. Religion does not consist of mere religious feeling; moreover, feeling itself is not simply the opposite of thinking, as Romanticism would have it. Religion is rather one expression of thinking *in form* of a human feeling:

> Religion, right and ethicality pertain to the human being alone, and only because s/he[3] is a thinking being. Therefore, *thinking* as such has not been inactive in the spheres of religion, right and ethicality—whether in the guise of feeling, belief or representation; in these, the activity and productions of thinking are *present* and *included*.[4]

In other words, Hegel classifies kinds of non-conceptual representations as species of the *genus* 'thinking in general'. Still, these species differ significantly from the *genus* they belong to: 'But it is one thing to have feelings and representations that are *determined* and *permeated* by *thinking*, and another to have *thoughts about them*.'[5]

Thinking as such, then, is not always articulated conceptually. But if, as Hegel maintains, the proper (or 'adequate') concept of any thing is its truth, then the concept of thinking will be the truth of thinking—a truth obtainable only by thinking itself, and only in its conceptual form. Indeed, while there may be sensible, and perhaps non-sensible, intuitions of various objects of consciousness, concepts can be represented only through concepts. The fact, therefore, that thinking is not always articulated conceptually amounts to the fact that thinking itself, like everything else that has a temporal dimension, is not always adequate to its concept or, to use Hegel's paradoxical expression, thinking is not always adequate to itself.

Hegel's notion of conceptual cognition has its point of departure in Aristotle's characterization of thinking mind as 'form of forms.' In the *De Anima*, while explicating the sensing and thinking soul, Aristotle elucidates the metaphysical relation of form and content in the soul by recourse to an analogy with the hand as 'tool of tools.' Both the hand and the mind 'grasp' contents that they themselves have helped to bring about. Thus, both apply their power to themselves, an activity that results in each playing the double role of form and matter: 'It follows that the soul is analogous to the hand; for as the hand is a tool of tools, so thought is the form of forms and sense the form of sensible things.'[6]

Hegel enriches Aristotle's notion of a 'form of forms' with a developmental conception of thinking,[7] a conception that is best understood in ontogenetic as well as phylogenetic terms. For Hegel, conceptual cognition begins at a relatively late stage in the genesis of subjectivity, and this applies to both individual development and to the history of the species. In this (relatively late) conceptual mode, thinking is both a representational form and its content, or thought-*content* that has acquired the *form* of thought. The paradigm of conceptual cognition is philosophic thinking:

> Now, since philosophy is a peculiar mode of thinking—a mode by which thinking becomes cognition, and conceptual cognition[8] at that—philosophical thinking will also be *diverse* from the thinking that is active in everything human and brings about the very humanity of what is human, even though . . . *in-itself* there is only *One* thinking . . . [T]he human content of consciousness,[9] which is based on thinking, does not *appear in the form of thought* straightaway, but as feeling, intuition, representation—which are *forms* that have to be distinguished from thinking *itself as form* (*E* § 2).

The inclusion of 'feeling, intuition, representation' within the category of thinking indicates the breadth of Hegel's conception of human thought. In Hegel, as in the philosophic tradition that nurtures his theory of mind, thought and experience are not separable elements of our cognitive activity. Rather, they are always already entwined with one another. On the one hand, experience is never reducible to sensory stimuli; on the other, thought is never devoid of experiential content. The 'thinking that is active in everything human' refers to the very structure of the whole of human experience. Thinking and experiencing share the same logical structure. The sections that follow offer a thematic reconstruction of Hegel's conception of human experience and its contents (sections 2.1 and 2.2). This cannot but be a selective reconstruction. Its function is to provide a framework for an understanding of Hegel's conception of individual subjectivity, which he identifies as the most concrete result of the logical and historical development of mind (or of 'thinking as such').

Section 2.3 reflects on the distinction between the two modes of thinking Hegel refers to as ratiocination (or the 'mere understanding') and reason, this latter being the mode in which thought ultimately thinks itself. This reflection is carried out by tracing Hegel's criticism of Kant's conceptions of these modes as faculties.

The last section of the present chapter (2.4) briefly outlines the various uses of 'concept' in Hegel's philosophy. This is done in view of the theory of the Concept (*der Begriff*) that is the central concern of the chapter that follows.

2.1 'Enmattered forms' or thoughtful sensibility

In a first approximation, we read in the introductory sections of the *Encyclopaedia*, different modes of thinking may be called forms, and their different objects, contents, of thought. Images, for example, may be considered contents of a form of thinking called imagination,[10] and aims or ends may be considered contents of a form called will.[11] Hegel refers to all these contents with the generic term 'representations' (*Vorstellungen*)—a reminder that the most generic feature of whatever is being thought is that it is simply present in consciousness or re-presented.

Objects of thinking are said to be 'external' to thought itself but, since thought is not a spatial entity, the externality in question must be rather *sui generis*. By entering the sphere of consciousness, spatial-temporal phenomena or events acquire a thinking-form: they become images or sounds of something external, desires for objects perceived as extraneous to consciousness, goals yet to be achieved, and so forth. When the object of thinking is itself a non-spatial subject matter, as is the case when thinking thinks of the representations themselves, spatial expressions referring to externality and inwardness are metaphorical at best.

Furthermore, there are different ways in which contents of thinking may be said to be 'in' consciousness. One basic distinction is that between kinds of representations that are merely present *in* consciousness and those that are also present *to* or *for* it. Though epistemologically distinguishable, these are not two separate sets of conscious presentations. While the first kind is often referred to as 'mere representations,' these may change into increasingly 'conceptual representations' of the second kind. Hegel describes the relations between mere representations, on the one hand, and conceptual representations, on the other, in various ways, whose common theme is the following. To say that mere representations are only *in* consciousness while concepts are *for* it amounts to saying, first, that concepts are the source of meaning for mere representations, and second, that non-conceptual representations may be viewed as metaphors (meaningless in themselves) for concepts: 'Representations in general can be regarded as *metaphors* of thoughts and concepts.'[12] The meaning of a representation is thus a function of the relation in which it stands to consciousness as a unitary whole. Without including, for example, a sensible representation's relation to the sentient consciousness as its center, one could only state (if at all) in wholly impersonal terms that *there is* a sensation, or—more awkwardly still—that a sensation *is taking place*. It would be inaccurate to describe the sensory event in terms of a subject (or 'we' or 'I') *having* a sensation.

The distinction between presentations in- and for-consciousness is one reason for the importance Hegel attributes to the overcoming of what he considers a fundamental but one-sided epistemological tenet of empiricism, namely the 'principle of *experience*' according to which 'in order to accept and hold true a content, man [der Mensch] himself must *be present*'—in body and mind, as it were.[13] In order to lose its trivial connotation, Hegel rejoins, the principle of experience must be specified as meaning that the human being not only must be present but 'must find any such [sensible] content to be united and compatible with *the certainty of his own self*.'[14] If the necessary condition of perception and ultimately of all cognition is the presence of a sentient human being endowed with the capacity to receive impressions from without, it is an equally necessary condition that she be endowed with an 'inner sense' by which truth is conferred (*Fuehrwahrhalten*) to what has been taken up.

The empiricist principle that all human cognition must originate in sensible experience has often been lent corroboration by the (philologically controversial) attribution to Aristotle of the statement *'nihil est in intellectu quod non fuerit in sensu* [there is nothing in the intellect that has not been in sensibility].' According to Hegel, this principle expresses however only one aspect of human experience. Already Kant corrected the empiricist principle by showing that, though inevitably beginning with experience, human knowledge cannot be entirely rooted in experience alone.[15] Without embracing Kant's *a priori* elements of cognition, Hegel appropriates his recasting of the question of knowledge by claiming that the other aspect of experience lies in its being rooted in thought: 'everything human is human because it is brought about through thinking.'[16] There is no meaningful way in which human sensations and feelings may be interpreted as mere collections of chemical-physical events or mere reactions to environmental stimuli. Human perceptions are rather always mediated by one or another form of thought. Speculative philosophy will therefore supplement the principle ascribed to Aristotle with its inverse: *'nihil est in sensu quod non fuerit in intellectu.'* This has two meanings: a metaphysical one, according to which subjectivity as such makes objectivity possible, and an epistemological one, to the effect that specifically human experiences are always already mediated by human thinking:

> Conversely, speculative philosophy will equally affirm: 'Nihil est in sensu, quod non fuerit in intellectu',—in the very general sense that *nous*, and in deeper determination *spirit*, is the cause of the world, and in the narrower sense (see § 2) that juridical, ethical and religious feeling is a feeling and hence an experience of contents that have their root and their seat only in thought (*E* § 8 Remark).[17]

Thus, Hegel does not disparage the idea that human cognition begins in sensibility. He specifies the *kind* of sensibility that this cognition must always proceed from. It is human, thought-ful sensibility. There is indeed an inevitable, though not fallacious, circularity in our cognitive activity.[18]

In adding the inverse to the proposition that captures the empiricist stance, Hegel builds upon one of Leibniz's fundamental insights against Lockean empiricism. Hegel distinguishes aspects of *sensus* in a way that empiricism does not. There are sensations or 'impressions' in all living organisms, of course, but not all are also experienced sensations; not all are representations *for* the consciousness *in* which they take place. The more highly developed the inwardness, that is, the degree of subjectivity or self-relation, of a finite consciousness, the more its sensations attain the status of experienced sensations or perceptions proper (*Wahrnehmungen*).[19]

An experienced sensation is a sensation become meaningful. Its meaning does not issue from a sudden act of intellectual reflection applied to it. This would reduce it to an abstraction. Rather, an experienced sensation is one that has become real to the consciousness in which it is present. As explained in the first chapter of the *Phenomenology*, for sensations to become part of the flow of experience they have to become *for* (or present *to*) the unity of consciousness. Their meaning arises precisely by their acquiring such a relation to a center: meaningful sensations are those that have become 'mine.'[20] The kind of self-certainty into which we see sensibility evolve in the course of the phenomenological description is consciousness's certainty about its own knowing and not, as naively assumed in the beginning, about its alleged object. Toward the end of the movement of sensible consciousness, the object becomes inessential. Truth belongs to it now only insofar as it is an object *for* knowing consciousness:

> When we compare the relation in which *knowing* and the *object* first came on the scene, with the relation in which they now stand in this result, we find that it is reversed. The object . . . is now the unessential of sense-certainty, . . . the certainty is now present in the opposite, namely in knowing. . . . The truth [of this certainty] is in the object as *my* object, or in the *meaning*, the object is, because *I* know of it (*GW* 9, 66/Miller 61).[21]

In the *Encyclopaedia* introduction, Hegel relies on the conception of a fundamental interpenetration of human sensible and intellectual activity in order to distance himself both from romantic and rationalist theories of knowledge. The Romantics' aversion to conceptualization, which they denounce as an abstraction from the concreteness of the senses, a depletion of experience, a slaying of life, is premised upon their own reductionist understanding of intellectual activity. They view the latter as an empty mechanism, an endlessly repeated algorithm, a form devoid of matter. They cast concepts as threats to the alleged virginal truth of mere representations, for example, to the assumed 'authenticity' of religious ecstasy or aesthetic intuition. But religious or aesthetic representations, Hegel counters, are not present in mere consciousness.

They rather exist only in and for human consciousness, that is, they embody forms of human thought.

Rationalism, in its turn, follows a logic only apparently antithetical to that of the Romantics. In its emphatic reliance on intellect's powers of abstraction, rationalism tends to ignore that common concepts are meaningful only as functions of non-conceptual representations or pre-conceptual thoughts. The rationalist extols inferential and calculative thinking (to which Hegel often refers as 'ratiocination', *das Raesonnieren*). Rationalism recognizes only (correct) judgment as the embodiment of truth. But the kind of thinking that 'brings about the humanity of what is human' must be distinguished from the kind for which it is a necessary condition, namely thinking that thinks about the first, or reflection (*das Nachdenken*).[22] To assume that non-conceptual contents of consciousness are heterogeneous in kind from concepts, and that the former contain no degree of knowledge whatsoever apart from their synthesis with the latter, is analogous to assuming that belief in the existence of god could not occur without familiarity with the ontological proof, or that digestion could not take place without previous study of human physiology.[23]

These preliminary considerations of Hegel's aim at overcoming cognitive reductionism—whether of the Romantic or rationalist persuasion. This he attains through the (inherently Aristotelian) recognition that no representation can be a mere form or a mere content of consciousness, but must rather be both at once. The distinction between thinking as formal activity on the one hand, and its content (a representation, an intuition and so forth) on the other, is only useful as a methodological device:

> [T]he *content* that fills our consciousness is what makes up the *determinacy* of our feelings, intuitions, images, and representations, of our purposes, duties, etc., and of our thoughts and concepts. Hence . . . [such] content . . . remains *one and the same,* whether it be . . . *only* felt, or felt . . . with an admixture of thoughts, or thought quite *without any admixture*. In any one of these forms . . . the content is *object* of consciousness. But in this objectivity the *determinacies of these forms join themselves onto the content*; with the result that each of these forms seems to give rise to a particular object, and that what is in-itself the same can look like a diverse content (*E* § 3).

On account of this incessant process by which formal determinations of consciousness affect its contents, representations in general are best thought of as form-contents of consciousness. Hegel's notion of human experience in general (*Erfahrung*) refers to the whole of these form-contents.

It is precisely in the principles of Hegel's overall account of experience that both his debt to Aristotle and his departure from him are most evident. The debt lies in the logical account of experience; the departure, in the historical-developmental conception of it.

The movement of experiencing consciousness displayed in the *Phenomenology* is not a pandemonium of wandering images, shifting perceptions or fleeting notions. It unfolds according to a describable logical pattern—the logic of thought itself. As a unitary whole, the movement is substantivized as '(the) consciousness' (*das Bewusstsein*). As noted above, just as the essential nature of anything is expressed by its concept, so also the essence of the movement of thought is captured by the concept most adequate to it. This concept, however, is not given *ab aeternitate*. It is arrived at through spirit's self-experience. Hegel describes the latter, in the *Encyclopaedia*'s Subjective Spirit, in terms of self-differentiation. In the Anthropology, this self-differentiation is the motor for the development of the natural soul into the ego, 'the *lightning* which strikes through the natural soul and consumes its naturality';[24] in the Phenomenology of Spirit, it is the principle of consciousness's development into reason; in the Psychology, of the evolution of spirit from intelligence into will and freedom.

As stated in the *Lectures on the History of Philosophy*, the series of phases through which spirit passes may be described as a succession of its self-particularizations (diremptions). In its form as consciousness, the fundamental particularization of spirit consists of its splitting up into externality and inwardness. This is a diremption by which consciousness takes some of its representations to originate from a separate source, while it takes others to belong to itself. Out of this original diremption (*Ur-theil*) develop other divisions, most prominently that between 'real' (external world-based) and 'apparent' (internal world-based) representations. But these seemingly mutually exclusive kinds of representation (either external or internal, either real or apparent) are dialectically opposite sides of one experience. In § 3 of the *Encyclopaedia* Hegel is insistent about the fact that one content of consciousness may take up many, even 'opposite' forms (as feeling, concept, intuition, but also as external, internal, real, apparent and so on) thereby giving rise to seemingly different contents: 'each of these forms seems to give rise to a particular object, and . . . what is in-itself the same can look like a diverse content.' Modern philosophy often succumbs to the misconception that differences in thought-forms are differences in thought-contents. Categories are then said to refer to contents utterly different from the referents of perceptions, or objects of the intellect are thought of as wholly heterogeneous with objects of sensibility. More generally, 'real' sense experience is misunderstood as referring to an utterly different world than that of 'mere' conceptual knowledge.[25] Hegel counters that both real perceptions and conceptual representations simply result from the incessant 'translation' of the same experiential content from one form into the other. Conceptual forms are the ones that confer meaning to all other forms: 'the genuine *content* of our consciousness is *preserved* when it is translated into the form of thought and concept, or is actually placed for the first time in its proper light by this translation.'[26]

To take the most primitive of representations as an example, even the truth of a sensation can ultimately be provided only by a concept. Every sensation has an external dimension (it is caused by an external agent and it consists of a physiological process), as well as an internal one (it is an event exclusively in me); and while it is mere appearance (it merely depends upon my sensibility), it is also actual (it does take place). Thus, grasping the nature of sensation implies grasping that it is outer and inner appearance (*Erscheinung*), outer and inner actuality (*Wirklichkeit*), and the unity of this appearance and this actuality.

Hegel's theory of representations as form-contents of consciousness preserves basic insights from Aristotle's account of *psyche*. In the first book of *De Anima*, the affections (or attributes) of the soul appear as having the same double nature as Hegel's 'general representations'. The Greek philosopher presents the affections of the soul as *logoi enuloi* ('enmattered accounts'[27] or 'forms or notions realized in matter'[28]). He states that in order to do full justice to the nature of the soul, its affects must be accounted for simultaneously 'by the physicist' and 'by the dialectician.' The physicist will explain the matter, the dialectician the form, of the soul's affections. Neither account alone is able to provide the truth about *psyche*, as its affections are form and matter at once. Like all other objects of rational contemplation, a soul's affection truly exists only as a composite of matter and form. In the first chapter of the first book, Aristotle explains:

> [T]he attributes of the soul appear to be all conjoined with body. . . . If this be so, the attributes are evidently forms or notions realised in matter [logoi enuloi]. Hence they must be defined accordingly. . . . Anger, for instance, would be defined by the dialectician as desire

> for retaliation or the like, by the physicist as a ferment of the blood or heat which is about the heart: the one of them gives the matter, the other the form or notion. For the notion is the form of the thing, but this notion, if it is to be, must be realised in matter of a particular kind (*De Anima* 403 a 15–b 3).

The same applies, according to the Stagirite, to an adequate account of virtually every object of knowledge: the dialectician may define a house as a shelter from natural calamities, but a physicist may call it with the same legitimacy an assemblage of bricks and timber. The adequate concept of 'house,' however, contains both definitions in their necessary interdependency, and teleological reason grasps the latter as a unity. Neither every kind of shelter, nor random heaps of brick and timber do qualify as houses, but only those collections of brick and timber do that are structured towards the end of providing shelter for humans.

As Aristotle's choice of examples shows, the teleological notion around which his argument is built is evidently not intended as an external goal of the entity it helps explain, but rather as an end intrinsic to it. In Hegelian terms, this inward 'end' is precisely the concept of the entity in question: its fully (or 'ideally') developed state. Even for Hegel, the latter is reached only to the extent that the concept in question is 'realized in matter of a particular kind.'

Hegel's main concern is to show how this realization is possible, not only for representations in general, but for mind itself. Indeed, Aristotle's treatise already points in this speculative direction. It shows how not only every object of knowledge and every affection of the soul, but the very substance (*ousia*) that knows, namely *psyche* itself, can only be fully grasped in accordance with this same principle. In the second book of *De Anima*, the principle by which life and then mind become actual in matter is specified not simply as *eidos* (form or idea) but as *entelecheia*, that is, as internal developmental goal of the body or, as the term is often translated, its 'completion': 'soul is substance in the sense that it is the form of a natural body having in it the capacity of life. Such substance is actuality [entelecheia]. The soul, therefore, is the actuality of a body as above characterized.'[29]

2.2 Historical subjectivity and absolute subject matter

The *Phenomenology of Spirit* can be described as a reflection of the progression of thinking (as conscious being: *Bewusst-sein*) from its first sensing and perceiving stages to its culmination as absolute knowing. Using the language of the *Encyclopaedia* one could say that the *Phenomenology* shows how the contents of representative thinking as such (the generic content of consciousness) are natural and social phenomena whose grasp (*Begreifen*) is first made possible by their articulation in conceptual form (*begreifendes Denken*). It is only in concepts that the phenomena of consciousness acquire meaning for it. Since philosophy is the purest form of conceptual cognition, philosophy can be defined as consciousness's reflection upon its own experience. This reflection is, then, the source of meaning *par excellence*. Moreover, since the experience reflected upon has taken place through the mediation of various forms of thought, then the subject matter of philosophy is ultimately thought itself. Thus, philosophic science is essentially speculative reflection.

Hegel, of course, is not the first to identify objects of knowledge with contents of consciousness. Already Aristotle's discussion of real substances in the first book of *De Anima* treats objects and thoughts ('matter' and 'form') as indissolubly connected. The same identity can be said to be implicit in Kant's discussion of intuitions in terms of 'matter' for thoughts. The chiastic formulation of his statement: 'thoughts without content are empty, intuitions without concepts are blind'[30] implies first of all the synonymy of concepts and thoughts on the one hand, intuitions and contents on the other. Secondly, since intuitions and concepts are said to be the 'elements of all our knowledge,'[31] the statement can also be taken to imply that the proper object of cognition is a content of consciousness (in Kant's terminology, of mind: *Gemuet*), namely intuition.

Hegel differs from the Aristotelian and the Kantian accounts of mind mainly with respect to the historical (in the sense of *geschichtlich*)[32] framework in which he places the relations of mind to its contents. The Aristotelian soul, its capacity for affections, its degrees of awareness and perception, its passivity and ultimate activity as *nous* mark divisions and transformations inside a perennially self-identical nature of individual substances. Kant's theory of mind abstracts programmatically from genetic accounts of any sort, as he understands the latter to belong to a branch of inquiry separate from a theory of knowledge. According to Hegel, instead, long before conceptual cognition makes its appearance, consciousness already knows in some way and to differing degrees its own representations—be they called intuitions or otherwise. In this perspective, non-conceptual representations are not blind elements of a possible knowledge, but themselves kinds of knowledge.

In general terms, Hegel characterizes the first and simplest way in which consciousness is always already endowed with contents as its familiarity or acquaintance (*Bekanntschaft*) with phenomena of nature and spirit. This is a kind of cognition akin to the manner in which a pious individual may be said to know his religion, tribal people to know their society, or a child to know the physical laws of a toy. Cognition proper (*Erkenntnis*) by contrast is reflected, conceptual knowledge of objects that are already known—albeit in different ways. Philosophy itself is inquiry into the conceptual truth of that with which thinking is already acquainted.[33] In this sense, philosophic science (and, strictly speaking, all science in its theoretical part) is indeed a circular enterprise.

The Greater Logic's introductory essay: 'With What Must the Science Begin?'[34] as well as the introduction to the *Encyclopaedia* both offer arguments for the claim that philosophy (which, it shall be recalled, Hegel identifies with the inquiry into what is true) is inevitably circular without being fallacious. After all, every valid deductive argument is ultimately circular. There are a bad and a true circularity, as there are a bad and a true infinity. Briefly put, the argument centers upon the consideration that a beginning in thought cannot be simply immediate, and thus cannot arise *ex nihilo*, because all thinking is essentially mediation. Thus, thought's beginning is mediated and, if it is to be a genuine beginning, it cannot be mediated by anything other than itself. Philosophic inquiry without presuppositions will have to start from some form of thought. Put somewhat differently: the circularity consists of the fact that thinking both is pure mediation and has pure mediation for its subject matter. This circularity need not (and indeed cannot) be represented as a circle. Both the fact that reflection takes place at more than one logical level, and the fact that later philosophic principles sublate earlier ones in the history of philosophy suggest that a three-dimensional, spiral figure is a better image of the circularity of science. In a spiral figure, each spire returns to its beginnings but at a different level, its end point never coinciding with the point where it began, though corresponding to it.

Matters of nature and of spirit, then, are objects of thought (or contents of consciousness) long before the advent of conceptual cognition—let alone of philosophic speculation. The *Encyclopaedia*'s preliminary definition of philosophy as a '*thinking consideration* of objects'[35] means that philosophy is an inquiry into the conceptual truth of the sensed, perceived, imagined, intuited, desired, or otherwise represented objects of human experience.

A careful analysis of even the most primordial (so-called immediate) kind of experience, namely sensation, discloses the presence in it of a differentiation between the fleeting and the permanent, the meaningless and the meaningful. This shows that something else but sensation is at work in sensing consciousness, something that paves the way to the more sophisticated differentiation between appearance and reality. If Hegel introduces the *Encyclopaedia* by claiming that conceptual knowing does not differ in kind from all other human activities, this implies as well that it does not even differ in kind from the first stirrings of human sensing—at least insofar as conceptualizing and sensing refer to the same object: *experienced* actuality. Philosophic thinking aims precisely at demonstrating the in-principle correspondence of conceptual cognition with experienced actuality.

Grasping the dynamic and circular nature of knowing is indispensable to understanding the meaning and function of Hegel's 'absolute knowing' and its philosophic correlative, 'speculative philosophy.' First, they help clarify Hegel's insistence upon the fact that philosophy's having thoughts for its objects neither implies a lack of experiential content nor remoteness from what is real. The opposite is the case: as explained in the preface to the *Philosophy of Right*, philosophy is and can only be about actuality itself. Since it is cognition of that with which consciousness in general is already acquainted, philosophy contains 'the outward and inward world of consciousness'—and that is precisely how actuality is defined in the *Encyclopaedia* Logic: '[Philosophy's] content is nothing other than the one originally produced and self-producing in the sphere of living spirit, the content made into the *world*, the outer and inner world of consciousness—in other words, . . . [philosophy's] content is *actuality*. The first consciousness of this content we call *experience*.'[36]

Second, the envisioned congruence of knowing and actuality implied by the circular nature of knowing is what prompts Hegel's use of 'reason' (*Vernunft*) to denote both the subject and object of rational cognition: 'it has to be seen as the supreme and ultimate purpose of science to bring about, through the cognition of this concurrence [Uebereinstimmung], the reconciliation [Versoehnung] of the reason that is conscious of itself with the reason that *is*, with actuality.'[37] Spirit's absolute knowing[38] signifies the explicit grasp of this concurrence of self-conscious or 'subjective' with existing or 'objective' reason. And since existing reason is as much part of spirit as self-conscious reason, absolute knowing amounts to a self-knowing of spirit.

Through their respective means, art, revealed religion and speculative philosophy embody absolute, that is, self-knowing spirit. Each dominates as expressive form of spirit one of the main epochs in its history. Art provides a concrete intuition of the coincidence of subjectivity and objectivity in the production of the aesthetic work ('the beautiful').[39] This form of intuition is the dominant form of self-knowing in antiquity, and the aesthetic arts are the principal vehicle of this knowledge. Revealed religion provides a self-conscious representation of the same coincidence in form of knowledge revealed by spirit as god to spirit as man. While it replaces art as the supreme form of self-knowing after the decline of antiquity, its own predominance eventually recedes, marking the advent of modernity.[40] Eventually, speculative philosophy grasps and enunciates explicitly the principle immanent to the other forms of absolute knowing, namely the unity of objective actuality and subjective thinking. Philosophic knowing, in other words, provides the conceptualization of the same congruence captured by aesthetic intuition and religious representation: 'This science [of philosophy] is . . . the unity of art and religion . . . elevated to *self-conscious thinking*. This knowing is thus the *concept* of art and religion cognized through thinking.'[41] It is the dominant form of absolute knowing in the modern world.

One of the most far-reaching consequences of the theory of absolute spirit and knowing sketched out here in broad strokes is Hegel's rejection of normativism in practical philosophy. In the introduction to the *Encyclopaedia,* he himself draws attention to the connection between dualistic presuppositions in theoretical philosophy on the one hand, and the establishment of ideal, unattainable norms in practical philosophy on the other:

> However, the severing of actuality from the Idea is particularly dear to the understanding, which regards the dreams that are its abstractions as something genuine, and is all conceited about the *ought* that it likes to prescribe, especially in the political field—as if the world had waited for it, in order to learn how it *ought* to be, but is not.[42]

Surprisingly, contemporary interpretations of Hegel attribute to him precisely the theoretical move he criticizes so explicitly. The claim is being made, for example, that Hegel construes the transition from knowledge of the objective world to knowledge of subjectivity mainly in terms of a transition from 'factual' to 'normative' consciousness. Even more radically, some interpreters maintain that mind's relation to objectivity in general, if it is to be an intelligible relation at all, must ultimately be essentially 'normative.'[43] Others claim that Hegel's absolute Idea is best interpreted as a 'normative whole of the "space of reasons".'[44] Readings such as these are due to an important philosophical *impetus*. Their intention would seem to be a broadening of contemporary epistemological inquiry from its narrow concern with the subject–object constellation to a more complex one in which relations among subjects mediate their relations to the object. The precise meaning and implications of this thesis would merit a broader treatment than is warranted here. What is doubtful is, however, the appeal to Hegel as corroboration of the thesis. Hegel's approach to the problem of knowledge includes indeed both kinds of relations at once: it purports to account for theoretical and practical cognition, for mind and will, and it may not fully account for one without the other. As seen above, Hegel explains thought's relation to objectivity by way of thought's internal diremption, that is, ultimately by way of subjectivity's relation to itself. The ethical dimension of this is made explicit in (among other places) the *Philosophy of Right*, where the full account of categories that express subjects' relations to objects is made possible only by an exposition of relations among subjects. 'Property' in general, for example, includes subjects' acquisition, use and alienation of the object, but 'rightful property' can only be grasped in the light of 'contract,' a relation of subjects.[45] Contrary to the assumptions of contemporary analytic interpreters of Hegel, however, relations among subjects (as well as their archetype: subjectivity's relation to itself) are not primarily normative relations. In the juridical and political realm, for example, they are relations inside objective spirit *as it exists*. For better or worse—and this could well be the least productive, least intellectually attractive aspect of his philosophizing—Hegel denies the *philosophical* relevance of the category of the 'ought to be,' except as a topic whose illusory and contingent character is the only thing worth philosophizing about. Explicit statements from the introduction to the *Encyclopaedia*, in addition to those already discussed from the *Philosophy of Right* and innumerable others, speak for themselves against the legitimacy of attributing to Hegel a 'normative discourse.' In closing the Remark to § 6 of the *Encyclopaedia*, he concedes a sort of worldly validity to morality-based critical ratiocination: 'When the understanding turns against . . . objects, institutions, situations, etc., with the "ought" . . . it may very well be in the right and . . . find much that does not correspond to correct universal determinations.' But he hastens to add that such considerations are outside the scope of philosophic science. The latter 'deals only with the Idea, which is not so impotent as that it merely ought to be and were not actual.' The establishment of norms simply does not figure in philosophy's 'thinking consideration' of actuality—unless such establishment is already part of actuality itself. Hegel even goes so far as to mock the notion of norms by identifying them with 'chimeras' and 'phantoms' which, needless to say, philosophy has no business dealing with. In the actuality that it grasps, philosophic spirit grasps its own realization. The philosophical Idea is always infinitely ahead of all normativity: it is thought that already coincides with what is true (and right and beautiful) in spirit's actuality.[46]

Hegel's rejection of prescriptivism is rooted, then, in the logical and metaphysical foundations of his thought. An in-principle contraposition of 'is' and 'ought' presupposes the impossibility of the absolute identity of actuality and ideality. If this identity, however, is postulated as intelligible and demonstrated as necessary (as in Hegel's brand of absolute idealism) then uncovering discrepancies between the structure of reality and that of its concept is a useful diagnostic tool for philosophizing, but hardly the philosophic truth on the matter. For example, a study of the inner workings of finite cognition has for Hegel mainly propedeutic function. Philosophy's concern cannot be just with the exposition of finite forms and contents of thought, as its goal is to provide a grasp of thinking itself as form of forms. Borrowing Aristotelian terminology, one may reformulate Hegel's concern here by saying that a study of *psyche* is of philosophic interest as necessary prolegomenon to an investigation of *nous*, the ultimate concept of *psyche* itself. To reduce philosophy to an analysis of various functions of *psyche* excluding its function as active *nous* is to renounce the scientific, truth-generating function of philosophy.

Hegel's criticism of self-limiting approaches to knowledge is best understood via his criticism of Kant's conception of rationality. This criticism plays an essential role in paving the way for Hegel's own theory of speculative knowing and of the subject of this knowing: the Concept (*der Begriff*). The next section (2.3) sets forth Hegel's interpretation of basic elements of Kant's conception of knowledge. It addresses Kant's focus on finite knowing, his allegedly rigid distinction of concept and intuition as elements of cognition, as well as of what Hegel sees as a conflation of reason and understanding (as 'faculties') despite their formal separation in Kant's explicit doctrine.

2.3 Reason and the rational[47]

True cognition presupposes for Hegel that the movement of knowing be adequate to its different types of objects, or that the form of knowing be adequate to its content. If thinking relates itself to objects limited and conditioned by other limited objects, then it is capable of forming true propositions of the understanding. But if thinking relates to objects that are unlimited and unconditioned, its activity as understanding becomes insufficient to grasp such objects in their wholeness, that is, in their truth. In the attempt to apply categories of the understanding to unlimited and unconditioned ('infinite') contents, thinking runs the risk of perverting what is true into 'untruth.'[48]

To conclude from this, however, as Kant and Jacobi do, that the attempt to grasp the unconditioned necessarily leads to hopelessly contradictory results, thus making it by definition into the un-knowable, constitutes for Hegel a *non sequitur*. This false conclusion is based on the assumption, common both to Kant and his critics, that human thought, precisely because it is human, is *ipso facto* an activity of finitization. In critical philosophy,

> to *grasp* an object means nothing more than to grasp it in the form of something *conditioned* and *mediated*. . . . In [Jacobi's] polemic, knowing is interpreted only as knowing of the finite, as the thinking progression through *series* from *conditioned* to *conditioned*. . . . To explain and to grasp, therefore, means to show something as *mediated* through *another*; hence, all content is only *particular*, *dependent*, and *finite* (*E* § 62 and Remark).[49]

While Kant, in accordance with this assumption, classifies notions of infinite objects as mere postulates, Hegel affirms that infinite objects may actually be grasped through concepts of reason. It is indeed a general claim of Hegel's to be able to show in the system's unfolding from nature to absolute spirit that human thinking, despite its being rooted in the finitude that is nature, can do justice to infinite objects, that is, that it can comprehend them conceptually. Sensible or mystical intuition, faith, or immediate, common-sense acquaintance with the world[50] are often invoked as the only alternatives to the shortcomings of the understanding. Hegel, instead, argues that infinite objects can be grasped conceptually, though not through concepts of the understanding.

In the Greater Logic, Hegel credits Kant for having 'reclaimed the expression *idea* for the *concept of reason*'[51] while in common parlance and in pre-Kantian philosophy 'ideas' have been conflated with 'concepts' or 'representations' all along. By claiming, however, that concepts of reason do not provide knowledge of the essence of appearances, Kant has restricted cognitive activity to a mere ordering of experience instead of grasping the truth in it. In criticizing Kant's ban of concepts of reason from knowledge of what is actual in favor of 'concepts of the understanding' (*Verstandesbegriffe*), Hegel uses the latter term to refer now to empirical or common concepts and now to the transcendental categories.[52] The first kind are classifications of perceptions or intuitions, the second kind are determinations of experience, also referred to as 'determinations of the understanding' (*Verstandesbestimmungen*).

Hegel prefers to reserve the term *Begriff* (without qualification) for contents determined by reason (*Vernunft*). One difference between concepts of the understanding and concepts of reason is that the former result from mediation with something that differs from them or, to use a Kantian term, they are discursive, while the latter are not. Concepts of reason show therefore an affinity and, Hegel insists, only an affinity with intuitions, in that both are non-mediated, non-discursive contents of consciousness.

An appreciation of Hegel's differentiated uses of concept, understanding and reason requires revisiting his reading of Descartes' as well as Kant's conceptions of rationality.

(i) Self-assertion and self-confinement of reason

In § 64 of the *Encyclopaedia*, Hegel identifies in Descartes' principle: '*cogito, sum*' the modern prototype of rational though non-discursive cognition. This 'proposition of immediate knowing', as he calls it in the Remark, does not express either a syllogism, blind faith, or sensory intuition, but rather rational knowledge. The self-certainty of thought is a concept of reason. All propositions of modern philosophy that assert the apodictic necessity of the agreement of certain representations with our experience are ultimately rooted in the Cartesian principle, namely the rational self-comprehension of human thinking.

In the main text of this section, Hegel outlines the 'speculative core' of the Cartesian *cogito* in the following way: every representation whose content is unconditioned or 'infinite'—for example, god, eternity, the ego or thinking itself—is 'immediately and inseparably combined' with 'the certainty of its *being*.'[53] In this sense, as long as it is not understood as proving a transcendent existence (that is, an existence dependent upon and limited by what is being transcended), the ontological argument states an indubitable truth.

Admittedly, the ways in which this speculative principle has found expression in the history of philosophy have often been (to use Hegel's expression) 'unphilosophical.' What is actually the self-certainty of thinking has been disguised as certainty of a transcendent existence, of the being-there of an external world, or even, in versions verging on the bizarre, of the thinker's own body, as in Friedrich Jacobi's 'Through faith we know that we have a body.'[54] According to Hegel, the rational core common to all these conceptions is the recognition 'that the nature of thought or of subjectivity implies that they are inseparable from being or from objectivity.'[55]

With the assertion that the grounding principle of modern philosophy is a form of non-discursive knowing, Hegel may appear to be making the intellectual intuition of mysticism into the cornerstone of philosophic cognition. He himself confronts this interpretation in a lengthy Addition to § 82. Here we find an explicit denial that the *concept* of thought's self-certainty is the same as an intellectual *intuition*. Both indeed 'transcend the understanding,' but while intellectual intuition is non-conceptual and thus unintelligible, the self-certainty of thought is grasped by reason. The intended content of intellectual intuition and of a concept of reason may well be the same, but only the latter provides the comprehensibility of that content:

> [T]he meaning of the speculative is to be understood as being the same as what used in earlier times to be called 'mystical', especially with regard to religious consciousness and its content. . . . Thus, everything rational can equally be called 'mystical'; but this only amounts to saying that it transcends the understanding. It does not at all imply that what is so spoken of must be considered inaccessible to thinking and incomprehensible (*E* § 82 Addition).

Thought's grasp of its own existence cannot be classified as one among many forms acquired by consciousness's contents but must rather be understood as the supreme form of those forms. Descartes' proposition expresses the notion of *noesis noeseos*[56] at the level of human thought. It expresses the actuality of 'thinking *itself as form*.'[57]

In relating speculatively to an object, knowing also relates to itself. In this kind of self-reflective cognition, as in the authentic beginning of thought discussed by Hegel at the onset of the Greater Logic, the difference between immediacy and mediation is sublated.[58] In order to fully understand Hegel's emphasis on the necessity of this sublation it is helpful to revisit, by contrast, Kant's effort at keeping concepts logically and epistemologically separate from intuitions.

In the introduction to the Transcendental Dialectic of the *Critique of Pure Reason*, Kant summarizes the 'hierarchy'[59] of kinds of representation that he has made use of throughout the Critique. Under the highest kind *repraesentatio* we are to subsume first of all conscious representations (*perceptiones*). Insofar as conscious representations are mere modifications of the representing subject, they are called sensations (*sensationes*); insofar as they contain objectivity, they are called cognitions (*cognitiones*). A cognition can in turn be either immediately related to an object, in which case it is an intuition (*intuitus*), or it can be indirectly related to objects, namely by means of a mark common to them—then it is a concept (*conceptus*). For their part, concepts can be either empirical or pure. Pure concepts originate in the understanding alone. (In this passage, Kant appears to be neglecting a mention of his just as fundamental distinction between empirical and pure intuition.) Finally, a concept whose content consists solely of pure concepts and thus can have no reference to any possible experience is called 'the *idea* or the concept of reason.'[60]

Thus, in this text the fundamental distinction between intuition and concept is explained primarily as a distinction between immediate and mediated knowledge (*cognitio*). This is in itself remarkable because in the introduction to the Transcendental Logic Kant has stated that knowledge can only arise from the interplay or synthesis of intuition and concept, and that it can never be embodied in one of them alone: 'Intuition and concepts therefore constitute the elements of all our cognition, so that neither concepts without intuition . . . nor intuition without concepts can yield a cognition'[61] and, a few lines later, more explicitly: 'Only from their unification can cognition arise.'[62]

In Kant's *Logic*, however, we find concepts as well as intuitions classified again as in the Transcendental Dialectic, namely as cognitions in their own right: 'All cognitions, that is, all representations consciously referred to an object, are either *intuitions* or *concepts*.'[63]

The relationship and distinction between intuition and concept is thus more complex than is suggested by the famous passages introducing the Transcendental Logic. While relying on the texts just mentioned, the following concise reconstruction of this complex relation makes use of further sections of the *Critique of Pure Reason*, in particular the Introduction,[64] the Metaphysical Exposition of the concept of space,[65] and the Transcendental Deduction of the categories.[66]

For cognition of any kind to occur, objects must first of all be 'given' to the mind (*Gemuet*). Cognition as *intuitus* would then consist in representing such 'givens' immediately, thus as wholes, *ergo* as singularities. In the Transcendental Dialectic, Kant writes that intuition 'is immediately related to the object and is singular.'[67] Due to its immediacy, however, intuition cannot (from an epistemological perspective) be distinguished from its object. Accordingly, intuitions must be singular because their objects are. Furthermore, singularity implies lack of determinacy—at least in the common acceptation of the latter as negative relation to different species of the same *genus*. This indeterminacy of the object of intuition in Kant is the equivalent of the infinity of the object of reason in Hegel.

Kant, then, contrasts intuitive cognition with cognition as *conceptus*. The latter is a representation of objects (or 'givens') through a common mark abstracted from them and fixed in the concept. In Kant's *Logic*, the general nature (*Allgemeinheit*) of concepts is identified with their discursivity and contrasted with the singular nature (*Einzelnheit*) of intuition. Thinking, moreover, is identified with the discursivity of concepts: 'Intuition is a singular representation (*represaentatio singularis*), the concept is a general (*repraesentatio per notas communes*) or reflected representation (*repraesentatio discursiva*). Cognition through concepts is called thinking (*cognitio discursiva*).'[68]

From these definitions follows that (a) no concept relates to objects in an immediate manner; therefore (b) no concept relates to a singular object (or else it would be a non-discursive representation, that is, an intuition); and thus (c) no concept can refer to an object with infinite determinations, or an indeterminate object.

In the Metaphysical Exposition of space, whose goal is to prove that space cannot originally be a concept but must be an intuition, Kant indeed states explicitly that a concept cannot contain an infinite number of representations but can only be superordinate to them.[69] It follows that concepts always represent classes of objects. They are 'discursive,' that is, abstracting, abridging and indirect representations. Moreover, the proper objects or 'givens' from which they abstract are intuitions: 'In whatever way and through whatever means a cognition may relate to objects, that through which it relates immediately to them, and at which all thought as a means is directed, is intuition.'[70] Sidestepping the difficult question of how this notion of aim-directed thinking is to be integrated into the broader context of Kant's theoretical philosophy, this statement seems to imply the following consequence. On account of its singularity, an intuition can only be the object of another intuition, not of a concept. Concepts can thus only relate to classes of intuitions which they represent by means of common marks.

The argument of the Metaphysical Exposition shows in an exemplary fashion that for Kant the unsuitability of certain representations to be originally concepts is due precisely to their involving infinity. The argument can be summarized as follows. If space were originally a concept, it would be *per definitionem* discursive, that is, it would have to refer to a plurality of spaces by means of a common mark. Accordingly, any concept of space presupposes a given plurality of distinguishable spaces. But these spaces can only be distinguished spatially from one another. Thus, a plurality of spaces presupposes in turn the representation of a singular, boundless space. According to the hierarchy of representational kinds made explicit in the Transcendental Dialectic, a representation of this latter kind can only be an intuition. And since (as remarked by Hegel in the *Encyclopaedia*)[71] understanding is an activity of finitization, Kant continues: '[Space] is essentially single; the manifold in it, thus also the general concept of spaces in general, rests merely on limitations.'[72] Space is thus an intuition that can be *rationally comprehended* in its singularity and infinity, though it can only be *understood* by division into a plurality of spaces and by abstraction of a common mark from them.

The difficulties that result from Kant's inconsistent classification of intuition and concept, on the one hand as modes, on the other hand as elements of cognition[73] get compounded by the further distinction he introduces between form and content of intuition, or between pure-sensible and empirical-sensible intuition. We are told in the Transcendental Logic that human intuition can only be sensible. Our sensibility consists of the capacity to be affected through sensations, thanks to the 'actual presence of the object'[74] that enables us to have representations. But since the so-called 'undetermined object,' that is, the '*appearance*' given to us through sensation,[75] exhibits order, and since the order of sensations cannot in its turn be a sensation, the philosopher must conclude that, in addition to the empirical content of our sensible intuition, we are endowed with a pure, non-empirical form of it.[76]

Whereas both form and content, as elements of intuition, should be characterized by immediacy, only pure-sensible intuition is said to take place with *a priori* immediacy in the human mind: 'extension and form . . . belong to the pure intuition, which occurs a priori, even without an actual object of the senses or sensibility, as a mere form of sensibility in the mind.'[77] By contrast, empirical-sensible intuition is said to take place through the mediation of our sensibility: 'The effect of an object on the capacity for representation, insofar as we are affected by it, is sensation. That intuition that is related to the object through sensation is called empirical.'[78]

The juxtaposition of these passages paints an inconsistent, if not paradoxical picture of the relation of knowing to its object. First, in this picture concepts and intuitions are classified now as types of cognition in their own right and now merely as elements of cognition proper.

Furthermore, whether intuition is meant as cognitive mode or mere element of cognition, it is said both to lie immediately in us, in its aspect as thought-form, and to reach us mediately, namely through sensibility, in its aspect as thought-content.[79]

(ii) Existing reason

In his early essay *Faith and Knowledge* (1802)[80] Hegel criticizes Kant's deduction of the categories in the *Critique of Pure Reason*. He maintains that intuition and concept in Kant's philosophy are *de facto* less heterogeneous than the explicit doctrine states.

The distinction of intuition and concept is already problematic in the Introduction to the *Critique of Pure Reason*. Here Kant discusses the epistemic nature of the principles of the sciences. These principles, he writes, are *a priori* syntheses of a thinking activity that 'adds' (*hinzutut*)[81] intuitions to concepts. Neither do such intuitions have their source in external experience, nor can the necessity of their connection with concepts be deduced from an analysis of the latter. Their connection (*Verknuepfung*) rather precedes any and all conceptual analysis. In physics, for example, the thought of permanence is said by Kant to adhere necessarily to the concept of matter in virtue of an *a priori* synthesis of the intuition of quantitative sameness with the concept of a 'bodily world' in motion. Kant contrasts this *a priori* synthesis to the connection of the notion of 'space-filling' with the concept of matter, a connection he claims to be one of analytic entailment.

On the status of synthetic *a priori* cognitions, Kant writes:

> But the question is not what we *should* think in addition to the given concept, but what we *actually* think in it, though only obscurely, and there it is manifest that the predicate certainly adheres to those concepts necessarily, though not as thought in the concept itself, but by means of an intuition that must be added to the concept (*CPR* B 17).

The obscure notion of such 'obscure thoughts' acting as fundamental principles recurs, according to Hegel's reading, in Kant's idea of the 'spontaneity of a capacity for representation' (*Spontaneitaet der Vorstellungskraft*),[82] later referred to also as 'pure' or 'original apperception' (*reine* or *urspruengliche Apperzeption*).[83] This spontaneity, Kant adds for clarification, is 'the self-consciousness' that produces the representation 'I think.'[84] Hegel argues that this idea does not emerge only at the end of the *Critique of Pure Reason* and with a merely regulative function. It plays rather a positive, constitutive role already in the Transcendental Analytic, namely as the ground of both intuition and understanding. The unity that this ground represents is called by Kant a transcendental idea, a representation that can be neither mere intuition nor mere concept of the understanding, since it represents precisely the unity of both. In the same way in which the categories constitute the unity of our experience, so transcendental ideas constitute the unity of our knowledge as a whole. Translated into Hegel's terminology: if 'intuition' signifies the immediacy or identity of representation and object and 'concept' indicates their mediation or difference, then the original unity of apperception signifies the original identity of identity and difference.[85] Such an identity expresses for Hegel a concept of reason *par excellence*, or 'the rational' (*das Vernuenftige*) as such.

Hegel uses Kant's criticism of the ontological proof of god's existence in order to illustrate the dead end entered by attempts to grasp objects of reason, or the rational, through concepts of the understanding. He writes that while Kant at first denounces 'the highest Idea . . . as if it were empty musing, nothing but an unnatural scholastic trick for conjuring reality out of concepts,'[86] he ultimately establishes this same idea as a necessary subjective postulate of pure practical reason.

In Hegel's view, the reason why Kant assigns to the idea, or original unity of concept and object, such an ambiguous role lies in the fact that he implicitly applies the same notion, 'concept,' equally to contents of the understanding and to contents of reason. Hegel does not contradict Kant's argument that the reality of one hundred dollars cannot be 'extracted' from the concept of one hundred dollars, for this latter concept consists only of the abstraction of common marks from sensible-empirical intuition—a classificatory operation that presupposes, as Kant rightly stresses, the 'actual presence of the object.'[87] But concepts of reason are representations of unconditioned ('infinite') objects, not of classes of perceivable ones. What is true of one hundred dollars does not hold true for freedom or for the I:

> This cognition may be satisfactory enough within its own field. But . . . another circle of *objects* shows up that are not part of this field: *freedom, spirit, god*.[88] The reason that these are not to be found upon that soil is not because they do allegedly[89] not belong to experience. It is true that they are not experienced by the senses, but everything that is in consciousness at all is experienced. . . . The reason is that these objects present themselves directly as infinite with regard to their *content* (*E* § 8).

Like freedom, spirit, or god, also the (originally Cartesian) concept of a subjectivity that knows itself to be 'inseparable from being or from objectivity'[90] cannot be comprehended in terms of the understanding. And neither can self-consciousness, the shape in which consciousness 'makes a distinction, but one that at the same time is for consciousness not a distinction.'[91] According to this formulation, the concept of self-consciousness implies precisely that its subjective certainty is immediately identical with the objective truth it refers to.

Infinite objects of reason are not dealt with only in philosophy. An Addition in the 1830 *Encyclopaedia* states, for instance, that

> whatever goes beyond the determinacy of the understanding . . . occurs first in mathematics. For instance . . . in geometry . . . one must represent[92] the circumference of a circle to consist of an infinite number of infinitely small straight lines. Determinations that count as utterly diverse for the understanding (straight line and curve) are expressly posited here as identical.[93]

The 'expressed positing' of diverse determinations as identical is an act of reason. But the supreme object of reason is, of course, what is in itself rational. This is the 'I think . . .' that, according to Descartes, is immune to even divine deception, or according to Kant, is a 'vehicle of all concepts in general,'[94] a representation that 'must be able to accompany all my representations.'[95]

The representation 'I think . . .' is neither obtained by abstraction from a plurality of representations of 'I,' nor of 'thought,' nor of hypothetical objects filling the blank in the expression—as would be the case for an empirical representation. 'I think . . .' is also not intuited through sensible affection. Still, as for representations in general, its truth does depend upon its corresponding to a real experience of consciousness. In this case, the representation's correspondence is not with external experience but with the inner self-experience of the consciousness that thinks 'I think . . .'[96]

On the one hand, Hegel does share the conception that a necessary condition of human cognitions is their ultimate relatedness to experience—in Kant's words, the condition that 'all our cognition commences *with* experience' without thereby having to 'arise *from* experience.'[97] On the other hand, Hegel thinks that Kant's notion of experience is still reductive in that, at least in its explicit doctrine, it includes only experience based on affection by external objects. Philosophy's notion of experience, Hegel claims, is more comprehensive than this.

For example, even the certainty of the 'I' is based on experience, albeit the inner experience of consciousness. Thus, the concept of concepts includes more than empirical concepts and transcendental categories for the determination of external experience. It includes conceptual determinations of objects that, though not experienced through the senses, are experienced nonetheless: 'everything that is in consciousness at all is experienced. (This is even a tautological proposition).'[98]

Human experience thus includes the representation of having representations of objects. It includes, in other words, the representation of the thinking self. As subject and object of thought, this is a 'truly infinite' representation.

While the objectivity of contents of the understanding is a discursive result of the latter's activity, the objectivity of contents of reason (freedom, spirit, god, self-consciousness) is their immediate corollary. It is the kind of immediate objectivity that Kant assigns to mathematical entities: while the deductions of mathematics take place 'according to the principle of contradiction,' he writes in the introduction to the *Critique of Pure Reason,* mathematical principles can never 'be cognized from' that principle.[99]

The same applies, in Hegel's view, to concepts and objects of reason. The ontological argument, for example, expresses such an object of reason in the concept of divine perfection: the very concept carries with it immediately and apodictically the certainty and truth of divine existence. Despite the immediacy, the proof is an inference. It is not an act of faith or intuition. Its conclusion contains a speculative insight, though in the guise of religion. It is the closest approximation of absolute knowing attainable by the religiously alienated consciousness. For modern consciousness returning to itself out of its religious alienation, the thought of itself is equally bound, immediately and apodictically, with the certainty and truth of its own existence: *cogito, sum.* Here as above, the conclusion is reached by immediate logical inference and not by intuition. Neither side of this relation of thinking being (*Bewusstsein*) to being (*Sein*), or of subjectivity to objectivity, is in any substantial sense distinct from the other: thinking being has no certainty without its being, and being as such has no certainty without thinking being. Yet they differ in that they can and must be separated for analytical purposes: only thus is *cogitari* a premise and *esse* its conclusion. Thus, their identity is both immediate and mediated. The reality of the ego is indeed not analytically contained in the concept of the ego (as little, indeed, as the reality of one hundred thalers is contained in their concept), but the reality of the ego is identical with the act of conceiving the ego. The ego *is* thus *the concept* of itself.

2.4 Concepts of 'concept'

Hegel's 1802 criticism of Kant contains implicit assumptions on the nature of conceptual thinking that are largely consistent with his explicit treatment of *Begreifen* and *Begriff* in the Logic. Hegel's overcoming of Kant's epistemic dualism is predicated upon a radical revision of the concept of concept. This revision implies on the one hand a qualified return to an Aristotelian understanding of thinking as activity (*energeia*), on the other hand a qualified accommodation of contemporaneous (Romantic and Schellingian) reactions to empiricist and rationalistic theories of knowledge.

Before engaging the details of 'the Concept' as defined in the Logic, it will be useful to distinguish schematically three fundamental meanings of 'concept' used by Hegel, meanings that have already surfaced on occasion in this and the previous chapter. 'Concept' may refer to (i) a determination (or concept) of the understanding (*Verstandesbestimmung* or *Verstandesbegriff*), (ii) a concept of reason (*Vernunftbegriff*), and (iii) the Concept (*der Begriff*).

(i) Determinations of the understanding

As mentioned above (section 2.3) Hegel uses 'determination (concept) of the understanding' in more than one sense. One is that of 'empirical concept' consisting of the abstraction of common features from other contents of consciousness (impressions, intuitions, or other representations). Another, negatively critical use of this term denotes a category that, though appropriate for the disclosure of the empirical world, is being wrongly applied to non-empirical contents. Such are for example the Scholastics' ascription of being-there (*Dasein*) to god, or the attribution of simplicity or complexity to the soul. These represent precritical, merely ratiocinating ways 'of determining the Absolute by attaching predicates to it.'[100] Finally, Hegel also uses 'determinations (concepts) of the understanding' to refer to Kant's transcendental categories. He acknowledges that, contrary to his predecessors, Kant does subject to critical investigation 'the *concepts of the understanding* that are used in metaphysics.'[101] But he criticizes him for making these (here called *Verstandesbegriffe*) into the sole source of objectivity: '[According to Kant], the thought-determinations or *concepts of the understanding* make up the *objectivity* of the cognitions of experience.'[102]

It is worth noticing that, in all its variations, Hegel's term *Verstandesbestimmung* implies a twofold sense of the genitive case of *Verstand*, namely as objective genitive—a determination of objects *by* the understanding—and as subjective genitive—a determination *of* the understanding itself. In the objective connotation, the understanding determines, that is, circumscribes or finitizes, the infinite ('abstractly undetermined') content of consciousness. In considering the content of consciousness as in-itself infinite, Hegel relies on Leibniz's philosophical psychology, according to which 'at every moment there is in us an infinity of perceptions'[103] and 'since each distinct perception of the soul includes an infinity of confused perceptions . . . each soul knows the infinite—knows all—but confusedly.'[104] This is echoed already in Hegel's account of the natural soul in the Anthropology: 'the soul itself . . . is a *totality* of infinitely numerous . . . determinacies' and 'we are also *implicitly* a *world* of concrete content with an infinite periphery, and have within us a multitude of numberless relations and connections . . . even without our knowing of it.'[105]

At the level of mind, the function of the understanding is to determine (or finitize) both the indeterminacy (or infinity) of its objects as well as of subjectivity itself. Since mind is nothing apart from its contents, one can see why the determination of objects of consciousness is at the same time a self-determination of consciousness.

It is equally worth noticing Hegel's consistent choice, in this context, of *Bestimmung*, an act or process of determination, instead of *Bestimmtheit*, a state of determinacy. As all representations, concepts of the understanding are not fixed determinacies (not states) but rather dynamic determinations (phases or 'moments') of the activity of thinking. 'Determination' implies also that this movement of thinking is not merely a process reflecting or mirroring its objects, but a teleological activity carrying its end in itself. Already for Aristotle, the distinction between *kinesis* and *energeia* is a fundamental one. As defined in the *Metaphysics*, *energeia* (activity) transcends all kinds of *kineseis* (movements) analyzed in the *Physics*. The latter are inherently 'incomplete' (*ateles*) processes. By contrast, *energeia* (the kind of movement proper to thought) carries its own 'completion' (*entelechia*) within itself.[106] In the context of Hegel's theory of thinking, the inherent end of the activity of the understanding is the finitization of the otherwise infinite contents of consciousness.

(ii) Concepts of reason

Other types of contents of consciousness, by contrast, elude determination in this way. Comprehending them implies grasping their inherent 'infinity,' or self-referentiality. Knowing these contents is a form of self-knowing. The concept of freedom, for example, refers to mind itself in its form as will. Introducing the notion of 'right' as derived from that of 'will', the *Philosophy of Right* explains that by 'making freedom its object, mind's purpose is to be explicitly, as Idea, what the will is implicitly.'[107] Grasping these mind-contents calls for the employment of a cognitive function different from the abstractive-classificatory one. This function is reason (*Vernunft*), its generic object is the rational (*das Vernuenftige*) and the concepts in which it articulates itself may be called 'concepts of reason' (*Vernunftbegriffe*).[108]

Reason is not employed only in grasping self-determinations of mind. It is already employed in accounting for experiential objects that exist according to principles internal to them: from living and sensible matter, through feeling, self-feeling and conscious organisms, all the way to the existing self. One feature all these have in common is the particular nature of their movement, namely development (*Entwicklung*), a kind of movement whose principle, impulse or cause is internal to what develops. In this sense, all development is strictly speaking self-development. The development that characterizes objects of reason is *energeia* directed toward its own completion.[109]

Concepts of reason denote precisely the internal principles that distinguish self-developing objects. And since internal principles contain the completion (maturity) of the objects they inhere in (albeit in potential form), to have the adequate concept of such an object amounts to knowing its internal principle. This is why concepts of reason for Hegel denote both the proper subjective representation of the object as much as its objective, inner structuring principle:

> In accordance with these determinations,[110] thoughts can be called *objective* thoughts; and among them the forms . . . which are usually taken to be only forms *of conscious* thinking have to be counted too. . . . since thought seeks to form a concept of things, this concept . . . cannot consist in determinations and relationships that are alien and external to the things. As we said above, thinking things over leads to what is universal in them (*E* § 24 and Remark).

The reason why determinations of the understanding are inadequate to explain objects of reason lies in the self-distinguishing nature of the latter. These objects of outer and inner experience are not passive substrata for the determining action of the understanding. They are not only distinguishable (determinable) but also self-distinguishing (self-determining) contents of consciousness. In this sphere, 'genuine cognition of an object . . . has to be *such* that the object determines itself from within itself, and does not acquire its predicates in this [the understanding's] external way.'[111] Thus, concepts of reason refer to the objective internal principles that are the ground of self-distinction of organic, and among these, living, conscious and self-conscious entities. The concepts of the oak tree, of personhood or of the state denote primarily the internal *telos* that directs the development of each towards the actualization of its principle. The expression 'concept in-itself' refers to the not-yet actualized principle. The teleological unfolding of these objects according to their inner principle is the actualization of their concept. This movement is the 'concept-for-itself.'[112]

An early awareness of what Hegel calls the inadequacy of the understanding to grasp the rationality of living organisms can be detected in Aristotle's search for scientific criteria of classification of the living world. Among all physical characteristics and behaviors, Aristotle identifies reproductive mechanisms as providing the ultimate criteria of classification. By choosing reproduction, the philosopher (inquiring both as physicist and dialectician)[113] grounds his definition on how the animal itself determines (to use Hegel's words) its universality.[114] By taking reproduction rather than shape or habitat as classificatory criterion, the philosopher finds the concept of his object in the latter's self-defining activity.

A fully conscious employment of Hegel's criterion can be found in the young Marx's definition of the human being as species-being (*Gattungswesen*): 'Men can be distinguished from the animals by consciousness, by religion, or by whatever one wants. They begin to distinguish themselves from the animals as soon as they begin to *produce* their means of life.' Even for the historical materialist, moreover, this productive activity does not have just a material function or merely material results. As humans' self-distinction from other species, it is a self-determination of life in specifically human form: 'This form of production is not to be considered solely as a reproduction of the physical existence of the individuals. Rather, it is a distinctive . . . form of expressing their life, a distinctive *form of life* of those very individuals.'[115]

(iii) A self-positing concept

The third use of 'concept' will be investigated in a chapter dedicated to it (Chapter 3). At this juncture, it will suffice to highlight its peculiarity by contrasting it with the previous two meanings of 'concept.' In its third use, 'concept' is preceded by the singular form of the determinate article: *der Begriff*. Thus, it refers to one and only one content of consciousness. The Concept[116] does not refer to a class of objects by means of a feature common to all and is therefore not discursive. It also does not circumscribe an otherwise infinite content and is thereby not the finitizing determination of an undetermined object. The Concept is rather the archetype of concepts of reason. Like these, it denotes the internal organizing principle of a self-distinguishing being. Unlike them, however, the Concept's object is none other than itself. Furthermore, it defines itself not just in practice (for example by growth, reproduction, or production of its forms of existence) but through an activity that is theoretical and practical at once: self-knowing and self-willing. Hegel says that the Concept 'posits' (*setzt*) itself because its existence coincides with its self-knowledge and self-will. The Concept is nothing apart from this knowing and willing. It does not come to grasp and to will what it already is. Rather, it becomes what it grasps and wills itself to be. It is self-conscious subjectivity, the speculative concept of the ego as unity of its own thought and reality.

3
Conceptualizing Thought

The *Science of Logic*, as announced in the Preliminary Conception of the *Encyclopaedia*, has the movement of pure, that is, free thinking, for its content:

> In the Logic, thoughts are grasped in such a way that they have no content other than one that belongs to thinking itself, and is brought forth by thinking. So these thoughts are *pure* thoughts. Spirit is here purely at home with itself, and thereby free, for that is just what freedom is: being at home with oneself in one's other, depending upon oneself, and being one's own determinant.[1]

Since pure thinking is not an empty syntactical framework for thoughtless contents, but a meaningful, semantic activity, the fact that the matter of the Logic is pure thinking does not make it a twice-removed abstraction, but rather a science of the most basic contents of human thought: 'Thus *logic* coincides with *metaphysics*, with the science of *things* grasped in *thoughts* that used to be taken to express the *essentialities* of the *things*.'[2] Hegel classifies these fundamental 'thoughts of things' into representations of being, of essence, and of thought itself.[3] This generates the three-fold division of the Logic in a Doctrine of Being, of Essence, and of the Concept.

Despite its notoriously difficult, some would say impenetrable character, the Doctrine of the Concept or 'subjective logic' (as it is titled in the Greater Logic)[4] is a clearly articulated theory of the logical structure of subjectivity, richly supported by commentaries and illustrations of the subject matter that do not make undue use of technical terminology. The difficulty of this text is quite obviously due to the objective complexity of its matter—a situation of which the reader is made immediately aware by the opening essay that centers on the problem of a pure, presupposition-less beginning of thought whose initial matter can only be itself.[5]

The difficulty of the subject matter is the same as the one already remarked upon by Aristotle with regard to the study of soul in general and of pure thinking in particular: 'But everywhere and in every way it is extremely difficult to arrive at any trustworthy conclusion on the subject,'[6] he warns in the opening of the *De Anima*. The greatest difficulty encountered in the general study of *psyche* is afforded by the study of the intellect (*nous*), first in its relation to other objects and then, more intricately yet, in its relation to itself:

> This part of the soul, then, must be . . . receptive of the form [of its object] and potentially like this form, though not identical with it. . . . Thus . . . the part of the soul which we call intellect . . . is nothing at all actually before it thinks. . . . Moreover, thought itself is included among the objects which can be thought. For where the objects are immaterial that which thinks and that which is thought are identical. For speculative knowledge and its object are identical.[7]

One way of approaching Hegel's theory of thought thinking itself is to see it as an inquiry into the logical structure of the ego. Under the heading 'Of the Concept in General' in the Greater Logic, Hegel volunteers some help for possibly bewildered readers of the third doctrine:

> I will confine myself . . . to a remark which may help one to grasp the concepts here developed. . . . The Concept, insofar as it has developed into an *existence* that is itself free, is none other than the *I* or pure self-consciousness. True, I *have* concepts, that is to say, determinate concepts; but the *I* is the pure concept itself, which has come into *being* [*Daseyn*] as concept (*GW* 12, 17/Miller 583).[8]

The logical-metaphysical inquiry into the nature of egoity provides the foundation for Hegel's exposition of the social and juridical dimensions of subjectivity as individual personhood.[9] As always, Hegel's ultimate concern is simultaneously logical and historical. He delivers both an analysis of the general concept of subjectivity as such as well as a reconstruction of the development of human subjectivity towards concrete universality, that is, towards self-knowing and self-willing individual subjectivity. Furthermore, the dialectical movement generated by thinking about thought (instead of thinking about being or essence) explains why the Concept, despite being the outcome of a process, is not a genuinely new category. Rather, it makes explicit a concept of thinking that has been implicit throughout the Doctrines of Being and Essence. The concept of the Concept, Hegel writes, provides a cognition 'through which only that is posited which in itself is already present.'[10]

The following section 3.1 provides a brief overview of the division of the Logic in 'objective' and 'subjective.' This is a necessary setting of the stage for the reconstruction of Hegel's logical explication of subjectivity, given in section 3.2.

3.1 How thought differs from being and essence

In the original editions of the *Science of Logic*, comprising a Doctrine of Being (1812 and 1832), a Doctrine of Essence (1813) and a Doctrine of the Concept (1816), Hegel titles the first two doctrines 'The Objective Logic,' and the third, 'The Subjective Logic.' Although the Lesser Logic does not make use of these headings, the closing section of its 'Conception and Division of the Logic' (*E* § 83) is particularly helpful for understanding the rationale of the distinction.

As a whole, Hegel states, the Logic is a 'doctrine of thought' (*Lehre von dem Gedanken*). It is, in particular, a theory of 'pure' (*reiner*, not *leerer* or 'empty') thought.[11] Depending upon pure thought's contents, the overall doctrine must be developed in separate parts. Each part defines a different way in which thinking relates to its objects, that is, to metaphysical categories.

First, the Logic is a theory of thought as referred (in a seemingly immediate manner) to kinds of 'being'—being as such, nothing, becoming, being-there, otherness, and so forth. Objects are being thought here without explicit inclusion of a reference to thinking itself. This constellation is investigated in the Doctrine of Being or of the 'Concept in itself.' Second, the Logic is also a theory of thought referred 'mediately' (or reflectively) to kinds of 'essence', that is, to objects that depend intrinsically and explicitly on their relation to thought itself: essence as such, appearance, existence, actuality, contingency, possibility, necessity and so forth. This constitutes the Doctrine of Essence or of the 'Concept for itself.' Third, the Logic is also a theory of thought referred to contents that do not merely depend upon, but rather are modes of thought itself: subjectivity, objectivity, and thought's actual existence—the Idea. This is the subject matter of the Doctrine of the Concept proper or of the 'Concept in-and-for-itself.' It focuses on pure thought as resulting from its immediate and mediated, relatively abstract phases, and 'returning' to a more concrete concept of itself. Since it results from the previous moments of logical thought, this doctrine preserves but also surpasses the preceding ones. Each category treated in the last part of the Logic is meant to sublate, and thus to contain, the immediate and the mediated character of the categories of Being and Essence, respectively. In the Doctrine of the Concept, the difference between thought and what is being thought is explicitly part of the very identity of thinking itself. This doctrine is meant to provide a rational grasp of the speculative identity of subject and object in thinking envisaged by Aristotle.

The distinction between objective and subjective logic, as well as the classification of metaphysical categories into concepts of Being, of Essence and of the Concept, are also reflected in the methodic differences among inferences in the three doctrines: Hegel presents concepts of Being as 'passing over' (*uebergehen*)[12] into the next, concepts of Essence as 'shining' or 'reflecting' (*scheinen*)[13] into one another, but only concepts of the Concept as 'developing' (*entwickeln*).[14] In the beginning of the *Encyclopaedia* Doctrine of the Concept, Hegel summarizes this point in the following way:

> The preceding logical determinations, the determinations of Being and Essence, are . . . only *determinate* concepts . . . , concepts in themselves or, what is the same, *for us*, because the *other* (into which each determination *passes over*, or within which it *shines* . . .) is not determined as a *particular*, nor its third moment as a *singular* or as *subject*. The identity of the determination in its opposite, [that is,] its freedom, is not *posited*, because it is not *universality* (*E* § 162 Remark).[15]

This dense, concise formulation is intended as a preliminary to the full-fledged formal definition of the Concept that follows in the next section 163. This will be discussed below. The contrast highlighted in the passage quoted here between objective categories and modes of inference (in Being and Essence) on the one hand, and subjective ones (in the Concept) on the other, can be elucidated as follows.

While ways of being are the generic object of thinking in the Doctrine of Being, and modes of essence are the object in the Doctrine of Essence, in the third doctrine forms of thinking must play both the role of object and subject. In the last section of the Doctrine of Essence (§ 159) Hegel remarks on the difficulties one encounters in making the transition from thinking in terms of Being and Essence to thinking in terms of the Concept. For example, one will be asked to advance from the category of actuality to that of an actualized concept, or from the notions of blind causality and universal reciprocal action to that of purposeful activity. One will have to abandon inveterate metaphysical prejudices and grasp that the thoughtless and the thoughtful, immediate being and mediated essence, and further, necessity and freedom, are in truth identical—albeit as moments of a differentiated unity that will now be called the Concept.

The difficulties in the journey from objective to subjective logic appear to lie primarily in subjective logic's self-reflexive constellation: the subject and the subject matter of thinking here are to be conceived explicitly as the same and yet they must also be distinguished. Thus, contrary to what is the case for categorial transitions in Being or Essence, the contradiction of identity and difference plays a central role in the inferential movements between categories of the Concept.

In the Remark just quoted from section 162, Hegel says that the relations among categories of the first two doctrines are not isomorphic to the relations among the logical notions of universality, particularity and singularity. He implies that, by contrast, the categories in the third doctrine are precisely so related. Since universality, particularity and singularity are traditional attributes of terms in a syllogism, the passage is emphasizing that the subject matter of the Doctrine of the Concept will be structured like a syllogism.

Hegel's theory of the syllogism distinguishes 'syllogism of the understanding' from 'syllogism of reason.'[16] In the first kind, the choice of the middle term (the particular) through which the subject term (the singular) is subsumed in the conclusion to a predicate (the universal) is arbitrary. Though formally valid, these syllogisms may yield true or false conclusions, depending upon the middle term being chosen to connect or con-clude (in Greek, *sun-logizein,* in German, *zusammen-schliessen*) the subject and the predicate. Hegel's examples (taken here from the Greater Logic) of what follows from arbitrarily chosen middle terms are instructive:

> If from the middle term of sensibility it is inferred that man is neither good nor evil . . . the syllogism is correct but the conclusion false, because . . . man in its concreteness belongs equally to the middle term of spirituality. . . . Similarly, from the middle term of sociality, one may deduce [the appropriateness of] citizen's community of goods, but from that of individuality, if pursued with equal abstractness, follows the [appropriateness of the] dissolution of the state (*GW* 12, 96–7/Miller 671).

In the syllogism of reason, the subsumption of one term under another through the mediation of a third is not arbitrary. The terms are not indifferent to one another. The correct syllogistic form is dictated by the very nature of the terms involved: 'Let's take for example the *syllogism* (not in the sense of the old formal logic, but in its truth). . . . This form of inference is a general form of all things. All things are particulars that con-clude themselves [sich zusammenschliessen] as a universal with the singular.'[17] 'The animal,' for example, does not denote an individual. It does not have singular existence but is rather the universal that effectively constitutes the essence of every particular species—the universal without which the living individuals of any given species would not be what they are: 'Were we to take animality away from the dog, there would be no more telling what it is.'[18]

To sum up this point: inferences of the understanding may be valid but unsound, but inferences of reason, if valid, are sound. The syllogism of reason yields only true conclusions.

Hegel considers the categorial transitions in the Doctrine of the Concept as 'syllogistic,' first in the generic sense that its categories are interrelated as universal, particular and singular terms are related to one another. However, he also thinks of this doctrine as embodying the syllogism *par excellence*, or syllogism of reason. Because of the self-reflexive nature of a thought that thinks itself, its singularity (or the thinking individual) is not in-itself extraneous to the universality under which it is subsumed. Rather, the ultimate singularity that Hegel calls the Concept subsumes itself through its own particularization under the appropriate universal term: 'The rational syllogism instead consists of the fact that through the mediation the subject concludes *itself with itself*. Only thus is it properly subject.'[19]

By contrast, categories of Being do not relate to one another in this kind of reciprocity: the abstract universal concept of being does not become particularized into nothing, nor does it ultimately become singularized as becoming. Rather, these categories are being brought into dialectical connection with one another by an external reflection. In the logical sphere of Being, concepts are indeed thought-determinations of Being but they are not its self-determinations. None 'posits' the others, none 'develops' into the next, but is merely made to 'pass over' into it. In subjective logic, instead, all determinations are transparently self-determinations of thought.

Hegel classifies these self-determinations under three headings: the subjectivity, the objectivity and the concrete actuality of the Concept (or 'the Idea'). By 'subjectivity of the Concept' is meant the whole of formal rules of thought (concept formation, judgment and syllogism); by 'objectivity' is meant the whole of the fundamental patterns of nature (mechanism, chemism and teleology); and by 'actuality' is meant the whole gamut of thought's self-expressions, from living to cognizing, self-willing and self-knowing beings.

The first part of the Doctrine of the Concept thus studies Subjective Logic's 'merely subjective' side. This part analyzes what are commonly considered formal rules of thinking, rules traditionally conceived as merely internal to thinking itself—hypothetical rules, as it were, whose validity stands in no relation to their content: 'The Logic of the Concept is usually understood as a merely *formal* science, in the sense that what counts for it is the mere *form* of concept, judgment and syllogism, but not at all whether something is *true*; truth is supposed to depend exclusively on the *content*.'[20] In this perspective, in other words, the certainty of thought appears to be wholly unrelated to the truth of its object. On account of their universal character, however, these same rules are at the same time paradoxically understood as necessary conditions of objective truth itself. By reducing thinking, and thus the Concept, to a partial contribution to knowledge, and by then defining thought's contribution as mere consistency with its own formal operations, one makes it impossible to explain why objectivity must ultimately be consistent with such merely subjective conditions. Indeed such consistency must ultimately appear to be a purely contingent matter. Truth then is a phantom or, at best, a mere *desideratum* of reason.

The second part of the Doctrine of the Concept counters this formalism by investigating Subjective Logic's 'objective' side. It delivers an account of the logical structures of the objectivity with which the Concept is faced—an objectivity imagined as filling up the supposedly empty matrix of thinking. The conception of thinking typical of this perspective is antithetical to that of the first part of the Doctrine. Thought-forms are treated here as structures of reality—and that means also, as real structures. Thus, they are not formal schemes, empty frameworks for possible application, but are themselves objects:

> If the logical forms of the Concept were really dead, inactive and indifferent receptacles of representations or thoughts, then, as far as truth is concerned, our knowing them would be a very superfluous and dispensable *description*.[21] In fact, however, being forms of the Concept they are *the living spirit of the actual;* and what is true of the actual is only *true in virtue of these forms, through them* and *in them* (*E* § 162 Remark).[22]

Forms of thinking are being investigated here as laws and processes of reality, that is, of what conceptual formalism views as a thought-less realm of merely external existence. In Objectivity, instead, thinking recognizes its own activity in the mechanical, chemical and teleological logic of the natural processes that confront it. The study of objectivity and the discovery of its logic are the equivalent of a historical *anamnesis* by which the Concept attains a new grasp of itself. It knows itself now as the source not merely of subjective certainty (validity) but also of objective cognition (truth). This recollection is part of the larger historical movement by which spirit inwardizes and remembers (*er-innert*) itself in the very same process in which it self-externalizes.[23]

Philosophic inquiry has long been understood as being centered upon the task of explaining the conformity of reality, conceived as content, with the intellect, conceived as form: truth must lie in the *adaequatio rei et intellectus*. In the history of modern philosophy, this consonance has been variously explained as a result of divine intervention, as a consequence of pre-established harmony, or as concerning the truth of appearances only. For Hegel, all these interpretations amount to an avowal that the adequacy of intellect and object is not to be accounted for rationally. In his view, instead, the riddle of this so-called adequacy is not at all irresolvable. The riddle is neither an eternal condition of spirit nor a perennial problem of philosophy. It has historically identifiable origins. To begin with, ancient philosophy never even faced this problem. The logic of the object and the logic of thinking the object were immediately understood as concerning one and the same *logos*. In the words of Aristotle that Hegel chooses as conclusion to the system:

> And thought thinks itself because it shares the nature of the object of thought; for it becomes an object of thought in coming into contact with and thinking its objects, so that thought and object of thought are the same. For that which is capable of receiving the object of thought and the substance [*ousia*], is thought. And it is active [*energei*] when it possesses this object (*Metaphysics* XII, 1072 b 20).

The third and final part of the Doctrine of the Concept (The Idea) is dedicated to developing this standpoint. However, contrary to what might be suggested by Aristotle's concise formulation, Hegel does not present the 'absolute standpoint' as immediate awareness of the coincidence of thought and object. For him, self-thinking thought's 'sharing the nature' of its object is not an epistemic or ontological *given*, but rather the *result* of a development. The latter consists of the process by which thinking first divides itself into 'subjectivity' and 'objectivity' and then mediates these same moments. The subjective and objective sides of subjectivity, themselves the result of this original division (*Urtheil*), are eventually brought together again, this time in a concrete speculative unity. In Hegel's usage, 'speculation' in general indicates the unification of opposite categories, predicates or 'moments', into one whole that he refers to as 'the speculative.' When this unification is conceptual, the resulting unity is 'the speculative' as concept. This denotes the highest developmental stage of thinking, the general subject matter of the third doctrine. Thought reaches this stage by sublating the antagonism (logically: the negative relation) between its subjective and objective moments. This negative relation, it will be recalled, consists in the alleged neutrality of subjective certainty towards objective truth (part one of the Doctrine of the Concept) as much as in the apparent indifference of objectivity *vis-à-vis* subjectivity's rules (part two). Hegel calls the overcoming of the negative relation between these two opposing moments 'the second negative' of thought. The indifference of subjectivity and the recalcitrance of objectivity are now sublated, that is, overcome and included, in the Concept that knows and wills itself:

> The *second* negative, the negative of the negative, at which we have arrived, is this sublating of the contradiction, but just as little as the contradiction is it an *act of an external reflection*, but rather the *innermost, most objective moment* of life and spirit, through which a *subject*, a *person*, a *free entity*, exists (*GW* 12, 246/Miller 835–6.)[24]

A juxtaposition of this passage with Aristotle's just-quoted proclamation of the identity of pure thought and its object reveals at once the affinity and the profound difference between the two conceptions.

If Aristotle's *nous* can at all be interpreted as having a subject (or even as being one), then this subject, despite being explicitly described as moving from potentiality to actualization through the mediation of objects, remains a passive substratum throughout this movement. It is passive not only, as Aristotle himself declares, in being receptive of objects, but also insofar as its highest form of activity consists of simply possessing them. This subject is properly speaking a substance, or rather sub-stratum (*hypokeimenon*), to which, not unlike matter, its physical analog, everything can be attributed, while it can never be attributed to anything else—let alone, to itself.[25] At no point in this process does the subject of *nous* (or the subject as *nous*) determine its object or determine itself. Its movement is not a development, but rather the eternal return to itself typical of circular motions. Completely self-contained, *nous* is, as Aristotle puts it a few lines later, 'a substance which is eternal and unmovable . . . impassive and unalterable.'[26] In its highest cognitive state, this substance acts as contemplation: active *nous*, as opposed to passive, 'is the divine element which thought seems to contain, and the act of contemplation [*theoria*] is what is most pleasant and best.'[27]

In Hegel's account, by contrast, substance develops out of and away from itself. It can do this because its intrinsic concept is being-subject, the overcoming of mere substantiality. It is this concept that eventually sublates its substantial existence and becomes in actuality the subject that, implicitly, it has been all along: 'the *truth* of the *substance* is the *Concept*.'[28]

Let us now return to the claim that the moments of the Concept relate to one another as universal, particular and singular terms interrelate in a syllogism of reason.[29] Bearing in mind the major subdivision of the Doctrine of the Concept in subjectivity, objectivity, and their simultaneous realization in the Idea, the syllogistic nature of the Concept means that its subjectivity is its abstract universality, that its objectivity is a particularization of that universality, and its actuality (its absolute, subjective-objective moment) is a singular instantiation of both. In other words: the subjective Concept encompasses abstractly universal notions; the objective Concept encompasses particularizations (and this means also concretizations) of those abstractions; the Concept as Idea, finally, encompasses its own abstract universality and particularity, that is, it unifies them into one singularity. Because of its internal differentiations, Hegel calls this singularity 'concrete.' This does not mean, he hastens to add, 'sensibly concrete.' Echoing Socrates' words in *Phaedo*,[30] he writes: 'the Concept as such cannot be grasped with hands and, in general, when the Concept is in question, hearing and seeing must have vanished for us.'[31] Hegel's use of 'concrete' is justified by its derivation from the Latin verb *concrescere*, 'to grow together.' This implies both internal differentiation and processuality. Contrary to the common use of the term, for Hegel what is concrete is not what is 'given.' What is given immediately, or found intuitively, are abstractions: unadulterated sensations, impressions devoid of thought, the 'here' and the 'now' of vanishing sensual certainties. These concept-less representations (as shown in the *Phenomenology of Spirit*) are artificial abstractions from the reality of knowing. Real knowing is always concrete, not only because it is a continuous process of unification of different forms and contents of representation, but because it is the permanent act of unifying all these with the subject of this knowing, the form of all thinking forms. In this sense, the Concept in its singular dimension is the most concrete reality of all:

> The antithesis between form and content, which is given special validity when the Concept is supposed to be what is only formal, now lies behind us. . . . Certainly the Concept must be considered as a form, but it is a form that is infinite and creative, one that both encloses the plenitude of all content within itself, and at the same time releases it from itself (*E* § 160 Addition).

The absolute singularity of the Concept, then, comprises its self-identity and its self-differentiations. This logical sphere is apt to explain subjectivity in a way that the spheres of Being and Essence do not. In these spheres, the thought-determinations that unify mutually opposing ones cannot be understood 'as a *singular* or as *subject*.'[32] Furthermore, the unity of opposite determinations in those spheres 'is not *posited*'[33] by thinking but found. Finally, none of those determinations recognizes itself (is 'at home') in the opposite and thus none attains its 'freedom.'

By contrast, the Doctrine of the Concept is an inquiry into thought-determinations that do have all these characteristics. Here, each category attains its meaning (its identity) in the opposite. This implies that categories do not relate to their opposites as to their limitations, but are rather enriched, made concrete by them. Notions are here 'free' in the logical sense defined in the Preliminary Conception: 'that is just what freedom is: being at home with oneself in one's other, depending upon oneself, being one's own determinant.'[34]

The dialectical identity of opposite categories in the sphere of the Concept fulfills, rather than limiting, the meaning of each. In this sphere, particularity does not simply oppose universality. They are united in the universal and concrete singularity that Hegel calls the Concept.[35] Through the mediation of particularity (that is, by undergoing a process of particularization) the abstract universality of thought acquires concreteness and thought becomes an existing singularity. This singularity is concrete because instead of excluding universality and particularity, it holds them together as moments of itself. Such grasped (*begriffen*) identity of an internally differentiated whole is the concept of a self-conscious subject: *der Begriff*.

One can see how this logical structure may define human individuality, but not animal singularity. The singular animal relates to its genus, and thus defines itself, through reproduction. Socrates instead relates to his own *genus*, and thus defines himself, through self-knowledge and self-will. The single animal is a simple, abstract singularity—a specimen—that does not need a relation to self in order to instantiate its generic nature. Socrates, instead, is a concrete singularity (better called an individual) whose essence subsists only through the mediation of his knowledge and will.

At several junctures in the system[36] Hegel insists that the meaning of the Delphic Apollo's injunction 'know thyself' is not psychological. The phrase does not recommend personal introspection or self-critical assessment. It does not refer to a special kind of empirical knowledge. It rather refers to the fact that the specific nature of human subjectivity results from the universalizing character of human thought. The Socratic command means that 'the human being *as such* [der Mensch *ueberhaupt*] must know itself,'[37] and this means, it must know the essence of being-human *as such*.

Hegel's interpretation of the Socratic exhortation in philosophic and historical terms is best exemplified by the account of the myth of Oedipus he gives in the *Lectures on the Philosophy of History*.[38] He explains here the fall of the Egyptian sphinx upon hearing Oedipus' solution to its riddle as symbolizing the fall of the 'oriental spirit' *vis-à-vis* the rise of the 'Greek spirit.' Hegel credits 'the orient' with having first raised the central concern of philosophy, namely the question of the nature of man, but he also imputes to it the failure of not having been able to answer its own question. Oedipus' answer to the riddle ('What is it that walks on four legs in the morning, on two at midday, on three at nightfall?' 'It is man') signifies the self-knowledge of the 'human being *as such*' dawning in Greek culture.

It is however also Hegel's view that neither the oriental nor the Greek world were capable of providing a rational grasp and practical fulfillment of the Delphic command. This is because the 'self' that is object and subject of the command had not yet built the ethical world that would first make possible self-reflective knowledge and self-determining action.

The tragedy that befalls Oedipus in the sequel to his encounter with the sphinx, spanning the gamut from lack of insight to self-inflicted blindness, signifies for Hegel precisely the epochal failure of the ancient quest for self-knowledge:

> But this ancient solution [of the riddle] by Oedipus, who thereby shows that he is in the knowing, is coupled with immense ignorance regarding his own deeds. The rise of spiritual clearness in the old kingdom is still united with the horrors deriving from ignorance, and

> this first dominion of kings, in order to become true knowing and ethical clarity, must transform itself through civil laws and political freedom (*W* 12, 272).[39]

According to Hegel, the logical analysis provided in the Doctrine of the Concept exposes the dynamic structure of one theoretically and practically self-determining 'substance.' Because of its self-relation, this substance is ultimately not just some-thing but some-one. In the end, what the analysis will expose is the structure of individual subjectivity. However, in its most general features (development, self-reference, and identity-in-difference) the Concept is already at work in the natural existence of organic unities: 'the Concept is the principle of all life, and hence, at the same time, it is what is utterly concrete.'[40] Living matter is thus nature's analog to the logical Concept. In the framework of his critique of biological preformation, Hegel illustrates the concreteness of the Concept in its existence as natural life in a manner not entirely foreign to contemporary notions of genetic 'in-formation':

> What corresponds to the stage of the Concept in nature is organic life. For example, a plant develops from its germ: the germ already contains the whole plant within itself, but in an ideal way, so that we must not envisage its development as if the various parts . . . were already present in the germ *realiter*, though only in a very minute form. . . . What is correct in this hypothesis, however, is just that the Concept remains at home with itself in the course of its process.[41]

As for the Concept in its more proper element, human thinking, Hegel detects representations of it in the earliest forms of philosophic reflection. These amount to intuitions of the ultimately speculative nature of all knowledge. For instance, the ancient thesis that knowledge is a kind of reminiscence expresses the awareness that knowing is predicated upon gnosis of self. The Platonic theory of knowledge as recollection indirectly presupposes the idea of an original identity of knowing subject and known object: the subject finds in itself the truth of the object or, in Hegel's words, 'the Concept remains at home with itself in the course of its process.' And yet, Hegel argues, ancient doctrines do not attain *conceptual* knowledge of subjectivity.[42]

With the dissolution of the ancient world, the Concept finds expression increasingly in the representative thinking of religious monotheism: one god unifying the opposite natures of the supernatural and natural world, or one individual unifying divine and human natures. In Christianity, that Hegel considers the paradigm of religion based on the revelation of this unity, the logical core of the representation of Jesus as both human and divine is precisely the absolute identity of opposites in one universal individual. Images and articles of faith, however, are still pre-conceptual representations of the Concept. Its conceptual grasp, devoid of intuition and allegory, can only be delivered by modern speculative philosophy.

3.2 How thought differs from itself

The laconic introductory sections of the third doctrine in the Lesser Logic outline the most abstract features of the Concept. The corresponding passages of the Greater Logic (as well as the Remarks and Additions in the Lesser Logic itself) expand upon the psychological and historical dimensions of the subject matter of this doctrine.

Logically, the central features of the Concept can be summarized as (i) inner determination, (ii) intrinsic negativity, and (iii) syllogistic articulation. Attention to these features is crucial for an understanding of Hegel's philosophy of individual subjects.

(i) Inward determination

In introducing the formal divisions of Logic in the *Encyclopaedia*[43] Hegel calls attention to three features of every object of logical reflection (every category in the Logic): each is at once abstract (the side '*of the understanding*'), dialectical (or '*negatively rational*') and speculative (or '*positively rational*').[44] Despite his assurance that all three features characterize every category as such, we learn in the following that the categories grouped under Being, Essence and the Concept do differ among themselves on account of the predominance of one or the other of these features in their respective sphere. Concepts of being are characterized by their relative abstractness; concepts of essence, by the negative dialectic they contain; concepts of the Concept are properly speaking speculative. As has been mentioned (in section 3.1), the first two groups acquire their meaning through a reflection exercised upon them, while the categories of the last group owe their meaning to self-reflexivity: the third and last subdivision of the Logic provides a concept of thinking not 'in its *immediacy*' nor 'in its *reflection*', but 'in its *being-returned-into-itself*',[45] that is, in its reflecting back upon itself. The opening line of the Doctrine of the Concept recapitulates this idea in the following way:

> The Concept is what is *free*, as the *substantial might which is for itself*; and it is *totality*, since *each* of the moments is *the whole* that *it* is and

> is posited as an inseparable unity with it; thus, in its identity with itself the Concept is the *in and for itself determinate* (*E* § 160).[46]

The Concept is 'what is *free*' in the sense that and insofar as it is what it determines itself to be. It is not just a thought-determination, but rather a self-determination of thinking. Biological, social, or economic determinations of subjects qualify for Hegel as external determinacies. Being an individual subject and, further, a person is a determinacy that results from subjects' internal (or self-) determination. The logical difference between the concepts 'human' and 'person' is an example of the distinctions in question. The first notion is the result of phenomenological or scientific observation. The second notion is produced by, and can only be grasped as, the subject's self-definition. Indeed, the logic of being-human can be meaningfully analyzed in categories of being, but the logic of being-person needs to be explicated in terms of existence (a category of essence). In the same way, Hegel explains, the living body can be said to be the determinate being or reality (*Dasein*) of the concept we refer to as soul; a particular juridical institution can be explicated as reality of the concept of right or freedom; or the world can be said to be the reality of the concept of god.[47] Being person, however, can only be explained as the self-given existence of human individuals conceptualizing themselves as persons. It is 'the *form* that the Concept gives itself in the process of its actualization.'[48]

The psychological form of the Concept is the existing ego, that is, the existence of the concept that I have of myself. Its theological form is expressed in the notion of an *ens perfectissimum* whose existence lies in its concept:

> [W]hen *singularity* is understood as I, when *personhood* itself—not an empirical I, a *particular* personality—is meant, above all when the personhood of god is present to consciousness, then what is at issue is *pure*—that is, *inwardly universal*—personhood; and this is a thought and pertains only to thinking (*E* § 63 Remark).[49]

The fact that the inner logic of individual personhood can only be given at the speculative level of the Concept has a historical parallel in the fact of the late emergence of a concept of individual personhood in the history of subjectivity. Human beings as such are creatures of nature, but the ego results from a spiritual development, and persons are products of history. Despite its existence, individual personhood is and remains a concept: it 'is a thought and pertains only to thinking.' Thus, what emerges from individual development and human history is a self-conception, and this is precisely what makes subjects into persons.

Inward determination is the metaphysical notion that lies at the center of modern psychological and political conceptions of individual personhood. This notion, according to Hegel, is being sought in vain in the texts of Greek antiquity. Among other examples, Hegel points out the narrow sense in which Greek gods may be understood as being personal gods. In an Addition of the Lesser Logic we read, for example: 'The gods of the Ancients were of course also regarded as personal; but the personhood of a Zeus, an Apollo and so on is not an actual but a merely represented one or, in other words, these gods are merely personifications that do not *know themselves,* but are merely *being known.*'[50] Greek gods, in other words, are merely determinate concepts, 'concepts-in-themselves—or, to say the same thing another way, concepts *for-us,*'[51] not for themselves. They reflect, as is the nature of all things divine, a self-representation of human subjects. These know themselves in their personifications as masters or slaves, Thebans or Athenians, wives or heads of household, warriors, merchants or philosophers. They do not know themselves as 'what is *free,*' that is, as 'the *in and for itself determinate.*'[52] The same then applies to their divinities. A few sections later, Hegel presents the lack of development of the concept of individual 'person' in Greek antiquity as ground of explanation for the ancients' moral and juridical acceptance of slavery:

> What the slave lacks is the recognition of his personhood; but the principle of personhood is universality. The master considers the slave not as person, but as a thing devoid of self [als selbstlose Sache]; and the slave himself does not count as I, for the master is his I instead.[53]

In the same vein, he remarks in the *Philosophy of Right* that '[t]he right of . . . *subjective freedom* constitutes the turning- and center point of the difference between antiquity and modern times.'[54] This is reiterated in the section on modern civil society,[55] where we read that the lack of recognition of a right to subjective individuality (based in turn on self-recognition) marks the watershed between ancient social hierarchies (including Plato's tri-partite *polis* and India's caste system) on the one hand, and modern class society on the other.[56]

(ii) Inherent negativity

If all determination is negation—and Hegel acknowledges explicitly his debt to Spinoza's principle[58]—then all self-determination is self-negation. Indeed the fundamental distinction between merely determinate concepts and the self-determining Concept may be characterized also as a distinction between external negation and internal negativity. A brief clarification of the methodological use of 'negation' and 'negativity' by Hegel will have to suffice for the present purpose, which is merely to outline the essential features of the Concept.

In the Logic, a concept is not engendered by the simple negation of another, but by the process of *negating the negative relationship* between other concepts. This is the reason why Hegel interprets concepts resulting from the dialectical relation of opposites as units of formerly incompatible notions. This unity must be thought at a different ('higher') conceptual level than that at which the incompatible notions are at first encountered. The alleged incompatibility of 'rest' and 'change of place' and their compatibility in the higher unity of 'motion' are the simplest, most classical examples of this relation.[58] Negating negative relations is the ground of our capacity to grasp logical as well as actual contradictions. Once more, the distinction between understanding and reason is a crucial factor in Hegel's argument. In the discussion of the logical nature of antinomies, for instance, Hegel maintains that while each thesis of an antinomy can be understood, the antinomy as a whole can only be grasped by reason. It is one thing to understand that there is a contradiction and what its terms are, quite another to grasp the common ground in virtue of which there is contradiction and both thesis and antithesis have validity.

In the first triad of categories discussed in the Doctrine of Being, for example, 'becoming' is neither the simple negation of its predecessor 'nothing,' nor simply the double negation of the original category, 'being.' The exact meaning of becoming implies its being a negation of the alleged mutual exclusion of being and nothing. Since it negates their logical independence, becoming turns out to be their logical ground. Without a notion of becoming, as is made plain at the end of the Logic's first chapter, being and nothing could not be thought as standing in any relation whatsoever—not even in that of contradiction. Becoming is the concept into which must necessarily pass the one-sided, purely positive conception of being and the equally one-sided, purely negative conception of nothing. Becoming denotes precisely the logical and ontological compatibility of being and nothing. In this sense, becoming is a genuinely *dialectical* concept. Still, it is not a properly *speculative* concept because it does not contain a moment of self-referentiality. That which becomes, of course, becomes or changes, but becoming itself does not. While it results from the negation of a negative relation between other concepts, it does not in turn negate itself. Becoming is Heraclitus' ever-living fire: while changing, it rests.

A properly speculative concept not only results from the negation of the mutual negation of others that differ from it, but it also reflects this negation back onto itself, that is, it contains negativity in its meaning or identity. In the *Phenomenology*, for instance, we read about the identity of self-consciousness (that is, about self-identity) that its logical structure is best described as identity of identity and contradiction. In this shape of itself, in other words, 'consciousness makes a distinction, but one which at the same time is for consciousness not a distinction.'[59] This contradiction is intrinsic to self-consciousness. In-itself, consciousness must be one in order to posit a difference. This positing consists of the fundamental judgment (*Ur-theil*): 'I think x, and I and x differ.' But as this judgment takes place, consciousness becomes for-itself: it recognizes that the distinction is its own.

In the framework of language theory, this constellation would have to be expressed as follows: if we accept as meaningful a concept of self-reference, we accept that it implies the sameness of self-identity and self-differentiation or, closer to Hegel's formulation, the identification of identity and difference.

Conceiving a speculative concept, then, differs in significant ways from conceiving non-speculative notions. This is why Hegel thinks that a re-evaluation of the ontological argument becomes necessary independently of its role in theology. In the attempt to conceive the identity of identity and difference we discover the absolute identity of the conceiver. To put it more simply: none but an 'I' can think the 'I' that must accompany all my representations.

(iii) The Concept as syllogism

The main text of section 163 of the Lesser Logic gives the formal definition of the Concept as follows:

> The *Concept* as such contains the moment of *universality*, as free equality with itself in its determinacy,—of *particularity*, the determinacy in which the universal remains transparently equal to itself, and of *singularity*, as the inward reflection of the determinacies of universality and particularity. This negative unity with itself is the *in and for itself determined* and at the same time the self-identical or universal (*E* § 163).[60]

This makes explicit the indirect definition Hegel has given in the preceding section 162 (discussed in 3.1). The latter highlighted the fact that the same logical features of universality, particularity and singularity defined here do not characterize the categories of Being and Essence. The opening phrase of the present passage: 'The *Concept* as such', indicates that the definition is, at this early stage in the exposition, purely logical. We are being introduced to the anatomy of the Concept, that is, to the formal concept of the Concept in abstraction from its existence as psychological ego, historical subject or juridical person.

From a logical point of view as much as in reality, the three main moments of the Concept cannot be separated from one another. Although they can be understood each in its own terms and in their mutual opposition (universality is not particularity, particularity is not singularity and so on) through reason we are able to grasp their interpenetration in one unity: 'in the Concept their *identity* is *posited*.'[61]

For the purposes of analysis, however, it is best to follow the rules of reflective understanding and dwell on the moments in their distinction.

(a) Abstract universality

Considered in isolation from the other two moments, the Concept's universality means at first simply the abstract sameness that accompanies all differentiation. (It is only by including in our consideration the fact that the Concept is mediated through particularity—its second moment—that we will be able to grasp it as the concrete universality that it actually is.) But the universality of the Concept is more than self-sameness. Equality with oneself or self-identity must be distinguished from the permanence that accompanies change in general. Permanence is a necessary condition for change, but is not sufficient for, and thus not the same as, change. Self-identity is rather both the necessary and sufficient condition of self-differentiation—and thus it coincides with it. Accordingly, the Concept's self-identity is not like the 'immediate' vacuous sameness of the 'thing in itself' that underlies the multiplicity of appearances. It also is not the identity of the ego of sense-certainty described in the *Phenomenology of Spirit*: 'The I [of sensibility] is merely universal like Now, Here or This in general.'[62] The Concept is also not mediated by another, like a child's developing identity may be said to be mediated by that of its adults. It is rather mediated by its own activity.

In nature, the Concept is prefigured in the self-sameness of organisms that actively preserve their ontological identity through change. An organism's unity is permanently challenged by its surroundings and permanently restored by the interaction of its organs through the medium of the whole. In the sphere of thought self-identity consists, more radically, of the activity of identifying oneself. In philosophical psychology, this is reflected in the fact that self-consciousness cannot be attributed to another unless the latter attributes it to itself. In developmental psychology, self-identification is a stage in individuals' growth, not a skill that can be taught. In the philosophy of law, freedom cannot be conferred to subjects who do not will it. Self-identification is the true universality (*das wahrhaft Allgemeine*) proper to the concept of individual person that Hegel contrasts with the mere commonality or the generality (*das bloss Gemeinschaftliche*) of concepts formed by abstraction of a common trait. The merely general dimension of human subjectivity may be and has been expressed in various ways: as biological trait in the Cynic's definition of man as featherless biped, as naturalistically political feature like the alleged 'natural egoism' of all human individuals, even as a linguistic 'universal,' exemplified by the utterance 'I' that all speakers share.[63]

Hegel criticizes the conflation of generality with universality in the following terms:

> The universal of the Concept is however not just something common . . . but rather the self-particularizing (specifying) that remains by itself in its other. . . . It is of the greatest importance, both for cognition and for our practical agency as well that the merely communal not be confused with the truly general, the universal (*E* § 163 Addition 1).[64]

The concrete universality of the Concept is, then, essential to it. This is not a trait 'given' to the Concept, but the essence 'posited' by it. Concrete universality is attained through self-particularization. Thus it includes, rather than excluding, particularity. In the relational activity we call knowing, thought's self-identity consists of the fact that thinking occupies all the functional places in the relation. It is subject, object, and medium of cognition.

For a full grasp of its logical structure, it is useful to reflect on the Concept in its reality, namely as the ego that the Greater Logic defines as 'the Concept . . . grown into existence.'[65] The ego's utterance 'I' does not denote a receptacle for that which all egos have in common. It signifies the absolute identity of the object meant by the utterance with the subject meaning it. Hegel has already argued this point in the *Phenomenology of Spirit* with regard to the emergence of the self-conscious ego:

> If we give the name of *Concept* to the movement of knowing, and the name of *object* to knowing as a passive unity, or as the I, then we see that not only for us, but for knowing itself, the object corresponds to the Concept. Or alternatively if we call *Concept* what the object is *in-itself*, but call the object what it is . . . *for* an other, then it is clear that [in self-consciousness] being-in-itself and being-for-another is the same . . . I is the content of the relation and the relating itself (*GW* 9, 103/Miller 104).[66]

Even at the close of consciousness's phenomenological journey (in Absolute Knowing) Hegel refers explicitly to the Concept's self-identity as being a concrete universality: 'The nature, moments and movement of this knowing have, then, been proven to be such that this knowing is a pure *being-for-self* of self-consciousness; it is I, that is *this* and no other *I*, and that, in the same immediate way, is a *mediated* or sublated *universal* I.'[67]

Let us summarize this moment. The relevant sense in which the Concept is a universal is the 'concrete' sense. Strictly speaking, a concrete universal means a self-universalizing entity. Paradoxically, self-universalization is pursued and realized through activities of self-finitization, or is, in Hegel's terminology, the self-determination of an initially abstract universal. Thus, the determination of the Concept is not caused by an external agency, but by itself. Self-determination is not merely its destiny but also its point of departure, present in it at every stage of its development. We could say that the Concept is that whose particular nature lies in its being universal, and whose universality comes about through particularization. The Concept is the universal mediator of all difference and multiplicity that it posits as its own.

(b) Particularity

As we have just seen, particularization is the activity through which the Concept determines itself into being a universal: particularity is 'the determinacy in which the universal remains transparently equal to itself.' The next section (§164) specifies this point: what is particular in the Concept is precisely its inherent universality: 'the particular is what is distinct or the determinacy, but in the sense that it is inwardly universal.'[68]

The movement through which the Concept becomes actually what it is potentially is an activity, rather than a process, of determination. From beginning to end, this movement does not happen *to* the Concept; the Concept makes it happen. The result is something determinate 'in the sense that it is inwardly universal,' that is, the result is a finite something with a non-finite inward dimension. Distinguishing between process and activity helps to clarify that the Concept's specific nature results neither from natural chains of causes and effects, nor from external (whether natural or social) processes of reciprocal action or community (*Wechselwirkung* or *Gemeinschaft*). Already in the transitional sections from Essence to Concept (in the Lesser Logic) Hegel remarks that causality and its proximate truth, reciprocity, despite being necessary conditions of the self-development of the Concept, are not sufficient for it:

> Reciprocal action certainly . . . stands on the threshold of the Concept, so to speak; but, just for this reason, we must not be satisfied to employ this relationship when what is at issue is conceptual cognition [das begreifende Erkennen] . . . Instead of being . . . an equivalent of the Concept, this relationship [of reciprocity] itself requires to be comprehended (*E* § 156 Addition).

The confusion between notions of causal and reciprocal (communal) determinacy on the one hand and the notion of self-determination on the other is effectively a hindrance to a genuine grasp of the ego's inward universality.

It is generally accepted that causal processes do not explain the emergence of subjectivity, but processes of reciprocal action (intended as reciprocal causality) are often credited with it. Reciprocity however, Hegel argues, is barely sufficient to explain the living organism. What may appear to be two-way causal processes between independent organs or between organ and organism is rather the internal self-determination of the living body (in the same way in which attractive and repulsive forces in Newtonian physics turn out to be sides of one and the same internal determinacy of the universe as a whole). The identity of the organs is the organism, the ground without which they are not organs. Thus, although reciprocity is indeed the 'next truth' of causality, it does not even fully capture the essence of live matter. More importantly, it thoroughly fails as ground of explanation of forms of spirit—for example, the body politic. Reciprocity 'stands on the threshold of the Concept,' but it cannot cross into its sphere. To state, for example, that Sparta's mores are the cause of its laws and that conversely its laws are the cause of its mores does nothing to explain the common ground of the mores and the laws—though it is perhaps a better description of Spartan culture than one that reduces it to either alternative.[69]

Reciprocal action is thoroughly inadequate to explain the identity of a 'substance' that results from the latter's own activities, or, to put it differently: reciprocal action cannot account for the ground of self-differentiation. This kind of 'substance' with these sorts of 'properties' is more aptly called a 'subject' with 'actions.'

(c) Concrete singularity

The definition of section 163 calls the singularity of the Concept its 'inward reflection' and describes this reflection in turn as the Concept's 'negative unity with itself.' To the understanding, the first two self-determinations of the Concept (universality and particularity) appear to be antithetical. Universality suggests absence of difference, while particularity implies difference. If these are taken to be moments of substance as it is understood in pre-critical metaphysics, their contradiction appears to be irresolvable: a complete and independent substance (a 'universal') is supposed to be the ground for incomplete and dependent accidents ('particulars'), or conversely, accidents are supposed to be determinacies of what is the undetermined and undeterminable *par excellence*. Hegel argues that the contradiction is resolved dialectically by grasping substance as subject. To be subject is neither to be merely the substratum (the *hypokeimenon*) of external determinacies, nor to be the determinacy of an independent substratum. To be subject is to be that one substratum that produces its own determinacies. The Concept's singularity refers to its being an absolute unity of self-identity and self-differentiation, a subject whose nature it is to act upon itself.

In its most generic sense, singularity can be predicated of everything that is, whether considered as a mere being (a thing, an event) or as the essence of some being (for example, as a force behind the thing or event). But the way in which the Concept is singular differs from the way in which things and forces are. In exactly the same sense, also the category of actuality found at the closing of the Doctrine of Essence differs from that emerging in the Doctrine of the Concept. Despite the fact that everything that is, is singular ('what is singular is the same as what is actual'),[70] the actuality of singular things and forces is in-itself-actuality (or reality) while that of the Concept is for-itself-actuality or self-actualization:

> The *actual*, because it is at first only *in-itself* or *immediately* the *unity* of essence and existence, *has the potential* to act; but the singularity of the Concept is absolutely what is *effective* [schlechthin das *Wirk-*

> *ende*], and that does not any longer mean a *cause* appearing to effectuate an other, but rather that which effectuates *itself* [das Wirkende *seiner selbst*] (*E* §163 Remark).[71]

The distinction is reflected in the different ways in which things and forces on the one hand, and subjects on the other, are active: single things and forces cause and condition other things and forces, but individual subjects produce themselves.

When applied to the Concept, then, singularity does not denote a single thing or a single human being but self-mediated existence—individual subjectivity or personhood. The singularity of the individual implies inwardness as well as universality. This singular 'thinking thing,' this individual 'substance' that is not given, but posits itself, is the unity of all the singularities that make up its world: it is 'the Concept *posited* as totality.'[72]

As mentioned in the beginning of this section (iii), the intricate analysis of the dialectical relations among the logical moments of the Concept provides us with the formal structure of thinking, not with an account of its actualizations. According to Hegel, the actual existence of the Concept, its being 'effective' as free individual subjectivity is a result of historical developments. The Concept's making itself into a singular embodiment of concrete universality is an epochal event: 'in its true and comprehensive significance, the universal is . . . a thought that took millennia to enter into men's consciousness.'[73] Indeed, the whole of antiquity failed to attain a consciousness of concrete universality, both in its theoretical and practical dimensions:

> The Greeks, although otherwise so highly cultivated, did not know god, or even man, in their true universality. . . . Consequently, for the Greeks there was an absolute gulf between themselves and the barbarians, and the human being as such [der Mensch als solcher] was not yet recognized in its infinite worth and infinite legitimacy [Berechtigung] (*E* § 163 Addition 1).

The many shapes in which ancient spirit objectifies itself have one economic, social and juridical phenomenon in common: slavery. The legal and ethical recognition of slavery as a rightful social arrangement or as an inevitable extension of nature into human society predates the Concept's recognition of itself. In this early world-view individuals are specimens, instantiations of ethnic, national, economic or social particularities, not entities existing in their own right. At this time, individuals are universal only in the abstract sense of being single embodiments of their particular, social or natural, species. They are not universal in the concrete sense of being self-conscious unities of particular circumstances with their own inherent universality. Thus for example individual personhood has no juridical validity in social interactions in antiquity. The recognition of slavery is only possible as mis-recognition of the Concept: 'What the slave lacks is the recognition of his personhood; but the principle of personhood is universality. The master considers the slave not as a person, but as a thing devoid of self [als selbstlose Sache]; and the slave himself does not count as I, for the master is his I instead.'[74] In several sections of the *Philosophy of Right*, Hegel discusses slavery (but also any other life-long exploitation of one's labor by another) in similar ways.[75] He views attempted justifications and moral condemnations of slavery as opposite theses of an antinomy, each one-sided in that each regards man as a natural entity—namely as either naturally un-free or as free by nature. Such arguments, however—for which antithetical passages from Aristotle and Rousseau respectively stand as paradigmatic witnesses—misunderstand the essence of spirit (subjective as much as objective) as if it were a mere outgrowth of nature. For example, Aristotle writes: 'he who, despite being human, is by nature not his own but another's man, is a slave by nature; and one may be said to be another's man when, despite being human, he is a possession.'[76] In the same vein, but arguing for the opposite outcome, Rousseau opens the *Social Contract* with the famous and dogmatic stipulation: 'Man is born free' and then goes on to maintain that 'renouncing one's liberty . . . is incompatible with the nature of man.'[77] For Hegel, instead, the attainment of self-determined subjectivity in the history of spirit consists of individuals' taking possession of themselves, including their bodies and affections—an act of acquisition that expresses the sublation of one's naturalness into a grasp of oneself. At the most basic level (in Abstract Right), the attainment of this threshold is externalized in the explicit will to become one's 'own property over against others.'[78] By embodying its will (quite literally: by putting its will in its body) a subject attains an unlimited right to itself—the very right annulled in the institution of slavery. The blunt naturalistic assumption of inborn dependency or independency from the will of others misunderstands, in Hegel's view, an act of determination for an external, factual determinacy. But if freedom, in Rousseau's own terms, is self-imposed necessity, human freedom can neither be understood as natural nor as conventional, external determinacy. It is the result of self-determination. An important Remark in the *Philosophy of Right* concludes by explaining how the struggle of lordly and servile consciousness described in the *Phenomenology of Spirit* is a necessary result of the internal dialectic of the Concept:

> This early, un-true phenomenon [of slavery] affects spirit that is only still at the stage of its consciousness; the dialectic of the Concept and of the at first only immediate consciousness of freedom brings about at that stage the *struggle of recognition* and the relation of *lordship* and *servitude*.[79]

This struggle is a logical necessity (it is an internal contradiction of the Concept as consciousness) as much as a historically necessary phase of spirit's movement. During this phase, man still regards himself as a creature of nature, that is, 'as an existent not in conformity with its concept.' The concept of a self-determined universality arises late in the history of the species. Its objectification in a really existent system of ethical institutions centered upon that concept is even later. Echoing his own words from the Lesser Logic, Hegel comments: 'that man in and for himself is not destined for slavery . . . this insight takes place only in the recognition that the Idea of freedom is truly actual only as the [modern] state.'[80]

4
Hegel's Reading of Plato's *Parmenides*

In interpreting Plato's *Parmenides* during the early Jena period, Hegel focuses largely on its methodological value as a radical exercise in negative skepticism—and, as such, as an introduction to proper philosophizing. In his 'Relation of Skepticism to Philosophy' (1801), for example, Hegel characterizes Plato's dialogue as exhibiting 'the negative side of the knowledge of the absolute [die negative Seite der Erkenntnis des Absoluten].'[1] According to this interpretation, the dialogue's role in the history of philosophy is twofold.

On the one hand, the negative dialectic of ideas that constitutes its backbone would exhibit the inadequacy of the understanding to provide true cognition. The dialogue would show that concepts—here understood as determinations of the understanding[2]—like 'similar' and 'dissimilar.' 'older than' and 'younger than,' 'continuous' and 'discrete' or, more crucially, 'same' and 'other,' are intimately (or logically) connected with their respective contradictory. In consequence of this, Plato would demonstrate that to attribute these determinations to finite, that is, non self-reflexive[3] objects of thinking implies attributing their opposites as well—a constellation that must ultimately lead to the utter unintelligibility of the objects of thought themselves.

On the other hand, Hegel believes also that the dialogue works as indirect proof of the validity of a different cognitive mode, namely reason, one that Plato intends to display and account for in a separate trilogy: the *Sophistes*, the *Politicos* and in the planned but never executed dialogue the *Philosophos*.[4] The *Parmenides*, then, would tacitly imply that 'truly infinite,' self-reflexive objects of thinking may actually be made intelligible precisely by the dialectic contradictions of which the dialogue shows only the negative results. On this interpretation, the dialogue would indirectly suggest that self-reflexive objects of thought share the characteristic of being knowable through reason, the faculty that enables the philosopher to grasp dialectical unities of opposites.

In this early interpretation, then, Hegel views Plato's *Parmenides* essentially as negative reflection only paving the way to a positive or speculative science of the absolute. But just six years later, his well-known remarks on this dialogue in the Preface to the *Phenomenology* extol it as containing more than potentially constructive but actually negative skepticism. Referring to the Plato interpretations of the Neoplatonists, Hegel speaks here sympathetically of a time in the history of philosophy when

> Plato's Parmenides, arguably the greatest work of art of ancient *dialectics*, was held to be the true revelation and *positive expression* of the divine life, and despite all the obscurity produced by the ecstasy, this misunderstood ecstasy was interpreted as nothing else but *the pure Concept* (*GW* 9, 48/Miller 44).[5]

In the following development of Hegel's thinking, as attested by his commentaries on this and other Platonic dialogues in the Greater and Lesser Logic[6] and in the lectures on ancient philosophy,[7] the *Parmenides* appears to approximate the status of *prima philosophia speculativa*. Hegel sees now in the dialectic of the ideas exhibited in it an embryonic form of authentically speculative thinking.[8] Thus, he reads Plato's text not any more as cathartic training for a future science, but as the first historical incursion into the science of the Absolute itself.

4.1 An ancient concept of 'idea'

This mature Hegelian interpretation of the *Parmenides* may at first appear to be untenable on purely textual grounds as much as on account of historical considerations. The following reflections aim at dispelling some of these doubts.

As a preliminary consideration, it may be stressed that Hegel's reading is at least consistent with his own metaphysics of the history of philosophic thought. A condensed formulation of this theory, taken from the 1820 Introduction to the *Lectures on the History of Philosophy*, has been discussed in a previous chapter.[9] Hegel's conception entails that the series of system-identifying principles (*Grundbegriffe*) arising in the history of philosophy, and consisting of the successive sublation of each in the next, is ordered according to the logical derivation of determinations (*Bestimmungen*) of the Idea (the latter being used here in Hegel's technical sense of unity of concept and actuality). But the system-identifying principle of Plato's philosophy is that of *eidos* or *idea*. Its implicitly speculative character consists in its being at once purely intelligible and the most real. The Platonic concept of idea, then, must be present in sublated form in the subsequent principles of the philosophies of the Middle Ages and of modernity, including their latest embodiment in the Hegelian system. In Plato's *Parmenides*, according to this view, this concept takes the form of a principle (*arche*) posited as ground of the dialectical analysis of all ideas as such.

The attempt to justify this reading of the *Parmenides* as an early philosophic work with speculative import requires, however, more than an acknowledgement of its compatibility with Hegel's general theory of philosophy. As the following discussion intends to make clear, it is necessary to show that it is both textually legitimate and logically advantageous to re-interpret the main subject matter of the dialogue in a way that differs markedly from traditional readings and translations.

The first step in this undertaking consists of showing that the subject matter at the center of the historical Parmenides' poem *About Nature*[10] is quite different from that of the fictional Parmenides' speech in the dialogue. While the poem's subject matter is—in Hegelian terms—the archetype of non-reflexive, 'badly infinite' objects of the understanding, the Parmenides of the dialogue appears to be concerned with a self-reflexive, 'genuinely infinite' object of reason.[11] On this reading, in other words, the subject matter of Parmenides' discourse in the dialogue is not the lonely impenetrable 'being' (or, more precisely, the 'to be,' *einai*) of the poem, but rather a unity of mind, or the self-conscious ego.

For a variety of reasons, most of the interpretive tradition of Plato's *Parmenides* has taken for granted the identification of the dialogue's topic with the topic of the pre-Socratic poem—with the notable exception of Hegel.[12]

In defense of Hegel's interpretation, this chapter intends to show that (a) there is no unequivocal textual basis for identifying the 'being' of Parmenides' poem with the 'one' of Plato's dialogue; (b) a comparison of semantic and syntactic features of the poem on the one hand, and the dialogue on the other, speaks against such identification; and (c) there are compelling philosophic reasons not to go along with the traditional reading.

Taken together, these considerations show that the almost infamous obscurity of the dialogue's second part is at least partially dispelled when it is understood as an original attempt at grasping the internally contradictory nature of thinking selfhood, or mind.

Hegel, of course, does not claim that the *Parmenides* (or any other Platonic dialogue, for that matter) contains a theory of the speculative Concept. But he does explicate the discussion of contradictions that forms its cornerstone as the earliest insight into the essence of the Concept—though still in an epistemic and psychological embodiment typical of the 'childhood of philosophizing.'[13]

On Hegel's reading, the dialogue does not exhibit 'external dialectic,' that is, a sophistic exercise in futility. Indeed, if one recognizes that the contradictions exhibited in it are not meant to be determinacies of an abstract pure being, but rather determinations of a more concrete essence, Plato's *Parmenides* actually loses the abstruseness that has led twentieth-century interpreters to attribute to it the very non-Platonic character of a parody.[14] If the contradictions are understood as pertaining to a subject matter, and potentially to a subject, much different from 'being,' their treatment sheds its appearance of a virtuoso display of pointless dialectic. The dialogue then acquires the dimension of authentic pursuit of truth through dialectic reason, because the discussants recognize the subject matter as being potentially an identity of identity and difference—an insight that is abandoned in the end, leading to the customary aporetical conclusion of Platonic dialogues.

After the following preliminary sketch of the overall trajectory of the argument pursued in this chapter, section 4.1 will be dedicated to analyzing a passage of the *Parmenides* that is essential to my thesis. This is the opening passage of the dialogue's second half, in which Plato introduces, through Parmenides' voice, the subject matter of the dialectical investigation to follow.

At the beginning of his main speech,[15] the old Parmenides singles out the notion of *emautos*, literally 'myself,' as the field of inquiry in which to challenge the dialectical skill of his younger audience. From a Hegelian perspective, *emautos* represents a psychological instantiation of Plato's own philosophic concept of 'idea' as that which, though supra-sensible, contains reality in the highest degree and is the ultimate cause of both knowledge and sensible existence.[16] To frame this in terms of Hegel's Logic, one could say that Plato's *emautos* embodies in antiquity, at the logical level of being, the notion of what would later find expression, at the logical level of essence, in Descartes' *res cogitans* or in Spinoza's *causa sui*. The immediate certainty of the Cartesian thinking substance, for which the formula '*cogito, sum*' is the most adequate expression, is due precisely to the fact that in- and for this substance, thought and existence coincide. As for Spinoza's self-caused substance, it is equally such as to be inconceivable unless existent: 'By self-cause I understand that whose essence implies existence, or that the nature of which is not conceivable unless as existing.'[17] If, in conformity with Hegel's theory of the history of philosophy, his own concept of the Concept is a sublation of logical and historical predecessors, then Hegel's Concept will contain also a version of Plato's original conception of 'idea.' It is not surprising, then, that Hegel takes quite seriously the dialectical 'exercise' displayed by a Platonic dialogue in which contradictory pairs of ideas are both denied and attributed to one and the same subject matter—provided this subject matter can be interpreted as being an object of reason.

4.2 With what must Plato's dialectic begin?

In the first part of the *Parmenides*[18] Plato examines the relations between the ideas (*ideai*), forms (*eide*) or kinds (*gene*) on the one hand, and the sensible things ('the visibles') that participate in them, on the other. In the second part[19] Plato investigates, through the voice of the old Eleatic poet-philosopher, the relations among the ideas themselves.

In the opening of the dialogue,[20] young Socrates boldly declares that the notion of a sensible thing's participation (*methexis*) in different, even contradictory ideas, for instance similarity and dissimilarity, is logically unproblematic: after all, each sensible thing can be like others in some respect and yet unlike them in some other respect, thus participating in likeness and its opposite at once. It is equally intelligible, almost a matter of course, that all sensible things (*panta*) may be one entity from one perspective (as when we speak of 'the whole' world) but many from another. Every thing and all things can rationally be said to 'partake of one-ness' as much as 'of multitude.'[21] Thus, the attribution of opposite predications to finite entities does not strike Socrates as irrational as long as the predications are meant to hold in different respects. The apparent contradictoriness of things can be resolved by appeal to perspectivism: I, says Socrates, am many because I am composed of parts, but I am also one because I am a unity, one man.[22]

Real problems arise, in the young man's view, only when one considers the (necessarily logical) relations of ideas among themselves. What is the relation of the 'form, itself by itself'[23] of equality to that of inequality, of motion to rest, of coming to be to passing away or, most crucially, of being itself to non-being?[24] The precocious metaphysician finds it absurd to claim that one-ness itself is or even partakes of multiplicity itself and *vice versa*. The ideas themselves escape perspectivism. Since they cannot suffer to have predicates different from themselves, they have no parts and thus do not admit of either aspects or points of view. Each idea, if properly understood, is fully and exclusively what it is. If it is to be known, then it can be known only simply or immediately as what it is. The reason that no predicate—let alone, opposite pairs of predicates—can attach to ideas lies in the discursive understanding of predication that would later become canonized by Aristotle: the predicates of any given individual denote the species to which the individual belongs (or in which it participates), each species being defined in turn by its own participation in a higher species and so forth until the highest categories are reached (Plato's 'highest kinds').[25] But the ideas, being the highest kinds in which everything participates, cannot in their turn participate in any other, higher kind. The ultimate *gene* cannot be defined by reference to genus and specific difference, that is, they cannot be known discursively. The way to a grasp of the ideas, so it seems to Socrates, is neither dialogical nor dialectical. They must, in some way, be known 'themselves by themselves.'[26]

Socrates, however, faced with Parmenides' relentless criticism of the ideas, of their cognizability, and of things' participation in them, does admit to difficulties inherent in the notion of participation as well as to potential tensions among connotations internal to one and the same idea: equality, after all, must differ from inequality and thus contains a moment of difference, and so forth for the other ideas.

First, Parmenides criticizes the notion of participation because it leads to self-contradiction in the ideas;[27] second, he develops the famous argument that participation requires a mediator between the idea and what participates in it, that this mediator requires another in order to mediate that mediation, and so on in a ('badly') infinite regress.[28]

Despite being duly impressed by these objections, Socrates still insists (rather timidly, given the age and authority of his interlocutor) that what is logically impossible for sensible things and their classes may not be unthinkable regarding events that 'occur only in minds' (*en psychais*): 'But, Parmenides, maybe each of these forms is a thought . . . and properly occurs only in minds. In this way each of them might be one and no longer face the difficulties mentioned just now,'[29] difficulties among which the paradoxes produced by the sensibles' participation in the ideas are only the most immediately evident ones.

In the following intricate lesson in dialectics (the dialogue's part two) Parmenides accepts *de facto* Socrates' distinction between determinations proper to sensible things and those proper to ideas. At the same time, however, he undermines Socrates' epistemological optimism regarding the intelligibility of the latter. For the Platonic character Parmenides, while apparent contradictions affecting sensible things may indeed after all be resolved by perspectivism, the contradictions that seem to beset things of thought offer insurmountable difficulties and even evoke the specter of a far too radical 'idealism': 'Given your claim that other things partake of forms, won't you necessarily think either that each thing is composed of thoughts[30] and that all things think, or that, though being thoughts [*noemata*], they are not being thought [*anoeta*]?'[31] The outcome of Parmenides' unrelenting exposure of the inherent contradictions of the ideas, those 'things graspable only by means of reasoning [*logo*],'[32] is their hopeless unintelligibility.

Prodded by his audience, Parmenides launches into a dialectical analysis that commences with a rhetorical question about his listeners' willingness to begin their thinking with what is most fundamental:

> Do you wish me, since we seem to want to play this difficult game, to begin with *myself* and the *hypothesis of myself*, taking as our foundation with regard to *the one itself* either that one is, or not one, and see what follows from there? (*Parmenides* 137 b; my emphasis).[33]

In this pivotal passage, Parmenides uses three different expressions to identify the original subject matter of the analysis: 'myself' (*emautos*), 'the hypothesis of myself' (*emautou hypothesis*) and 'the one itself' (*to hen autos*). His strategy consists now of raising a disconcerting prospect regarding this subject matter, a prospect that becomes articulated in a series of seemingly rational, but ever more perplexing, hypotheses whose outcome will be that the very intelligibility of the initial subject matter must be called into question.

Parmenides proposes that two equally plausible but contradictory claims may be made about this original subject, namely (i) that it may only be one and (ii) that it may also be not-one, or many. From these two follow, in a sort of logical parthenogenesis, four further pairs of mutually contradictory theses.[34] If, according to the first claim, the beginning as foundation of everything is only one, then this one can be shown to be nothing (thesis 1) as well as everything (thesis 2); but if the principle is only one, it follows also that the many are nothing (thesis 3) as well as everything (thesis 4). *Vice versa*, if, as assumed by the second claim, not-one is the foundation of everything, then it follows, with regard to the one, that it both is everything (thesis 5) and nothing (thesis 6); and again, under the same assumption it also follows, with regard to the many, that they are everything (thesis 7) as well as nothing (thesis 8).

Each of these eight claims is then applied to the fundamental determinations of reality, that is, to the ideas in which all things allegedly participate. What results from this operation is the unsettling realization that the subject matter at issue (however vaguely it might have to be defined at the start) can neither be said to be continuous nor discrete,[35] neither finite nor infinite,[36] neither contained in itself nor in another,[37] neither moving nor at rest, neither changing nor unchanging,[38] neither identical with nor different from itself or another,[39] neither equal nor unequal to itself or to others,[40] neither spatially nor temporally determined,[41] and so forth. There is no escaping the intrinsic negativity and contradictoriness of the matter at hand. The outcome of the dialogue, as we have come to expect, is aporetical. In the last lines, Parmenides' contradictory conclusion finds the unreserved (if perhaps nonsensical) approval of his interlocutor: '[Parmenides:] whether one is or is not, it and the others, both in relation to themselves and in relation to each other, are and are not everything in every respect, and they appear and do not appear.—[Interlocutor:] Very true.'[42]

Much of the sense of the dialectic played out here actually depends on how one interprets Plato's first formulation (*via* Parmenides' voice) of the subject matter to be investigated. This must be stressed especially in view of the controversies in the literature spanning decades about the precise target of the dialogue's criticism: Is the dialogue pro-Eleatic or anti-Eleatic? Is the first part against Platonic 'idealism,' the second against Parmenidean 'monism,' both, or neither? Does its dialectics embody a logical exercise or an ontological doctrine? Is it 'serious' logic, fundamental ontology, or a parody of Parmenides' poem—a kind of literary criticism *avant la lettre*?

The actual formulation of Plato's announcement of the subject matter of the inquiry (at 137 b) has received surprisingly little attention in the vast and detailed literature on this work,[43] but for the purposes of our present concern, the clarification of this matter is pivotal. With this in mind, it is worth focusing on the passage in as literal a translation as possible, with the decisive Greek phrases given in brackets. This is, once again, how Plato formulates Parmenides' rhetorical question:

> Do you wish me, since we seem to want to play this difficult game, to begin with myself [*ap' emautou arxomai*] and the hypothesis of myself [*kai tes emautou hypotheseos*], taking as our foundation

> [*hypothemenos*] with regard to the one itself [*peri tou henos autou*] either that one is, or not one [*eite hen estin eite me hen*], and see what follows from there? (*Parmenides* 137 b.)

Given the semantic and syntactic ambiguities of this passage, one cannot simply go along with commentaries and translations that in fact neglect the double emphasis on 'myself' in the main clause and, in addition, crudely disambiguate the phrase 'the hypothesis of myself' by simply rendering it 'my own hypothesis.'[44] Neither is there a clear reason why we should follow the seemingly unremarkable rendering of the Greek *hypothesis* with the English 'hypothesis' (whose subjective connotation Cornford radicalizes as 'supposition'[45]) or its French or German equivalents. All these renderings denote a theoretical assumption and suggest therefore that Parmenides is starting out, like a modern scientist, by formulating a hypothesis to be subsequently tested.

A review of the principal modern translations of this passage indicates that most (with two exceptions)[46] are seemingly literal renditions of Marsilio Ficino's fifteenth-century Latin text.[47] One of the earliest editions of Ficino's translation (1491) renders the phrase 'to begin with myself and the hypothesis of myself' with '*a me ipso meaque suppositione in primis exordiar.*'[48] In the Ficino edition possessed by Hegel (the so-called Bipontina edition of 1787)[49] the prefix of *suppositione* has been dropped and the text reads *meaque positione*,[50] thus better rendered with 'my positing' (German: *setzen*) than 'my presupposing' (German: *voraussetzen*).

Friedrich Schleiermacher's 1817 translation[51] (one that Hegel does not seem to have used) starts out by rendering (*sup*)*positione* with *Voraussetzung*: 'Or do you wish me . . . to start from myself and my hypothesis . . . ? [Oder wollt ihr, . . . dass ich von mir selbst anfange und von meiner Voraussetzung . . . ?]'—a formulation echoed in countless variations ever since. But already in the next line, Schleiermacher strays from Ficino's text. When translating the second instance of *hypothesis* in verb form (*hypothemenos*), Schleiermacher does not use the German verb *voraussetzen*, as one might expect, but rather *zugrunde legen*, 'to take as foundation' or, literally, 'to place under.'[52] Thus, Schleiermacher's interpretation of the speech's beginning is appropriately ambivalent: Parmenides announces his 'presupposition' as if it were hypothetical, but he regards it also as the foundation of the dialectical analysis to follow.

Auguste Diès' very influential French text from 1923 follows a strategy similar to Schleiermacher's: 'myself' is translated with *moi-même*, 'the hypothesis of myself' is interpreted as 'my own hypothesis' (*ma propre hypothèse*), but the verb form *hypothemenos* is understood as meaning, indeed, 'to take as our foundation': *posant*.[53]

It is crucial to notice that, in addition to a shift in the meaning of 'hypo-thesis' in these classical readings, Parmenides is also presented as announcing, oddly enough, not one but two beginnings: himself, and a theoretical hypothesis with which his name is widely associated. The significance of the first instance of 'myself' (in 'to begin with myself') is largely ignored in the literature that seems to view it as purely rhetorical and logically superfluous. The second instance of 'myself' (in 'the hypothesis of myself') is taken to be the grammatical equivalent of a possessive adjective: '*my* hypothesis.' By neglecting the first and focusing on the second alone, the dialectical analysis carried out by Parmenides appears to apply to the 'being' of the Parmenidean poem, which in turn is understood as a working assumption.

There are at least five problems with interpreting the Greek passage in this way. The least of these is stylistic in nature, but still worth mentioning. It ought to strike one as uncharacteristic of Plato's elegant prose to first introduce the subject matter of an argument as if it coincided with the author of the argument (let's 'begin with myself'), to then specify that the topic is of course a thesis of the same author ('my hypothesis') only to finally formulate the thesis at stake (whether 'one is, or not one').

The second difficulty is grammatical: 'my hypothesis' would be expressed more effortlessly by the Greek *he eme hypothesis* rather than by the more complex formulation used by Plato: *he emautou hypothesis*. The first uses a straightforward possessive adjective; the second, a possessive pronoun in the notoriously ambiguous genitive form that may indicate a subjective or an objective relation to its noun: either 'my own hypothesis' (subjective genitive) or else 'the hypothesis of/about myself' (objective genitive).[54] One exception to the classical readings that makes use of the objective sense is the Italian translation by Enrico Pegone: '*l'ipotesi di me stesso*'—'the hypothesis of myself.'[55] Agreeing with this reading of the text does not amount to maintaining that the construction with the personal pronoun 'of myself' is never used in Greek to express the adjectival 'my.' By themselves, the syntactical and grammatical ambiguities of a text can only be circumstantial evidence, not definitive proof, for or against a philosophic interpretation. This example of a reading that strays from the traditional ones is only relevant in concomitance with the other objections listed.

The third problem arises from reading Plato as allegedly referring the so-called hypothesis in question to 'the one' of Parmenides' poem. As a matter of fact, however, contrary to what happens in the dialogue, where instances of *hen esti, peri tou henos* and *to hen* abound,[56] Parmenides' poem *About Nature* contains no reference at all to an 'existing one,' to a 'one that is,' or to 'the one.' The entire poem contains merely one instance of 'one' (*hen*) where it is used not as noun, but as an attribute in a cluster of three: 'whole, one, continuous' (*'pan, hen, syneches'*).[57] These in turn are predicated of that which the poet consistently refuses to name while alluding to it circuitously through various tenses of the verb 'to be' (*einai*).[58] The poem's expressions for what is commonly translated in English with the participial 'being' are mostly the infinitive 'to be' (*einai*), the present 'is' (*estin*) and on occasion the participial 'being' (*eon*).[59]

In the first part of the dialogue, Socrates initially characterizes Parmenides' famous doctrine quite faithfully as simply stating 'that the whole is one,'[60] a declaration in which, it should be noted, 'one' is the predicate and 'the whole' is the subject to which it is attributed via the copula 'is.' But a few lines later we are suddenly faced, through Zeno's intervention, with an original rewording ('if the one is') where 'one' has suddenly become a propositional subject and 'is' acquires an existential function: 'The truth is that the book comes to the defense of Parmenides' argument against those who try to make fun of it by claiming that, if the one is [*ei hen esti*], many absurdities and self-contradictions result from that argument.'[61] This new existential meaning of 'is' is at work in the passage under our scrutiny: let's take as our foundation, we are told, with regards to the one itself, either that it is or that not-one is.

To sum up this point: while the historical Parmenides' concern appears to be the declaration of the uniqueness of the whole ('all is one'), the dialogue's characters Parmenides and Zeno argue about the existence of a 'one.' The discrepancy at the very least suggests that the dialogue's reference to an unequivocal, well-known hypothesis of the poet-philosopher about an existing 'one' is doubtful.

A fourth criticism of the traditional readings must focus on the clause: 'either that one is, or not one.' Ever since Ficino, this is rendered in the (inherently Hamletic) version 'either the one is or it is not,' in which 'not' (*me*) negates the existence of the 'one' (as if the text read *me estin*) rather than negating, as Plato's text does, simply the 'one' (*me hen*). The Platonic formulation implies the possibility that what there is may be the negation of oneness, that is, multiplicity. The alternative presented is not between being or nothing, but between the existence of 'one' and that of 'not-one', that is, of many—or also perhaps of a 'one' that is many. The translations, however, only imply that the Platonic Parmenides' 'one' may or may not exist: either being, or nothing, but not both.

Taken together, these four considerations alone lend plausibility to the Hegelian interpretation: the announced subject matter of the dialogue is an object that escapes the boundaries of the customary logic of the understanding. The topic, in other words, cannot be the 'being' of the famous poem but is rather a novel conception: '*emautos*.' This is not only the more plausible denotation of the only instance of 'the one' in our passage ('the one itself') but it is also the more plausible subject matter of the following inquiry into contradictory predications of one and the same substratum.

The fifth and final reason for revising traditional readings of this Platonic text is connected with the meanings of the Greek *hypothesis*. To begin with, if the dialogue were indeed referring to a hypothesis, then it could hardly be meant to refer to the Parmenidean 'being,' and this for a simple reason: *About Nature* is utterly devoid of any hypothetical thinking whatsoever. As has been remarked by others, the poem is, as befits its genre, 'prophetic and apodictic'[62] throughout.

Furthermore, the complex semantics of *hypothesis* in Greek at the very least allows for alternative interpretations. *Hypothesis* is a substantivation of the verb *hypotithemi*, whose original meaning (in Homer, for example) is 'to place under' (Schleiermacher's *zugrunde legen*) and which indeed is used as such in countless pre-classical and classical texts including other dialogues of Plato.[63] The economic meaning of *hypotithemi*, namely 'to put down (a sum),' with its corollary connotation of pledge or wager on future developments[64] may very well have contributed to the secondary metaphorical uses of the verb as 'to propose,' 'to suggest,' 'to assume' and even 'to suppose,' all of which are indeed equally well documented in Plato's works.[65] Thus, only contextual considerations may decide in favor of interpreting *hypothesis* as an assumption or, as is being proposed here, as a subject matter or even as ground.

As for Ficino's translation, it must be remarked that the Latin *suppositio* does not denote primarily a theoretical assumption. Like its corresponding Greek term, *suppositio* denotes primarily the act of 'placing underneath,' as for example in the planting of seeds or in the laying out of grounds.[66] If Ficino had understood Plato as introducing a theoretical supposition in our sense, it is probable that he would have translated *hypothesis* with *assumptio*, *opinio* or *coniectura*.

In conclusion: there is no clear etymological reason why Plato's use of *hypothesis* and *hypotithemi* would require us to choose only one pole of the alternative between a metaphysical ground and a theoretical hypothesis. The ambivalence (conveyed by the Schleiermacher and Diès translations) may well be integral to Plato's conception. The disjunction reflected in modern languages' semantic separation of (objective) ground from (subjective) assumption may rather force itself upon the modern reader, but need not be projected back onto Plato's thought.

4.3 The one that is not one

At various junctures in the *Science of Logic*[67] we are reminded that, while the separation of so-called objective (ontological) from so-called subjective (epistemic) meanings of categories is a useful analytic distinction of modern philosophizing, it must eventually be overcome in order for the two moments of each category to be grasped as what they are, namely connotations of one and the same concept. This process culminates in the Absolute Idea, that is, in a really existing thought that thinks itself:

> As unity of the subjective and the objective Idea, the Idea is the Concept of the Idea, for which the Idea as such is the object, and for which the object is itself—an object in which all determinations have come together. This unity, therefore, is the *absolute truth and all truth*, it is the Idea that thinks itself (*E* § 236).

Before this stage, the progressive unification of the subjective and objective dimensions of logical concepts has been taking place all along in the movement of the Logic. For example, in the Doctrine of Essence we refer to 'essence' as a 'reflection' and we analyze the dialectic of objective 'essentialities' in parallel to that of subjective 'determinations of reflection.'[68] It is precisely by sublating the distinction between this subjectivity and this objectivity that we are enabled in the end to find their common ground.[69] The same happens again in the analysis of this last concept of ground: we must first distinguish objectively sufficient conditions from subjectively sufficient reasons before eventually being able to recognize their unity in the 'absolute relation' we call actuality (*Wirklichkeit*). And again, in the kind of actuality we call substance, we have to distinguish passivity from activity, effect from cause, in order to comprehend (once faced with the instability of each of these) that the truth of cause–effect relations is universal reciprocity, and that the truth of substance is its being a relation (*das Substanzverhaeltnis*) between moments internal to it. Ultimately, even 'substance' or 'substantiality' as names for this absolute relation are misnomers. What we have here is rather the completion of substance (*die Vollendung der Substanz*), namely 'the Concept, the subject.'[70]

For Hegel, the distinction between subjective and objective connotations of logical-metaphysical categories and, more radically, the separation of logic from metaphysics, are at once historical achievements of modern philosophy and its self-imposed limitations. Whatever the strengths and weaknesses of this separation, to assume it tacitly in the interpretation of texts that historically precede the differentiation must necessarily hinder our comprehension of them.

Applied to Plato's *Parmenides*, this means that a grasp of the principle from which arise the dialogue's contradictory deductions will be hampered by the assumption of the following disjunction: either this principle is the object of, or it is a presupposition for, the dialectical analysis that follows. Put differently: either the *hypothesis* is an objective *hypokeimenon* or it is a subjective conjecture, but not both. But this way of proceeding would be equivalent to presenting Plato with the alternative: either the ideas are real, or they are ideal, but they cannot be both. If we take Hegel's perspective, it becomes plausible, instead, that Plato's main character intends to begin the dialectical investigation from what is both real and ideal, being and thought. This is not just a 'one,' but an existing 'one' that thinks the 'one'—not unlike, though on a more abstract level than, another beginning of philosophy: *cogito, sum*.[71] If Parmenides is made to call this beginning 'myself and the hypothesis of myself,' then the more straightforward interpretive strategy will be to acknowledge this point of origin as the *thinking* of being, the ego that both deduces itself and lays down itself as the ground of all deduction. In this sense, and with these qualifications, Plato's *Parmenides* can reasonably be said to display the beginning stage of genuinely speculative philosophy.

Hegel maintains that the transition from objective to subjective logic provides a richer, more 'concrete' concept of reality than could be delivered by either the logic of Being or the logic of Essence alone. The logic of the Concept provides a notion that is the unity of the being- and essence-connotations of that which the notion signifies. This object of thought is (exists) only insofar and as long as it is 'reflection into itself' (*Reflexion in ihm selbst*): a self-reflective reality. According to Hegel, self-reflective reality marks in turn 'the highest possible determination' (*die hoechste Bestimmung*) to which anything can attain. Indeed, if reciprocal reflection is the kind of relation by which everything acquires its essential determinations (that is, the relation by which beings acquire their essence) then self-reflection is the kind of relation by which an entity acquires its essential determinations from itself alone. Thus, Hegel calls self-reflection not only the highest form of determination but also 'the absolute relation' (*das absolute Verhaeltnis*). In this kind of logical relation, the *relata* are such that their roles are indistinguishable. This is neither because the poles of the relation take turns in switching roles, nor because a beholder external to the relation may be unable to distinguish them. The absolute relation holds objectively between poles that 'turn into one another' (*ineinander ueberschlagen*) simultaneously and in the same respect.

In self-reflection or absolute relation, therefore, there are actually no two opposite poles, but rather a self-opposing one. This one, far from shunning contradiction, is itself essential contradiction: it is its own object, and thus its own subject; it determines itself, and is thus determined by itself; it posits its own identity, and thus, its own difference—exactly as envisioned by Parmenides in Plato's dialogue: '[Parmenides:] Nor will it [the one] be the same as itself. [Interlocutor:] Why not? [Parmenides:] The nature of the one is not, of course, also that of the same. . . . Therefore, if the one is to be the same as itself, it won't be one with itself; and thus it will be one and not one.'[72]

'Absolute relation' characterizes for Hegel that first, abstract, in-itself determination of the Concept we call the ego: 'The Concept . . . is none other than the I or pure self-consciousness. I do have concepts of course, that is, determinate concepts; but I is the pure Concept itself that has come into *determinate being* [*zum Dasein*] as concept.'[73]

From this Hegelian perspective, the second part of the *Parmenides* represents Plato's ultimately unsuccessful attempt to outline the logic of the Concept as it is in-itself. The dialectical inquiry must begin from a foundation, a substance of some sort, a one. But this substance cannot be dogmatically presupposed. A beginning in radical philosophizing can only be a beginning without presuppositions. But how can such a beginning be made? To any arbitrarily agreed upon principle, sophistry and philosophy can always find another one preceding it. Appeals to intuition or faith are not an option in Greek philosophy. The only available choice is a rational one, and here this means to begin from that which has itself for its presupposition. But the 'being' of the poem, while defined as 'ungenerated, . . . imperishable, . . . undivided,' is also described as being held by 'mighty necessity' in inexorable bonds.[74] It dwells in utterly passive dependence upon necessity—a determination it has not given itself. The poet's 'being' is, then, absolutely dependent upon an other, rather than depending upon itself alone. Indeed the very reason this 'being' does not relate to itself is that it has no self to relate to. Neither does it endure differences from what is external or other, nor does it sustain internal differentiation. Thus, it would make no sense at all to both deny and affirm of it, as done in Plato's dialogue, that it is one and multiple, similar and dissimilar, old and young, continuous and discrete. In this scenario indeed Plato's text would have to strike us as rather uncharacteristic of its author: a display of sophistic intellectual coquetry.

It is advisable, then, to be skeptical of readings of the dialogue in which Parmenides is seen as offering the principle of purely external 'being,' lacking all inward dimension and self-differentiation, as ground of the dialectic deductions. It will rather be helpful to take Parmenides to be announcing as starting point the principle of his self, *emautos*. What follows from this is an ineluctable series of contradictions that, although they cannot hold simultaneously if they are merely determinacies of being or merely determinations of essence, may well be rational determinations of the unity of both: the Concept. Thus, modern philosophy may come to understand how the ideas displayed in the dialogue, taken as a whole, form a web of dialectical relations by which a wholly new substance is being explained: a subject.

Needless to say, Hegel does not anachronistically attribute his theory of individual subjectivity to Plato. Quite apart from historical considerations having to do with Hegel's judgment of Plato's philosophy as expressing a *Zeitgeist* in which subjectivity is still underdeveloped, Hegel is well aware of Plato's consistent rejection of any thought involving the self-contradiction of a subject matter. No amount of dialectical reasoning, whether *ex negativo* or *ex positivo*, will convince Plato that a 'one' exists that is subject and object of itself, simultaneously and in the same respect. The point of Hegel's mature reading of *Parmenides* is rather that he detects in it an objective logic leading inescapably, even against Plato's intention and self-understanding, to the recognition of such a self-contradictory 'one.' This 'one' is not subject to the same determinations as the 'visible' things are. It is, actually, subject to no one-sided determination whatsoever and precisely because of this it is, for Plato though not for Hegel, both unintelligible and nonexistent. While the *Sophistes* will provide some evidence for an affirmative form of the dialectic of the real (though still to the exclusion of an authentically self-contradictory entity), the *Parmenides* provides merely negative arguments about what *cannot* belong to 'the one.' In a particularly dramatic passage, the philosopher stresses that 'the one' is impervious to all formal and quantitative determinacies: it is neither another from others nor from itself,[75] neither identical with others nor self-identical.[76] If indeed it were self-identical, Parmenides explains to his astonished audience, this 'one' would actually have to be in some strange sense double—even self-contradictory. In this passage, Parmenides argues that 'the one' cannot have two different determinations without becoming different from itself: the idea of one-ness and that of sameness are different ideas, because 'the nature of the one is not . . . also that of the same.' Thus, if it is self-same, the one cannot be one, and if it is one, it cannot be self-same. It follows that 'it will be one and not one. But this surely is impossible.'[77]

This is the most radical consequence that derives from Parmenides' self-destructive analysis. Self-contradiction is and remains in Plato's thinking an inadmissible feature if something is to be intelligible and existent at all.[78]

Thus, even Plato's *Parmenides* must end aporetically. While envisioning a concept of individual subjectivity, in the end Plato and his world must turn away from 'the realm of *freedom*'[79] that can only be disclosed by grasping substance as subjectivity.

5
Greek Moral Vocabulary: 'Shame is the greatest compulsion'[1]

The theory of spirit's 'experience' from the *Phenomenology* describes this experience as spirit's movement from a 'substantial form', in which it is an objective content of consciousness, towards a 'conceptual form,' in which it is a subjective self-reflection of consciousness. Hegel summarizes this complex evolution in the chapter on Absolute Knowing as a theory of spirit's transformation from its '*In-itself* into the *For-itself*, of *substance* into *subject*, of the object of *consciousness* into object of *self-consciousness*, that is, into a . . . sublated object, or into the *Concept*.'[2]

This concise formulation of spirit's experience as metamorphosis from substance to subject provides a most useful framework for understanding Hegel's assessment of the significance of Greek thought *vis-à-vis* the history of philosophy as a whole. Once we know that for Hegel the history of philosophy expresses human thought's unfolding in self-knowledge (Chapter 1 above), we can see why he would interpret the transition from ancient to modern conditions of spirit as a process of increasing subjectification. This is not identical with claiming spirit's allegedly progressive individualization. For Hegel, increasing subjectivity actually implies the advancing universalization of the subject away from mere singularity. His overall claim regarding ancient philosophy is that it harbors intuitions (mostly voiced by pre-Socratic philosophers) or conceptual precursors (foremost in the classical epoch) but never full-fledged conceptual accounts of the speculative notion of universal individuality as explicated in his own Doctrine of the Concept. We find the formal definition of 'universal individuality' embedded in the main text of § 163 of the *Encyclopaedia* Logic:[3] this concept of individuality refers to a singular 'negative unity with itself,' namely 'the *in and for itself determined* and at the same time self-identical or universal.' This formulation needs further unpacking, but a first approximation of its meaning can be obtained by pointing out that in ancient philosophy, the absence of a conception equivalent to this theoretical notion of individual subjectivity is most glaringly reflected in the virtual absence of a conception of universal individual rights in their ethical and juridical texts.

An exemplary precursor of the speculative notion of universal individuality can be found in Plato's figure of the marvelous parallelism of the good soul and the just city in the second through fourth books of the *Politeia*. Despite the important fact that this parallelism takes center stage in Socrates' discussion of the main subject matter of the dialogue (justice), no attempt is made to ground the purported kinship of individual city and individual soul either logically or metaphysically.[4] The reasons given for it are merely hinted at in form of repeated appeals to an intuitive analogy, to its didactical advantages, even to its persuasive force in Greek popular culture.

The analogy is used in the second book to introduce Socrates' inquiry into the parts and virtues of the republic:

> The investigation we're undertaking is not an easy one . . . [S]ince we aren't clever people, we should adopt the method of investigation that we'd use if, lacking keen eyesight, we were told to read small letters from a distance and then noticed that the same letters existed elsewhere in a larger size. . . . We'd consider it a godsend . . . to be allowed to read the larger ones first and then to examine the smaller ones, to see whether they really are the same . . . [L]et's first find out what sort of thing justice is in the cities and afterwards look for it in the individual, observing the ways in which the smaller is similar to the larger (*Politeia* 368 d–369).[5]

This strategy is then briefly recalled in the fourth book, when the time has come to summarize and conclude this phase in the investigation of justice:

> [Socrates:] We thought that, if we first tried to observe justice in some larger thing that possessed it, this would make it easier to observe in a single individual . . . [If] we do this, and compare them side by side, we might well make justice light up . . . [A]re things called by the same name, whether they are bigger or smaller than one another, like or unlike with respect to that to which the name applies? [Glaucon:] Alike. [Socrates:] Then a just man won't differ at all from

> a just city in respect to the form of justice; rather he'll be like the city (*Politeia* 434 d–435 b).

In light of Glaucon's doubts about the persuasive force of the parallel, Socrates appeals to what we would consider, with suspicion similar to Glaucon's, as popular wisdom about alleged cultural or ethnic facts.

> [W]e are sure compelled to agree that each of us has within himself the same parts and characteristics as the city? Where else would they come from? It would be ridiculous . . . to think that spiritedness didn't come to be in cities from such individuals as the Thracians, Scythians, and others who live to the north of us . . . or that the same isn't true of the love of learning, . . . mostly associated with our part of the world, or of the love of money, which one might say is conspicuously displayed by the Phoenicians and Egyptians (*Politeia* 435 e–436).

In Plato's text, the deeper identity of the unity of *polis* and the unity of *psyche* remains a mystery. In Hegel's terms, one might say that while Plato is the first to give voice to the bold thesis that objective spirit and subjective spirit are moments of one Idea, he does so only at the abstract conceptual level the Idea could attain in his epoch. This abstraction characterizes a stage at which spirit is only beginning its journey from substance to subject: the 'childhood of spirit'.

The logic of the speculative notion of universal individuality has been treated in Chapter 3. Here it suffices to say that the idea of a self-transforming activity of spirit towards growing subjectivity is the metaphysical framework for Hegel's account of objective spirit, that is, for his explanation of the historical rise of political institutions, legal systems, religious doctrines and moral theories in which subjectivity ('the independent development of particularity'[6] and its attendant 'right of subjective *freedom*'[7]) plays an increasing, though never unchallenged role. Human spirit's movement towards self-knowledge and self-will[8] is reflected through social and political upheavals, restorations of old orders, long periods of latency, and new upheavals, in the real history of jurisprudence, economy, state-building, positive science, art, religion and philosophy.[9]

This chapter focuses on Hegel's postulate of the absence from Plato's thought of any notion equivalent to that of a right to subjective freedom. The reading offered here of relevant passages from the *Apology*, *Crito* and *Politeia* is meant as the kind of 'external touchstone of the truth of a philosophy' that Hegel himself invokes in the Introduction to the *Encyclopaedia*.

The theory of the history of philosophy that has been outlined in Chapter 1 does not only inform thoroughly Hegel's *Lectures on the History of Philosophy* but is equally at work, as the following discussion shows, in the *Philosophy of Right*. Here as well, Hegel's references to ancient representational and conceptual thinking consists primarily in his interpreting the principles of Greek philosophy in light both of their own systematic context (when one exists) and of the subsequent systematic history of philosophy.

Hegel's treatment of Plato's ethical conceptions takes on the form of a critical reconstruction of the latter's notion of ethicality (*Sittlichkeit*). While I do not discuss here the sublation of 'abstract right' and 'morality' into 'ethicality' in Hegel's theory of right or law, I simply presuppose the unity of right and morality in expounding his reading of Plato. After all, Hegel's use of *Sittlichkeit*[10] to interpret ancient ethical theory and *ethos* needs far less justification than his use of the same notion in the explication of modern ethical theories and sensibilities. His choice of this term to refer to notions of the good as well as of right in Plato is apt to capture the latter's intention precisely because the theoretical and disciplinary separation of moral and juridical philosophy is largely alien to ancient thought.

The theme of the difference and continuity between ancient and modern conceptions of ethicality arises in countless places in Hegel's work. The present chapter deals exclusively with his assessment of Plato's ethical conceptions in view of later historical developments, but one should bear in mind that pivotal concerns of this assessment play a major role also in Hegel's interpretation of stoic and skeptic philosophy—foremost his concern with showing a speculative potential in the abstract character of ancient thought.

Furthermore, in his critical discussion of ancient authors Hegel tends to highlight differences rather than the common ground between ancient and modern philosophy. For example, he tends to stress quite often the conspicuous absence, but rarely the embryonic presence of an individual-subjective dimension in the Idea (that is, in the reality and concept) of Greek ethicality. His reason for focusing on discrepancy rather than continuity between antiquity and modernity in this respect lies in what he sees as the historically privileged position of modern philosophy. By surveying what constitutes their own past, later thinkers can achieve a comprehensive perspective on features, scope and limitations of ancient philosophy precisely by reflecting on their own differences from it.

The difference at issue here is of the kind for which the Logic uses 'distinction' (*Unterschied*; often translated simply as 'difference') as opposed to mere 'diversity' (*Verschiedenheit*). Diversity is the quantitative and qualitative otherness (*Anderssein*) of *Dasein* in the Logic of Being. The concept of distinction is introduced in the Logic of Essence as dialectical antonym of identity. Distinction is the kind of difference that results from a process of self-differentiation (*sich unterscheiden*) of what was previously simply or immediately an identity. Applied to the development of the moral and juridical sphere, this implies that modern experiences and conceptions differ from ancient ones not only in the trivial sense that they have other (diverse) connotations, scope and perspectives. This latter kind of difference applies equally to the diversity among modern conceptions themselves—for example those based on divine will *versus* autonomy-based ones. Rather, the non-trivial aspect of the difference between the ancient and the modern ethical mind is that the latter results by self-differentiation from the former.

For instance, modern juristic theories of retributive justice (such as Hegel's) derive their notion of the state's right to retribution by a process of self-differentiation from ancient conceptions of individual or tribal retaliatory privilege, while the inverse is of course not the case. In keeping with the theory of the progressive unfolding of universal individuality, the justification of modern state's coercion of the wrongdoer in the *Philosophy of Right*[11] is based by Hegel on the idea of a process of 'universalization' of pre-modern conceptions of 'particular' revenge. From the perspective of modernity, retribution is made necessary and is justified when it is required by the *volonté générale* (in its acception as universal, not merely common, will) expressed by the constitutional state, and not by the particular will of parties more or less immediately affected by the actions of the wrongdoer.

Relations of mere diversity are characterized by the passive indifference (*Indifferenz* or *Gleichgueltigkeit*) of the poles being related. In diversity, the *relata* are in a symmetric, because reciprocally indifferent, relation to one another. It is thus that the apparent paradox of diversity without difference can arise. Relations of distinction, by contrast, are characterized by active differentiation (*Differenz*). Thus, in distinction the poles are not symmetrically related: distinction arises solely from the fact that one side of the related poles differentiates itself actively from the other. Accordingly, modernity and antiquity are not merely diverse with respect to one another. Rather, a continuity runs deep between them, as modernity attains and maintains its identity by the permanent effort to distinguish itself from its past.[12]

Despite the stress put on the divergence between ancient and modern ethicality, then, Hegel must also hold fast to the principle of their continuity: after all, they are shapes of one and the same spirit. Indeed, self-differentiation is only possible in a context of continuity. The dialectical notion that helps describe how one moment—here: one epoch—gives way to the next, namely sublation, expresses precisely this continuity-in-difference. To cognize the ancient mind is for us to recognize an essential dimension of our own.

In a sense, Hegel's emphasis on the relation of past and present philosophic theories runs counter to the intuition and methodology of many contemporary interpretations of ancient philosophy. These tend to project modern problems, presuppositions and controversies back into ancient texts. In this way, Platonic dialogues (for example, the *Crito*) have been described as struggling with the predicament of the individual citizen, conceived as the bearer of rights, *vis-à-vis* the right of the state—despite the obvious anachronism of this interpretation. Similarly, Aristotle has been presented as the earliest of the empiricists despite the central role played by the unmoved mover, the *nous*, or the identity of *nous* and *noetos* in his philosophy.

For Hegel, at any rate, the study of antiquity is part of the historical process of spirit's fulfilling its Socratic destiny: know thyself. In view of the popularity attained by the Delphic Apollo's injunction over the centuries, Hegel stresses repeatedly that its relevance lies in its philosophical, not psychological meaning. The ultimate aim, essence or concept of spirit, thus of its absolute forms as art, religion and philosophy, is succinctly formulated in the Greater Logic and the Philosophy of Spirit as spirit's knowledge of its own actuality:

> The most important point for the nature of spirit is the relationship, not only of what it is *in-itself* to what it is *actually*, but rather [the relationship] of what *it knows itself to be*. This self-knowing is thus, since spirit is essentially consciousness, the fundamental determination of its *actuality* (*GW* 21, 15–16).[13]

And:

> Knowledge of spirit is the most concrete knowledge, therefore the highest and most difficult one.[14] *Know thyself*, this absolute

> command, does not mean, either in itself or where it appears in its historical expression, mere *self-knowledge* of the *particular* abilities, character, drives and weaknesses of the individual, but means rather knowledge of the true in man [Mensch] as well as of the true in and for itself,—of *essence* itself as spirit (*E* § 377).[15]

Hegel's conception of spirit as self-differentiating activity rests on the logical category of difference-in-identity. As has been discussed in Chapter 1 above, the dynamics of spirit is of the same kind as the organic movement of a living cell, which is primarily a self-differentiating unit. The result of spirit's self-differentiation is a plurality of spiritual modes. Hegel calls the most basic form of self-differentiation an act of 'primary judgment' (*Ur-theil*), that is, of division or critique (*teilen* is the German rendition of the Greek *krinein*). The primary judgment of spirit is both a theoretical and practical act: cognition in general dirempts itself into knowing an other and self-knowing, will in general into willing an other and self-will. (In Aristotle, we find the dialectic of identity and difference in cognition, or the dirемptive character of thought, expressed as follows: 'That which judges [that two are different], judges then instantaneously and hence as an inseparable unit in an inseparable time.')[16]

Hegel's thesis with respect to Plato's understanding of ethicality is best understood against this logical and metaphysical background. Plato's vision represents one of the earliest phases in the self-knowing and self-willing of spirit. There is in Plato's work, Hegel claims, an ambiguous precursor of the modern idea of the right of subjective individuality.

In the *Philosophy of Right*, in the wake of Rousseau's establishment of an indissoluble connection between *droit* and *volonté*, Hegel defines right in general as a function of the will. Thus, the moderns' conception of individual right grounds in their conception of individual will. The latter is thought of as the spring of particular motives of action and particular interests. The universalization of individual will means that the fact of the inherent particularity of the will becomes a recognized universal right. Hegel claims, now, to find in Plato's thought an early form of this notion of a right to one's particularity, that is, to one's will and its satisfaction. He also claims, however, that this notion and the reality it denotes play in Plato's work a negative role: they are recognized as a threat to the harmony of true ethical life. Individual will is therefore an 'idea' whose elimination is essential to guaranteeing a state of rightfulness: the just state. To Plato, subjective freedom in the *kallipolis* appears as the enemy emerging from within the universal itself.

5.1 *Apology*: hearkening to the few

Hegel's hypothesis of the absence (or perhaps negative presence) of a conception of the right to particularity in Greek ethical world-views goes hand in hand with his claim that the criterion of an individual and autonomous insight into right and wrong is largely absent from the moral philosophizing of the ancients.

In Plato's case, this interpretation is borne indeed by a careful reading of passages and arguments from Socratic dialogues that bear most immediately on this topic.

Readers of Plato's *Apology* or *Crito* are familiar with the feeling of disconcertment afforded by Socrates' glaring lack of interest in individuals' sense of guilt or their capacity for autonomous judgment—in contrast to his obvious familiarity with, and repeated appeals to, the authority of ethical experts, feelings of social shame (*aidos*) or a desire for fame or good reputation (*kleos*).[17]

A survey of the criteria for the ethical assessment of actions and motives in both dialogues reveals three implicit definitions of ethical wrong: wrong is (a) defiance of existing authority, (b) incompatibility with *élite* opinion and (c) breach of agreement—whose prototypical form, for example in the *Apology*, is the implicit agreement between the moral agent (Socrates) and state rule (the Laws). In Plato's political philosophy, as is well known, state authority must reside with a capable and educated *élite*, the philosopher-kings; furthermore, what could be called contractualism in the *Apology* does not refer to a horizontal agreement among individuals to found the state, but is confined to a vertically structured compact between single citizens and the existing state. It follows that the three definitions of the infringement of ethical right are intimately connected. They are really three elements of one definition: wrong is (a) defiance of the authority of (b) a minority of experts with whom (c) the wrongdoer is tied by an agreement.

Despite the apparent paradox of Plato's sympathizing with his teacher's defiance of authority, the equally sympathetic description of Socrates' ultimate refusal to escape state 'justice' shows that Plato's conception of wrong (and thus, indirectly, that of right) is perfectly consistent with the three elements of the definition just given. Plato's obvious admiration of the dissenting, 'anti-authoritarian' aspect of Socrates' behavior is easily explained by the circumstance that, before his acceptance of the Laws' verdict, Socrates has been resisting the authority of *demokratia*, not that of a (philosophic) oligarchy. As pointed out by scholars of classical antiquity, Plato's attitude in this point corresponds largely with that of prominent intellectuals of his time. The following comment of J.K. Dover on the comic poets, for example, applies equally well to Socrates' and, with qualifications, to Plato's position: 'the most eminent comic poets may well have been, by temperament and upbringing, critical of democratic politics, particularly since the democratic constitution was "the establishment" and revolution could only come from the right.'[18]

It is also worth noticing that Socrates' dissention does not consist of straightforward noncompliance but of the continuous attempt to engage the powers that be in a sort of *ante litteram* rational community of debaters—with truly democratic intent but in total oblivion of real relations of power. In *Crito*, the Laws insist that they merely issue proposals, not savage commands.[19] And yet they will condemn Socrates despite the fact that his entire life has been devoted to the open, public and argued criticism of these so-called proposals. Socrates' death sentence can only lead us to conclude that the Laws' tolerant attitude (and Plato's in principle sympathy) is limited to attempts at persuasion that turn out to be successful and does not extend to the very concept and practice of public argumentative persuasion as such, independently of success or defeat.

In the *Apology*, the appeal to a minority of ethical experts for the sake of distinguishing between good and corrupt men and their respective actions is carried out through a strident analogy between the moral educators of young men and the breeders of horses:

> All the Athenians, it seems, make the young into fine good men, except me, and I alone corrupt them. . . . Tell me: does this also apply to horses do you think? That all men improve them and one individual corrupts them? Or is quite the contrary true, one individual is able to improve them, or very few, namely, the horse breeders, whereas the majority, if they have horses and use them, corrupt them? (*Apology* 25 b–c).

Despite his castigation of Homeric figures in the *Politeia*, here Plato does not refrain from presenting archaic heroes as models of Socrates' obstinately insubordinate attitude. In Greek literature, while heroes are hailed because of their physical and spiritual courage, their virtue is ultimately explained as being rooted in, and fed by, their overwhelming fear of social disapproval. The pursuit of honor is the main motivator of the hero, and honor is measured on the scales of social reputation and posthumous fame. Achilles, for example, is the greatest of heroes mainly because, as Socrates says borrowing from the *Iliad*, he is 'so contemptuous of danger compared with disgrace.'[20] In other words: Achilles' choice is the hero's choice between fear and terror, between the natural fear of pain, death or captivity, and the terror instilled by social repudiation, the complete withdrawal of recognition by peers and posterity.

Plato makes Socrates quote approvingly Achilles' self-diagnosis about what motivates his righteous actions—or rather, as Plato puts it, his 'doing the deeds of a good man.'[21] The inward spring of action is for Achilles neither conscience nor personal insight into what is objectively right. It is not even the prospect of future pangs of conscience for having neglected to do what a good man would do. It is rather, in the hero's own words, the fear 'to live a coward who did not avenge his friends,'[22] words for which he earns the unconditional moral approval of Socrates. This fear, in turn, is explained as grounding in the horror of becoming the object of public derision and contempt:

> Someone might say: 'Are you not ashamed,[23] Socrates, to have followed the kind of occupation that has led to your being now in danger of death?' However, I should be right to reply to him: '. . . a man who is any good at all . . . should look to this only in his actions, whether what he does is right or wrong, whether he is acting like a good or a bad man.' . . . the son of Thetis . . . despised death and danger and was much more afraid to live a coward who did not avenge his friends. 'Let me die at once,' he said, 'when once I have given the wrongdoer his deserts, rather than remain here, a laughing-stock by the curved ships, a burden upon the earth' (*Apology* 28 b–d).[24]

Thus, despite Socrates' dismissal of Crito's initial argument that nonconforming conduct is reprehensible because it brings shame upon an agent, he does after all endorse reliance on popular opinions about cowardice, retaliation and ridicule in the justification of a hero's stance. This is one point in which philosophical insight and popular wisdom do not diverge noticeably.

What has been rightly characterized as 'the universal Greek fear of humiliation'[25] finds expression, even more than in philosophic argument, in popular epics, in lyrics, in tragic and comic literature, in court records or political oratory. In ways that are more familiar to modern readers than we like to admit, victims of fate or wrongdoing are widely (though not universally)[26] considered blameworthy. Before and during the classical age, losing a case in court or losing a military battle is deemed shameful for the loser no matter what the objective odds were against him or her to begin with. The same judgment is often extended in Greek literature to one's illegitimate birth, advanced age, physical disability, death by murder, and even dismemberment after death or lack of proper burial. It is important to keep in mind that the Greek word for 'disgraceful' (*aischros*), so widely used in Greek moral discourse, means originally 'repellent *for any reason*,'[27] not just, as in contemporary use, blameworthy because of the personal responsibility involved in the action. For the ancient mind, the array of circumstances that make agents and actions morally repellent is much wider than for the modern mind, as it includes material and physical factors: financial misfortune, ugliness or bodily inability are, more often than not, imputed negatively to the subject whose worthiness is being assessed.

Plato's own unwillingness to distinguish fear of external consequences from fear of internal feelings of guilt constitutes no exception to this context. The overall judgment given by Dover on the reasons for the inconclusive character of Socrates' arguments for virtuous behavior in the *Politeia* is worth quoting in full:

> Plato's Socrates, attempting to demonstrate that virtue is better than vice for its possessor, irrespective of the consequences . . . succeeds only in demonstrating that good men will earn honor, and bad men contempt, from those whose psychological and philosophical standpoint is Socratic. He suggests reasons for which a good man, though persecuted, may sometimes be happier than bad men who enjoy power and success, but he cannot show that this must necessarily be the case; one single tyrant dying in old age content with a lifetime of oppression and self-indulgence would be enough to refute such a contention. Not surprisingly, the *Republic* ends with a story about reward and punishment of the soul after death.[28]

Despite claiming repeatedly that his wisdom consists of awareness of his own ignorance, Socrates does after all lay claim to one positive piece of wisdom. This is the knowledge that what constitutes wrongdoing is insubordination to authority—with little distinction made between legitimate and illegitimate authority:

> And surely it is the most blameworthy ignorance to believe that one knows what one does not know. It is perhaps on this point and in this respect, gentlemen, that I differ from the majority of men . . . I do know, however, that it is wicked and disgraceful to do wrong, to disobey one's superior, be he god or man (*Apology* 29 b).

As in numerous other passages, here Socrates qualifies negative moral qualities (ignorance and wrongdoing) primarily by the negative reputation they are known to engender: ignorance is blameworthy (*eponeidistos*: literally 'worthy of being thrown an insult at'), wrongdoing is shame- or disgraceful (*aischron*). The recurrence of these and equivalent formulations suggests the conclusion that the wrong and the disgraceful are, even in Socrates' mind, coextensive. Furthermore, Socrates lays claim to only one, and for this reason fundamental, ethical insight. Since in the context of a discussion of knowledge and ignorance 'one's superior' must refer primarily to superiority in knowledge, then wrongfulness must be a deviation from the (ethical) knowledge of an educated *élite*.

Nowhere does Socrates claim to have intimate knowledge of good and evil or to be able to deduce moral concepts' meanings; nowhere does he provide rational proof of actions' worth, of the rightfulness of agreements, or of the legitimacy of authority. At most, he mentions the demonic voice—originating in an undetermined, utterly impersonal source—that prohibits certain courses of action but remains silent on others:

> I have a divine or spiritual sign that Meletus has ridiculed in his deposition. This began when I was a child. It is a voice, and whenever it speaks it turns me away from something I am about to do, but it never encourages me to do anything (*Apology* 31d).
>
> At all previous times my familiar prophetic power, my spiritual manifestation, frequently opposed me . . . but now . . . my divine sign has not opposed me . . . Yet in other talks it often held me back in the middle of my speaking (*Apology* 40 b).[29]

5.2 *Crito*: hearkening to a *daimon*

An understanding of ethical wrong as inadequacy to the authoritative opinions and expectations of experts is also implicit in much of the text of *Crito*.

Due to Socrates' scorn of his friend's 'slavish' dependency upon the opinions of the many, a modern reader may at first be misled into thinking that the philosopher is advocating the moral superiority of personal insight. Yet, the criterion Socrates offers to Crito for distinguishing right from wrong action is not the alternative we would expect to submitting to majority opinion. Socrates' alternative is still very far from what the Enlightenment would call an individual's 'emergence from self-imposed tutelage' or enfranchisement from 'the inability to use one's understanding without guidance from another.'[30] According to Socrates, the alternative to tutelage of the many is simply tutelage of the knowledgeable few:

> My good Crito, why should we care so much for what the majority think? The most reasonable people, to whom one should pay more attention, will believe that things were done as they were done [that is, they will have the true belief] (*Crito* 44 c).
>
> [D]o you not think it a sound statement that one must not value all the opinions of men, but some and not others, nor the opinions of all men, but those of some and not of others? . . . The good opinions are they not those of wise men, the bad ones those of foolish men? (*Crito* 47 a).

These rather circular formulations acquire relevance only when these and like passages are read against the background of the epistemic and ontological distinctions between opinion and cognition drawn in the fifth book of the *Politeia*[31] and illustrated by the Divided Line and the Allegory of the Cave in the sixth and seventh books. The distinction drawn is one between thought that refers to what is intermediate between being and non-being, and thus more appropriately called opinion, and thought referring to what actually is, and thus legitimately called knowledge. And yet in all relevant passages, whether dealing with cognitive, aesthetic or ethical matters, Plato links ignorance, mere opinion and actual knowledge directly to the differing natures of the *bearers* of ignorance, opinion and knowledge respectively. The following excerpts from Socrates' speech in the fifth book will suffice to illustrate this point:

> So, I draw this distinction: On one side are those you just now called lovers of sights, lovers of crafts, and practical people; on the other side are those . . . whom one would alone call philosophers. . . . The lovers of sights and sounds . . . their thought is unable to see and

> embrace the nature of the beautiful itself. . . . In fact, there are very few people who would be able to reach the beautiful itself and see it by itself. . . . So we'd be right to call his thought [of him who can see the beautiful itself] knowledge, since he knows, but we should call the other person's thought opinion, since he opines? (*Politeia* 476 a–d).

As it befits Plato's elitist worldview, the truthfulness of cognitions and the moral goodness of actions appear to be here almost inversely proportional to the number of people holding them. This is evident also in Socrates' choice of analogies in *Crito*: the moral hero facing an ethical dilemma should seek the advice of him who knows best, just like the athlete should rely only on his doctor's or trainer's judgment.[32] Furthermore, the reason for following the expert's ethical judgment lies in the fact that by defaulting on the expert's expectations the moral trainee will face even more dread and embarrassment than by facing the disapproval of the masses:

> With actions just and unjust, shameful and beautiful, good and bad, . . . should we follow the opinion of the many [*ton pollon doxe*] and fear it, or that of the one [*te tou enos*], if there is one who has knowledge of these things and before whom we feel fear and shame more than before all the others? (*Crito* 47 d).

An important element of the Laws' definition of 'wrong' in the *Crito* is as well 'breach of agreement,' though not in any sense the modern reader would be familiar or comfortable with. Plato's choice of analogies reveals at once how far removed *homologia* (agreement) and *homologeo* (to hold the same language or to agree) are from modern or contemporary contractarian conceptions. One of the most revealing passages in this regard is where the Laws, apparently oblivious to the juridical logic and actual relations of slave-keeping societies, liken the citizen who is running away from the responsibilities accrued to him by previous agreements with the runaway slave—precisely one who, we must assume, has not stipulated any such agreement:

> Whoever of you remains . . . has in fact come to an agreement with us to obey our instructions . . . you act like the meanest type of slave [*doulos ho phaulotatos*] by trying to run away, contrary to your commitments [*sunthekas*] and your agreements [*homologias*] to live as a citizen under us . . . you are breaking the commitments and agree-

> ments that you made with us without compulsion or deceit (*Crito* 51 e–52 e).

Even Socrates' rhetorical device of quoting the Laws' speech, instead of presenting arguments as his own, is in keeping with the impersonal character of the source of ethical criteria in Plato's thought. For Plato, the objectivity of an ethical stance (what the moderns would call its 'moral truth') neither lies in its genesis (for example, in its issuing from a personal god's infallible will or from an individual's conscience), nor does it result from a kind of argument that every rational being could share. The 'proof' of ethically right deliberation resides rather in the impersonal authority of the Laws, and the force of the Laws' argument in turn resides, once more, in the coercive power of the foreseeable social consequences of unethical action:

> Will you then not now stick to our agreements? You will, Socrates, if we can persuade you, and not make yourself a laughingstock by leaving the city . . . all who care for their city will look on you with suspicion, as a destroyer of the laws. . . . Will you have social intercourse with them and not be ashamed to talk to them? . . . Do you not think that Socrates' action will appear an unseemly one?[33] . . . [M]any disgraceful things will be said about you (*Crito* 53 a–e).

Socrates' final assurance that he is, rather than the author of his convictions, merely their resounding board, is perhaps the most striking expression of the impersonal nature of Plato's criteria for moral discrimination: 'Crito, my dear friend, be assured that these are the words I seem to hear, as the Corybants seem to hear the music of their flutes, and the echo of these words resounds in me, and makes it impossible for me to hear anything else.'[34] The very choice of the phrases 'the words I seem to hear'[35] and 'the echo of these words resounds in me'[36] well conveys the ambiguous status (psychologically speaking, the almost schizophrenic character) of Socrates' convictions, a status that, from a critical perspective, makes it difficult to qualify them as being 'his own' in the full sense.

Against this background, Hegel also judges the aporetic ending of the dialogues to be grounded in a substantial philosophic issue, rather than in their literary or pedagogical vocation. The *aporiae* of the dialogues can be traced to the epistemic and logical inadequacy of appeals to ethical expertise, social renown, fear of ostracism and other extrinsic criteria for adjudicating the ethical dilemmas raised in them. In other words: the problems Socrates formulates appear to require for their solution a theoretical framework that is not historically available to him or to Plato. This framework would have to include the psychological idea of an *individual* consciousness with *universal* content (whose logical counterpart is in Hegel's terms 'universal individuality')[37] and a faculty of reason to make this contradictory notion intelligible and acceptable. But although we may glimpse these concepts, and others deriving from them, in Plato's recurring metaphors of gods, *daimonia* and voices, they never find explicit recognition in his work.

Hegel does recognize that Plato's silence on the ethical relevance and potentially universal dimension of particular subjective motives and personal convictions is occasionally broken by somewhat incongruous, positive allusions to individual judgment and even to something akin to conscience—of which Socrates' *daimonion* is perhaps the only explicit sign. One is tempted indeed to find in these rare passages textual evidence for the struggle of the ancient philosopher against a seemingly inevitable development of spirit from knowing substance into self-knowing subject. In the Preface to the *Philosophy of Right* Hegel writes:

> In the course of this treatise I have remarked that *Plato*, . . . conscious of the deeper principle breaking into [Greek ethical life] but appearing in it immediately only as a longing still unfulfilled and thereby only as depravity . . . had to seek a remedy against it by which he thought to overpower that depravation and by which in fact he did the greatest injury[38] to its deeper impulse, namely free infinite personhood (*W* 7 p. 24).[39]

In this passage, the collapse of antiquity's dominant, relatively stable form of social and political life is being diagnosed as resulting from an internal imbalance or, as Hegel puts it in other contexts, from an inward contradiction.[40] Repeatedly, spirit comes to be at variance with itself in the course of history. At the turning point of each of its transitions from one major developmental phase to the next, the two phases confront and oppose one another, prompting spirit to alienate itself from itself. The self-alienation of spirit concerns of course as much material history as the history of thought. It is precisely as an epochal moment of the latter that ancient philosophy can be seen as the most 'natural' form of philosophic thinking. Thus, the self-alienation that spells the demise of the ancient world and its thought is analogous to the self-alienated stage of the most natural form of spirit: soul.

In the Anthropology Hegel defines the soul's alienated state or illness (*Seelenkrankheit*) as a relapse onto the level of 'spirit existing in a subordinate and more abstract form,'[41] namely as a regress to a merely natural stage of soul. The description of this 'deranged' state of spirit in the transition from soul to consciousness[42] is an apt illustration of how Hegel views the discord of Plato's world (and Plato's thought) with its foe:

> Since at this standpoint it [the soul] appears at variance with itself, we shall have to consider it in its *diseased* state. A contradiction between freedom and un-freedom of the soul is predominant in this sphere, for while on the one hand it is still fettered to its substantiality . . . on the other hand it is already beginning to separate itself from its substance, its naturalness, and so to raise itself to the intermediate stage between its immediate natural life and objective free consciousness (*E* § 402 Addition).[43]

5.3 Contradiction in the city: the enemy within

In the Preface to the *Philosophy of Right*, in a passage leading up to the discussion of the inherent rationality of the 'ethical universe' (*das sittliche Universum*) or the state as 'in-itself rational entity' (*ein in sich Vernuenftiges*),[44] Hegel offers Plato's *Politeia* as an example of his thesis that philosophic theories are fundamentally interpretive descriptions[45] of their own epoch rather than normative theories about political life, morality or knowledge.

This thesis, as has already been argued here (Chapter 1, 1.3), is not equivalent to the simplistic one of a merely mirroring or even recollective function of philosophy. Moreover, it is well known that Hegel holds this thesis to be true despite other philosophers' own understanding of the nature of their craft, which some of them may view as a creative act of genius providing, in its ethical articulations, original moral instruction for the improvement of mankind:

> It is just as foolish to imagine that any philosophy may go beyond its contemporary world as that an individual may overleap his own age, jump over Rhodes. If the individual's theory really transcends that, if he builds for himself a world *as it ought to be*, then this world will exist indeed, but only in his opinion—a soft element.[46]

A long tradition, beginning already in Hegel's own time, has interpreted Hegel's use of 'contemporary world' in this passage (and of 'actuality' elsewhere) as referring to *Dasein*, that is, to being-there or even to what happens to be the case. In a Remark in the 1830 edition of the *Encyclopaedia*[47] Hegel rebuts, in a somewhat bitter tone, these kinds of interpretation with regards to his (by then already notorious) statement from the *Philosophy of Right*: 'What is rational, is actual, and what is actual, is rational.'[48] In defense of this earlier statement he now writes: 'These simple propositions have seemed shocking to many. . . . But . . . we must be able to presuppose enough education to know . . . that, quite generally, being-there [Daseyn] is partly *appearance* and only partly actuality.'[49] It cannot be stressed enough that for Hegel the mere being of the world is precisely not what is rational in it. It is the 'what' of the world, its in-itself rationality, not the 'how,' that philosophy aims at uncovering.

In a polemic move, Hegel chooses to illustrate the idea that the essential character of philosophy is not implicit nor explicit prescriptivism with none other than the archetype of all utopian literature: 'even the *Platonic* Republic, which has become the paradigm of an *empty ideal*, has essentially apprehended nothing but the nature of Greek ethicality.'[50]

Prima facie, this verdict is astounding. One is hard pressed not to read the *Politeia* as prescribing an ideal division of labor and a lifelong separation of individuals in classes as ultimate guarantors of virtue and of justice. After all, Plato understands justice as the harmonic ratio resulting from the diversified social allocation of individuals on the basis of needs and talents that pertain to their natural souls. The harmony is supposed to result from the lower class's sharing the conviction of the ruling classes that their rule is legitimate:

> [Socrates:] If indeed the ruler and the ruled in any city share the same belief about who should rule, it is in this one [the temperate city]. . . . And when the citizens agree in this way, in which of them do you say temperance[51] is located? In the ruler or the ruled? [Glaucon:] I suppose in both. [Socrates:] Then, you see how right we were to divine that temperance resembles a kind of harmony? . . . It spreads throughout the whole. It makes the weakest, the strongest, and those in between . . . all sing the same song together. And this unanimity, this natural agreement between the worse and the better as to which of the two is to rule both in the city and in each one, is rightly called temperance (*Politeia* 431 e–432).

This harmony, Plato insists, is not a simple given, but a condition to be achieved. Yet Hegel insists that Plato's philosophy of the state is carried out as a *conceptualization of the essence* of Greek ethical life.

Essence, we learn from the Logic, is 'the sphere of *posited contradiction*.'[52] Considering that 'posited' (*gesetzt*) is the antonym of 'given' (*gegeben*), this means that the logical structure of the essence of every given implies a contradiction generated internally to each: essence is a contradiction for the being whose essence it is. In essence, mere being-in-itself has begun to self-relate and has thus begun, to this extent, to transcend itself:

> Everything is posited in it [the sphere of essence] in such a way that it relates itself to itself, while at the same time it has gone beyond this—as a *being of reflection*, a being within which another shines while it shines within the other.—Hence, the sphere of essence is also the sphere of *posited contradiction*.[53]

In other words, the essence of anything is its being, but being in a state of reflection. This reflection, however, is precisely the object of philosophic science. In this sense, Plato's philosophic description of the essence of Greek ethicality can be said to exhibit the essential contradiction of the Greek city. Thus, the question arises: what is the essential contradiction of the *polis*?

One way of assessing the claim that, instead of presenting a utopian alternative to the realities of his epoch, Plato is really expressing the contradictions between the epoch's being and its essence, is to compare ethically significant notions from Plato's work with the available historical evidence of Greek ethos. The following brief discussions of social class, of the twin notions of slavery and personhood, of property and of happiness aim at such a comparison and assessment.

(i) What the city lacks: a universal without individuality

Contemporary scholars of antiquity know as much as Hegel does that Athenian society in the classical age is not a place of harmony and unbroken continuity with the past. It appears rather as a relatively self-contained world of antagonism and strife, some of it bearing the unmistakable marks of class struggle—not the contradiction Hegel focuses upon—and some of it closely resembling forms of antagonism typical of modern civil societies, especially the conflicts among particular interests and between particular interests and the common good.

Attention has been drawn repeatedly to what some have called Plato's 'obsessive' references to class struggle in the city.[54] Indeed, in the eighth chapter of the *Politeia* we find oligarchy (here used to denote the rule of the wealthy few) characterized in terms of the mutual re-enforcement of hostile classes:

> [O]ligarchies . . . reduce people of no common stamp to poverty. And these people sit idle in the city . . . some in debt, some disenfranchised, some both—hating those who've acquired their property, plotting against them and others and longing for a revolution [*neoterismou erontes*]. . . . The money-makers, on the other hand . . . create a considerable number of drones and beggars in the city (*Politeia* 555 d).

As is well known, democracy fares no better in Plato's eyes. He uses explicitly the notions of internal strife and civil warring (*stasiazei*) to portray the kind of social body from which, to the philosopher's dismay, democracy results:

> [A]s a sick body . . . is sometimes at civil war with itself . . . , so a city in the same condition needs only a small pretext . . . to fall ill and to fight with itself and is sometimes in a state of civil war even without any external influence. . . . And I suppose that democracy comes about when the poor are victorious, killing some of their opponents and expelling others (*Politeia* 556 e–557).

Regarding class, scholars have long debated whether the rulers, the military and the third state of the *Republic* ought to be understood as social-economic classes or as castes. It has been argued quite persuasively that, as far as the social reality of Western antiquity is concerned, 'Caste is a phenomenon which we do not encounter at all in the Greek and Roman worlds.'[55] This does not exclude, however, that Plato's conception of hierarchy in the *kallipolis*, being critical of Athenian society, may instead exhibit strong connotations of caste—especially if caste is being conceived by him as the authentic, more stable because 'natural,' form of class.

Plato's vision of the city's social hierarchy exhibits indeed features that do not necessarily belong to a rational account of class society—not even an ancient one. His recourse to the Phoenician 'myth of the metals,' so far-fetched for Athenian audiences as to cause Socrates embarrassment for introducing it in rational discourse, is a case in point: 'How, then, could we devise one of those useful falsehoods, . . . one noble falsehood? . . . I'll tell it, then, though I don't know where I will get the audacity.'[56] The noble lie to be told to the members of the city consists in the explanation that the educational criteria assigning individuals to classes (as just presented in the second and third books) are rather an illusory dream, while the real ground of class membership lies in birth—the gods' admixture of gold, silver or bronze into the bloodstream of individuals assigning to each his place in life.

The life-long adjudication of citizens to one status rooted in their natural endowments excludes by itself social mobility. While this exclusion is one central feature—though by no means the only feature—of caste societies and their self-understanding, it does not play the same role in class societies, and it is certainly not part of their self-image. In modern class society, as long as the reproduction of class structure is guaranteed, individuals and groups may in principle move up and down the hierarchy, depending upon conditions indifferent to their 'natural place' in life—indeed the very existence of such a natural place is questioned in class society, where biological, ethnic, national or gender-characteristics are theoretically 'indifferent' variables for class membership. Not so in the theory and self-image of caste society. Though the real world of classical Athens may perhaps be successfully analyzed in terms of class relations,[57] the myth of the metals can be understood as an attempt to envisage a city that would embody the essential core, though not the developed reality, of Athenian society. In this light, Plato appears to be thinking of caste as representing class stripped of its surface mobility and accidental appearance: caste as the essence of class.

Hegel's view of what constitutes the essential contradiction of Plato's city is, however, not the antagonism of classes or castes. He locates the contradiction in the conflict between particular and universal interest. That such a conflict does indeed exist in the ancient *polis* and is there widely perceived as a fact of civilized life finds as much support in textual and other historical evidence as does the thesis of the centrality of class struggle.[58]

Athenian civilization presents indeed anachronistically premature forms of what modern philosophers would call 'civil society.' The rise of an aristocracy of wealth joining the ranks of the aristocracy of birth, a modest degree of inter-class mobility, the establishment of popular juries, the successes of political satire or the documented existence of skepticism in religious matters, are all ingredients of Greek *demokratia* that for Hegel (though certainly not for Plato) represent embryonic forms of existence of 'the *independent, intrinsically infinite personhood* of the individual, of subjective freedom.'[59] On this interpretation, legal institutions, economic realities, and cultural phenomena of Greek ethical life like the ones just mentioned carry within them the dawning, still abstract consciousness of a right to recognition of such freedom. In themselves (though not yet for the agents engaged in their practices) they imply that particular and possibly even individual interests or will have relevance and legitimacy *vis-à-vis* the substantial existence and absolute validity of the state's universal interest or will. This is what Hegel identifies as the main contradiction inherent in Plato's social world. Particular interest and individual freedom, to which Hegel sometimes refers as 'right of subjective *freedom*,'[60] is the 'other' emerging from within, and threatening the harmony of, the ancient state. As such, subjective right becomes the target of Plato's condemnation.

From a logical point of view, Plato's attitude is explained by Hegel as resting on the conviction that what is singular and particular is absolutely incompatible with what is universal—a belief grounded in turn in the principle that self-contradiction is a figure of thought lying outside the realm of intelligibility. On the plane of political philosophy, this doctrinal belief translates into a rejection of the hypothesis that singular or particular interests may imply and be implied by the universal interest.

To the contrary, Hegel's analysis of 'singularity' in the Logic leads him to the conviction that not only are singularity and particularity compatible with universality, but that this compatibility translates, in the juridical and historical sphere, into the insight that the complete development of individual personhood lies precisely in its universalization: 'the principle of personality is universality.'[61] As one ought not to confuse Rousseau's *volonté générale* with a mere *volonté de tous*, so Hegel's use of 'universality' (*Allgemeinheit*) ought not to be confused here with mere 'generality' or 'commonality' (*Gemeinschaftlichkeit*). It is the first, not the second meaning that constitutes the principle of personhood—individuality as a right. Furthermore, the ability to make this logical distinction is the result of a historical development:

> The universal in the Concept is however not just something common against which the particular stands on its own, but rather the self-particularizing (specifying) that remains by itself in its other . . . in its true and comprehensive significance, the universal is a thought that took millennia to enter into men's consciousness (*E* § 163 Addition 1).[62]

Hegel is insistent that lack of recognition of the concrete universality of individuals is a structural feature of ancient thought and practice: 'The Greeks, although otherwise so highly cultivated, did not know God, or even man, in their true universality. . . . Consequently, for the Greeks there was an absolute gulf between themselves and the barbarians, and man as such was not yet recognized in his infinite worth and his infinite legitimacy.'[63]

(ii) What the slave lacks: an individual without universality

The broad acceptance and recognition of the institution of slavery (intended as ownership of human individuals) in antiquity is one of the most striking common features of its many social formations. In these, slavery is generally viewed and, where necessary, justified, at once as a legitimate privilege of the master, a natural state of the slave and an unavoidable economic device.[64] Hegel interprets these views as resulting from the failure to grasp that the objective nature (the truth or concept) of being-human (*Menschsein*) is personhood (*Persoenlichkeit*). The ancient mind contains in itself, but does not posit for itself, the universality of the ego: 'What the slave lacks is the recognition of his personhood; but the principle of personhood is universality. The master considers the slave not as a person, but as a thing devoid of self;[65] and the slave himself does not count as I, for the master is his I instead.'[66]

In an introduction compiled by Griesheim from Hegel's lectures on the history of philosophy, the historic failure of ancient spirit as such is categorically (if succintly) summarized in a sweeping comment that is worth being quoted in full:

> The Greeks and the Romans, not to mention the Asiatics, knew nothing of this concept [of freedom], did not know that man as man is born free and is free. Neither Plato and Aristotle, nor Cicero and the Roman jurists, and still less the Greek and Roman peoples, possessed this concept although it alone is the source of right. They knew well enough that an Athenian, or a Roman citizen, an *ingenuus*, is free and that there are free men and slaves; therefore they did not know that man *as man* is free . . . , that is, man as apprehended in thought and as he apprehends himself in thought.[67]

As mentioned in Chapter 3, in the *Philosophy of Right* Hegel discusses the social institution of slavery along these same lines. The section on Abstract Right centers upon the external embodiment of the will (which, it will be recalled, is the source of right) in property. Here, Hegel brings up the topic of slavery in the context of property acquisition ('Taking Possession').[68] Hegel explains both the 'asserted justification of *slavery*'[69] and the opposite 'assertion of the absolute injustice'[70] of property in human beings as theses of an abstract antinomy. Historically, the thesis can be located within Aristotle's *Politics*: 'he who . . . is by nature not his own but another's man, is by nature a slave.'[71] The antithesis is epitomized by Rousseau: 'Man is born free, and everywhere he is in chains.'[72] But Hegel maintains that the antinomy is merely abstract: thesis and antithesis both regard 'man' exclusively as a natural being. The concept or truth of 'man,' however, contains more than its immediate existence as a natural creature. It is the concept of a natural creature's ability to own its own nature through the act of willing itself, body and soul, over against any other claimant:

> Man [der Mensch], in conformity with his *immediate* existence, is in himself something natural, external to his concept. It is only through the *formation* of his own body and mind, *essentially* through *his self-consciousness's apprehension of itself as free*, that he takes possession of himself and becomes his own property over against others. This taking possession . . . is the positing into *actuality* of what he is according to his concept (as a potentiality) (*W* 7 § 57).[73]

The ancient world is a world in which man still regards himself exclusively as a creature of nature, that is, as an entity 'external to its concept.' This kind of being can only be conceived (because it can only conceive itself) as a mere '*existence* . . . that is not adequate to its concept.'[74]

The problem with the use of man as a 'tool for tools' as codified by Aristotle[75] does not consist of its alleged incompatibility with nature, but rather of its incompatibility with the essence (only metaphorically called 'the nature') of man—what Hegel prefers to call 'the concept' of man. This concept implies that man is to become a subject of free will. Slavery is common and legitimated by custom and positive law at stages of human thinking that precede man's grasp of his own concept: 'This early, un-true phenomenon affects spirit that is only still at the stage of its consciousness.'[76] The new standpoint is attained late in the history of the species. It is the standpoint of self-consciousness. From this moment on, there unfolds a dialectic that eventually brings about the subjectivity of persons who will their own freedom and the objectivity of a state that guarantees and legitimates their free will:

> [T]he dialectic of the Concept and of the at first only immediate consciousness of freedom brings about at that point *the struggle of recognition* and the relation of *lordship* and *servitude*. . . . It is only in the knowledge that the Idea of freedom is actually true exclusively as

> *state* that objective spirit, the content of right, is no longer taken in its subjective concept alone, and that thereby man's in-and-for-himself incompatibility with slavery is no longer taken as a mere *ought to be* (*W* 7 § 57 Remark).[77]

5.4 Gifts of fortune, not deeds of will

Plato's role in suppressing subjective particularity is first discussed in the first major subdivision of the *Philosophy of Right* (Abstract Right). As has just been mentioned in conjunction with Hegel's treatment of slavery, Abstract Right deals with property as an outward expression of personal will. Property is the first—also the most primitive—form in which the will of individuals becomes objective to them, namely as embodied in a thing. Hegel argues that as long as this kind of externalization of the will, however rudimentary, is proscribed, development into more sophisticated, concrete forms of personhood cannot begin. The prohibition for guardians and auxiliaries of the *polis* to own property stems, Hegel maintains, from Plato's awareness of the connection between the first externalization of the will in objectivity (here used in the sense of thing-hood) and potentially more sophisticated and subversive forms of the will:

> The idea of the *Platonic* state contains as general principle a wrong against the person, namely its unfitness for private property. The idea of a . . . fraternization of all human beings with *communal goods* and of the proscription of the private property principle may offer itself readily to the kind of mentality which fails to recognize the nature of spirit's freedom and of right (*W* 7 § 46 Remark).[78]

The second part of this Remark, incidentally, seems to be aimed at Hegel's contemporary (and predecessor of Hegel's academic position in Heidelberg) Jacob Friedrich Fries, rather than at Plato. Fries' social ideals are characterized in the Preface to the *Philosophy of Right* as 'the broth of "heart, friendship and inspiration".'[79] Plato, who advocates the elimination of private property only for the ruling classes, certainly does not advocate the fraternization of all human beings. Be that as it may, this interpretation of the *Politeia* as containing in a prominent role a principle that denies the necessary (though not sufficient) embodiment of personal will in property is paradigmatic of Hegel's reading. Thus, it is worth reflecting on some influential ways in which this passage has been understood. In T.M. Knox's translation of the quoted passage, the first sentence is paraphrased as follows: 'The general principle that underlies Plato's ideal state violates the right of personality by forbidding the holding of private property.' This formulation suggests, through the use of 'violation,' the previous existence of a right of persons. Hegel's point, however, is precisely that the right in question has no place in Plato's ethical universe. Plato's principle violates no established right, but rather pre-empts such establishment in the face of unruly social realities. More important, however, is Knox's pertinent comment that Hegel's reading is in need of factual rectification, if indeed he is assuming here that private property is entirely excluded from Plato's idea of the *polis*: 'If Hegel has Plato's *Republic* in mind, then he fails to notice that it is the Guardians only who are there precluded from holding private property. But he may be thinking of *Laws* V 739.'[80] Rather than presuming, however, a hasty reading of the *Politeia* on Hegel's part, it may be more useful to recall that Hegel is concerned with pointing out in Plato's text a precursor of the notion of 'citizenship' in the modern sense, and that it is indeed the guardians who come closest to the modern idea of a self-knowing and self-determining citizenry. Because of their particular position, Plato is emphatic about the need to keep the guardians from participating in degrading forms of life typical of the lower classes. The foremost of these is the practice of objectifying their particular will (that Plato conceives as necessarily antagonistic to the common will) in the acquisition and holding of private possessions. The ideal state of which Plato talks in the fifth book of *Laws*[81] represents a generalization to the whole of the *polis* of the principle that in *Politeia* holds for the ruling class alone. And it is precisely this principle—whether applied to a few or to all—that Hegel holds to be 'a wrong against the person.'

The specific role attributed in the *Politeia* to those who embody their particular interests in private possessions seems indeed to confirm Hegel's interpretation. The lowest ranking members in the city's hierarchy, namely manual workers, merchants, builders and so on, are characterized altogether as 'money makers.'[82] In contrast to the auxiliaries and the philosopher-kings, money makers may privately own, accumulate and trade currency and material possessions. Hegel's point is that Plato's endorsement of money makers' privilege to buy and sell material goods relates directly to his low estimation of their soul's nature and their way of life. Private property in the city is not a matter of right but both an indemnity for and a symptom of the third state's congenital and definitive lack of power, that is, of self-control and control of others. In Plato's vision, a life dependent on money making marks one's permanent exclusion from power. Here, once again, his views are quite consistent with those of contemporaneous orators and poets. Demosthenes and Aristophanes, for instance, present essentially anybody who makes money for survival, for the improvement of his quality of life, or out of sheer greed, as either a servile nature or an irredeemably dishonest *nouveau riche*.[83] In sum: what in Hegel's theory represents the simplest, most abstract incarnation of free or self-determining personhood, namely the externalization of the will in property, is precisely what Plato considers incompatible with active citizenship. By denying the guardians the most basic embodiment of their will, Plato means to destroy in them, and thereby in the *polis* as a whole, the first awakening of free personhood.

In the second part of the *Philosophy of Right* (Morality), Hegel presents modern concepts of the good and their philosophic accounts as based on the historically novel recognition that the motives (*Beweggruende*) of human action have a double aspect: they are simultaneously objective or general purposes (*Vorsaetze*) and subjective or particular intentions (*Absichten*).[84] The recognition of the particularity of intention or 'right of intention' (*Recht der Absicht*)[85] as essential constituent of the moral worth of actions derives from the recognition of a more concrete, that is, internally complex form of subjectivity than the kind of subjectivity presupposed in considering only the general objective purpose.[86] What is being recognized by allowing subjectivity in the guise of intention to play a role in the ethical assessment of an action is the '*right* of the *subject* to find his *satisfaction* in the action'[87] or, according to a formulation already cited, the 'right of *subjective freedom*.'

Hegel's interpretation of the ancients' understanding of subjectivity in its ethical dimension can thus be specified as follows: it is a claim that neither intention nor a right to the satisfaction of one's particular interest (whether in the form of desire or of will) plays any pivotal role in ancient authors' assessment of individual agency. This claim ought of course not to be confused with similar sounding but quite different ones. For example, it ought not to be taken to mean that ancient individuals do not in fact seek personal satisfaction in their actions. Neither does it constitute a denial that this fact is reflected in the literary, juridical, or artistic products of ancient civilizations. Hegel's point, once again, concerns the ethical recognition of a right to subjectivity, not the factual acknowledgment of subjectivity's existence.

Indeed, Hegel stresses that the high place Greek authors accord to happiness reflects their active concern with and promotion of the satisfaction of 'needs, inclinations, passions, opinions, fancies etcetera.'[88] In the *Lectures* on pre-Socratic philosophy he points out for instance that already the sayings of Solon, by extolling the lifelong satisfaction of human drives and needs, really do conceptualize its quintessence as happiness or, as Hegel sometimes refers to *eudaimonia*, 'welfare': *das Wohl*. 'Happiness' does not indicate the satisfaction of this or that particular need or wish, but rather refers, in a manner forecasting conceptual universalization, to a state of control over the particularity and multiplicity of one's desires: 'Happiness as a state for the whole life, represents totality of enjoyment. This [totality] is something universal and a rule directed to the single enjoyments . . . [a rule] to restrain desire, to have [a] universal standard before one's eyes.'[89] Solon's legitimization of happiness marks a transition from the factual acknowledgment of individual desire and the (much later) philosophic-juridical notion of a right to individual satisfaction.

Hegel is thus not alleging that the ancients ignore individual subjectivity but rather that they neglect or, as in Plato's case, actively oppose the *idea of its universalizability*. They neglect or oppose the ethical and juridical quality of subjectivity, of what the modern epoch would call a 'freedom to' or 'right of' fulfillment of the individual's will. The satisfaction of particular subjectivity is taken by ancient thinkers to be a gift of nature (or of the gods) and therefore largely subject to contingency—something that may or may not happen to individuals depending on fortune, divine favor, or personal gifts. The original referent of *eudaimonia* is indeed a condition of life resulting from the 'good will of a *daimon*' and is mostly used to indicate not a state of mind as much as a social condition buttressed by wealth—a condition which, of course, may well be accompanied by a 'happy' state of mind. Solon's 'happiness' is universal in form, says Hegel, but not in content; it is not a deed of free will, but a gift from an external source. In Solon's world, individuals do not claim a right to realize their happiness through actions issuing from their will, simply because happiness is not dependent upon their will. Referring to a conversation Herodotus alleges to have taken place between Croesus and Solon, Hegel explains:

> In happiness . . . the form of universality is already present, but the universal does not yet emerge for itself. This is what issues from Croesus' conversation with Solon. Man as thinking is not solely concerned with the present enjoyment, but also with the means for obtaining the future one. . . . This edifying story wholly characterizes the standpoint of the reflection of that time (*W* 18, 187).[90]

This is restated in the *Philosophy of Right*,[91] where Herodotus' report is mentioned again: the generalization of happiness as subjective end in antiquity amounts to a prudent reflection about means for ends, essentially an endorsement of the short-term sacrifice of pleasure for the sake of the long-term attainment of happiness. Neither freedom of choice nor a right to that attainment, however, are part of this picture. Historically, the recognition of subjective freedom is a gradual process expressed in the most diverse phenomena of spirit's transition from antiquity through the Middle Ages to modern civil society and the state. (As is well known, when Hegel speaks of antiquity he mostly refers to the Mediterranean region, and when he refers to the feudal world he means the European Middle Ages. He understands, however, the structural features of ancient and medieval mind or spirit as going beyond particular geographic regions. He believes that the same features subtend non-European ancient and medieval worlds.) These phenomena are also useful focal points for the modern observer's identification of radical changes in the continuous stream of history: 'The right of the subject's *particularity* to find itself satisfied, or, in other words, the right of *subjective freedom* constitutes the turning- and center-point in the difference between *antiquity* and *modern* times.'[92]

Knox's interpretation of Hegel's overall assessment of this world-historical difference is very well taken: 'Hegel was far from supposing that subjective freedom is just freedom to satisfy what Plato called *to epithumetikon*—desire pure and simple. . . . On the contrary, he held that subjective freedom never came within the Greek purview at all.'[93] Although the utter denial that subjective freedom was ever part of the Greek spiritual horizon is perhaps an overstatement of Hegel's thesis, still the latter's judgment on Plato's leading role in warding off the unfolding of subjective individuality, and with it, subjective freedom, is unambiguous. Plato, Hegel maintains, inflicts enduring harm to the development of personhood by depriving the paradigms of citizenship, his guardians, of property and privacy (family) privileges as well as by stripping everybody else in the city of the 'choice of social status.'[94] The principles denying to subjects in the city access to property, family or social mobility constitute the philosopher's answer to forms of freedom that are already at work, albeit in embryonic form, in the real world of Athens' body politic.

Plato's famous characterizations of life in a democracy are symptomatic of his attitude towards emerging expressions of subjective freedom in the (real) city. In reading his descriptions, one must of course be mindful of the fact that the term he uses for 'freedom,' *eleutheria*, is the common Greek term for 'doing as one pleases,' that is, the kind of agency resulting from personal discretion or arbitrariness (*Willkuer*) and not from rational will (*Wille*). But even while referring only to the free pursuit of individual satisfaction, Plato's thinking about its possible legitimacy transpires forcefully in this famous caricature of Athenian democracy:

> A democratic city, athirst for freedom [*eleutheria*], . . . praises and honors . . . rulers who behave like subjects and subjects who behave like rulers. . . . A father accustoms himself to behave like a child . . . while the son behaves like a father. . . . A resident alien or a foreign visitor is made equal to a citizen. . . . The utmost freedom for the majority is reached . . . when bought slaves, both male and female, are no less free than those who bought them. And I almost forgot to mention the extent of the legal equality of men and women and of the freedom in the relations between them (*Politeia* 562 d–563 b).

Equally important is Plato's bitterly satirical conclusion regarding the freedom of dogs and asses in the democratic city, because it culminates in the disparagement of a citizenry incapable of enduring any kind of bondage (*douleia*)—the very ideal of citizenry extolled in the constitutions born from modern revolutions: 'No one who hasn't experienced it would believe how much freer domestic animals are in a democratic city than anywhere else . . . all these things together make the citizens' souls so sensitive that, if anyone even puts upon himself the least degree of slavery, they become angry and cannot endure it.'[95]

In the third and final part of the *Philosophy of Right* (Ethicality) Hegel contrasts the ancient reverence for order and harmony with the modern exaltation of choice and antagonism. In modern civil society, he says, self-conscious particularity[96] perpetually asserts itself against the controlling and containing power of the state's universality. If left unchecked, the self-assertion of particularity will produce and reproduce an economic and social polarization that undermines civil society itself. Hegel's description of the social and cultural manifestations of this dialectic shares both in the Platonic disdain of the arbitrary freedom of 'the many' and in the Rousseauian contempt for that of 'the few'—without of course sharing Rousseau's romantic attachment to the social figure of the destitute. If Hegel's judgment on civil society appears close to Plato's judgment on *demokratia*, we have to remember that in the *Philosophy of Right* modern civil society embodies a necessary, though not sufficient condition for freedom: it is a '*state* of *need* and *of the understanding*' (Not- *und* Verstandesstaat),[97] not, by itself, the incarnation of reason, *das Vernuenftige*. Hegel attributes 'depravity' to both extremes of civil society's spectrum: 'In these oppositions and their entanglement, civil society offers a spectacle of excess, misery, as well as of the physical and ethical depravity common to both.'[98] The ancient world, he comments, whether founded on patriarchal, religious, or as in Plato's case, philosophical principles, cannot but view the potentially subversive consequences of particularism as a menace to its *ethos*, which it understands in terms of a static balance or 'harmony.' With realistic foreboding, the philosopher of ancient society fears that the emergence of that subjectivity may become its doom.

In sum, there is no sweeping claim on Hegel's part about antiquity's general lack of awareness of or even concern with the particular or the idiosyncratic. He does not deny that the ancient world is able to discern and willing to acknowledge individual personality, group interests or other aspects of 'particular' existence. His allegation is that antiquity and its philosophers are not willing to acknowledge the moral and political *legitimacy* of such particular existences.

Whereas the breadth and depth of individual characterization in Greek tragedy are indeed very limited (undoubtedly because of the exemplary, archetypal role played by its characters and required by the archaic setting of their lives and deeds), characters in other literary forms of the classical age, mainly comedy and oratory, are often highly individualized. Comedy writers delight in the study of peculiar and diverse human types, whose eccentricities they associate with gender, social position, age, or sexual proclivity. Nothing is sacred to comedy, especially not the moralistic typology of human agency embodied in the Hero, the Heroine, the Patriot, the Philanthropist or the Philosopher. Comedy's characters are bluntly anti-heroic. Bullies and opportunists, immoralists and philistines, superstitious fools and cunning atheists, rogues and their victims: what they all share is their independence from literary, philosophical or religious models of the tradition. If Menander could elicit laughs at the elated reaction of the cook whose enemy has fallen into a well: 'There *are* gods, by Dionysus!'[99] his audiences must have recognized widespread skepticism towards established religious belief. Several extant fragments of literary works of the classical age are testimonies of ideas and attitudes stunningly divergent from what can be found in Plato's dialogues. A fragment by Antiphanes, for example, contains the extraordinary thought that the educated man forgoes retaliation when wronged and is motivated by compassion in all circumstances.[100] Comedy's dislike of *clichés* is of course at its best when it parodies the divine intervention schemes of traditional epic and tragedy. In Aristophanes' *Knights* the archetypal anti-hero, namely the sausage-seller, accompanies his gift of a hare to Demos with a parody of religious beliefs in the divine origin of human thought: 'The idea was Athena's, but the theft was mine.'

Hegel is of course familiar with this picture. His point is that the ancient world could have given ethical acknowledgment to, and thus a philosophical account of, 'the independent development of particularity' only in a self-defeating mode. The foe of ancient ethical thought is not the factual existence, awareness and enjoyment of individual subjective interest, but the inward free will whose expression it is. The foe is the potential development of the *fact* of individuality through its ethical *recognition* into a *right* to the satisfaction of it: the actualization of free will. This is the novelty that, as we have seen, Hegel judges to be the most significant difference between the ancient and the modern mind. His pronouncement on the form of consciousness upon which ancient civilization and its philosophic articulations rest is ultimately severe: 'These states . . . could not endure in themselves the diremption [of their ethicality] nor the infinite reflection of self-consciousness in itself. They succumbed to this reflection, as it began to appear first in mental disposition and then in actuality.'[101]

Plato's *Politeia*, then, accords merely negative recognition to the potential significance of the 'infinite reflection of self-consciousness in itself.' By preemptively outlawing this infinite reflection, Plato reaffirms the pre-eminence of ancient, originally Eastern ethicality. The so-called Eastern world—Hegel's chosen examples are India's caste system[102] and ancient Egyptian society[103]—is based on the 'allotment of individuals to classes according to *mere* birth.'[104] Plato's political philosophy incorporates this same principle, though on the potentially more rational basis of the rulers' selective educational system. With the inclusion of the so-called myth of the metals, however, Plato seems ultimately willing to accept the accident of birth as selection criterion, if only because of its usefulness as political propaganda—a 'noble lie' borrowed from non-Greek, barbarian mythology. Through this principle, citizens' right to seek their personal welfare is excluded from the rational organization of the state.

Though Hegel himself views the right to individuality only as a moment in the overall 'progress in the consciousness of freedom'[105] that is world history, it still is a necessary moment in it. While it already emerges in the purely substantial state of antiquity, it cannot but be conceived in it as a destabilizing factor of the social order: 'Thus, not being integrated in and unified with the organization of the whole, subjective particularity shows itself . . . as an enemy, as corruption of the social order.'[106] It is individual will, though still in its form as arbitrary will, that appears in the ancient world as violation of its harmony and threat to its very subsistence: 'The independent development of particularity . . . is the moment that appears in the states of antiquity as intruding corruption of the *ethos* and as the ultimate ground of their decline.'[107]

Despite the deep and long-lasting wounds inflicted by Plato to this first stirring of individual insight and self-determination in Athens' social world, Hegel maintains, this shape of spirit re-appears later, phoenix-like, as 'the pivot on which the . . . impending world revolution has turned.'[108]

The development from knowing substance to self-knowing subject takes place in human history (and is reflected in the history of philosophy) as a gradual recognition of the species' freedom. After the disintegration of the slave-holding world of antiquity, it is at first religious monotheism, then its inwardization, and finally its secularization that make it possible for subjective singularity to be conceived as being universal—first in its shape as unique god, then as god-man, finally as man.

At first, the universal dimension of individuality emerges abstractly in the formal notion of the juridical equality of every citizen of Rome. It then resurfaces in the early Christian notion of the equal worth[109] of individuals as one god's creatures. In modernity, this same universality is embodied in the recognition of free will or a right of individual subjectivity. This recognition is a gradual process that moves through the emergence of feelings of individual love, the romantic ideal, the juridical recognition of previously ignored social figures, and the development of a moral sphere distinguished from the ethos of tradition and custom.

Together with the rise and acknowledgment of conscience (*Gewissen*), the recognition of egotism in civil society, and other self-expressions of the ego in art, religion and philosophy, these phenomena of spirit are what the Logic refers to as process of self-recognition of the Concept as free. All modern arguments in favor or against the possibility of 'autonomy' understood as self-imposition of the moral or political law have been at heart arguments about the intelligibility of the dialectical concept of a universal individuality. The personification of god's will, the enlightened exaltation of personal insight, the conceptualization of freedom as subjection to self-imposed law, or the proof of the autonomy of the will: these are for Hegel variations upon the theme of the rational intelligibility of the speculative Concept.

It will be obvious by now that despite the metaphysical terminology with which he describes the transition from 'substance' to 'subject,' Hegel's theory of the real history of this transition includes as a matter of course its concrete, social and economic dimension. Indeed, in the last major section of Ethicality, 'The State,' the *Philosophy of Right* locates the transition in the phenomenon of the mediation of labor through the volition (*Willkuer* or *besonderer Wille*)[110] of the individuals who perform it. This means that labor becomes for the individuals a means to further their particular ends. Instead of performing work only according to another's will, one's work is increasingly seen as individual possession (much like one's body, talents, religious belief or inclinations) to be employed according to one's own will. In a decidedly materialistic vein, Hegel adds that the recognition of the right to one's work and thus, in the end, to one's will, explains among other things why contributions are exacted by the modern state not in form of personal services but in form of an equivalent as their 'universal value,' that is, in form of money.

> In *Plato's* state the rulers are left to assign individuals to their particular stands and to impose on them their *particular* tasks . . . in the feudal monarchy vassals had to carry out equally undetermined services, though in their *particularity* as well. . . . What is missing in these contexts is the principle of *subjective freedom*, namely that the substantial activity of the individual . . . be mediated through his *particular will*—a right made possible only by the requirement that services be provided in form of universal value (*W* 7 § 299 Remark).[111]

Neither ancient nor feudal social orders require that an individual's life activities be mediated through her will. The material side of the mediation in the modern order is represented by the exchange of wages (in universal currency) for the labor performed. Wages represent the abstract equivalence (the abstractly universal value) of particular, qualitatively different labors.[112] It is through this mechanism that individual volition begins to be integrated into the all-encompassing necessity of the general interest. This, Hegel notes, is one of the most striking features of the spectacle offered by modern civil society—the realization of freedom in its most abstract dimension: 'The egoistic end in its actualization, conditioned in this way by the universality—grounds a system of all round dependency.'[113]

Plato, Hegel maintains, cannot countenance the incipient phase of this dialectic. Fearing the destructive potential of free particularity, the extremes and degeneration to which it may lead, he repudiates it altogether. But if human history is the development of the Idea itself then, 'the infinite right' of particularity being one moment of the Idea,[114] this right cannot be banned from history. The ancient world pays for the suppression of this moment with its own dissolution.

Hegel therefore sees the *Politeia* as a work that, far from pitching a lofty ideal against a supposedly monolithic reality, rather gives voice to this reality's inner contradiction—and that is a dynamic contradiction between 'substantial' and increasingly 'subjective' experiences of the good and of justice. In this context, the 'substantiality of spirit' refers to an abstract, rather undifferentiated experience and conception of the common good; the 'subjectification of spirit' refers to evolving experiences and conceptions of the good as containing as well the particular good of groups and individuals. The dynamic contradiction between these ideas of the good finds expression in the controversies between Socrates and his contenders throughout the *Politeia*. While the single disputes remain unresolved, Plato aims at resolving the fundamental antagonism between knowing substance and self-knowing subjectivity by depriving the latter of any validity. The subjective particularity of desires and interests that threatens to tear the ideally rigid fabric of his society will bring about, with historical and logical necessity, an epochal revolution of social agency that is beyond Plato's grasp. In time, precisely the principle of a right to subjectivity will show itself to be the main factor in the collapse of Plato's world, enabling spirit to move on to new forms of its existence.

Among the intellectuals in Plato's time, the Sophists are the clearest ideological impersonation of an emerging (right of) subjectivity. Rather than conceiving the true and the good as objective or substantial goals, the Sophists take them to be the result of competent argument, acquired skill or—more scandalously still—personal interest or conviction. Sophistry embodies for Plato the paradigm of the corruptive, subjective element developing within the ethicality of a peaceful society of mutually segregated classes. To this threatening degradation of *ethos* Plato opposes his interpretation of communal life as a substantial one, that is, a life ideally devoid of all recognition of 'the right of individuals to their particularity.'[115]

Plato's idea of the state thus excludes precisely the principle that is constitutive of the modern—in explicit form, Rousseauian—idea of legitimate authority: self-rule. On the political plane, self-rule describes the principle of the necessary role of individual will and insight within the supreme legitimacy of the universal interest of the sovereign. Insofar as the modern concept of state includes the concept of free individual will, it embodies the logical figure of an identity of differences. Hegel calls it a concrete concept (or concrete universal), in contrast to which Plato's *polis* is an undifferentiated, abstract concept (or abstract universal):[116]

> In the states of classical antiquity, universality is already present, but particularity had not then been unfastened and let free. . . . The essence of the modern state is that the universal be bound up with the complete freedom of particularity and with the well-being of the individuals, . . . the particularity, whose right must be given its due (*W* 7 § 260 Addition).[117]

There is no place in Plato's work for the thought of a concrete unity of individual subjectivity with the objectivity of the state. He conceives individual goals largely as arbitrary or accidental and thus as naturally contradicting the city's rational goal, namely justice as balance. He sees no role for a universalization of individuals' interest to encompass, that is, to freely will, the goals of the whole, nor does he allow for the whole to make individual interest into its own principle, a non-alienable 'right.' When Plato does acknowledge subjective particularity, it is ultimately not as something (as Hegel puts it) 'whose right must be given its due,' but rather as the regrettable phenomenal expression of the social *hybris* of his time.

6
Dialectic Matters: Starting Out with Simple Motion

One aspect of Hegel's appraisal of ancient philosophy is directly linked to his interpretation of Greek antiquity as being pervasively involved in an epoch-defining struggle against incipient developments of individual or particular independence ('the independent development of particularity'),[1] that is, against tentative expressions of subjective freedom. According to Hegel's view, the struggle ends with the ancient world's succumbing to its foe, namely 'free infinite personhood,'[2] the same principle that will then provide 'the pivot on which the . . . impending world revolution turned.'[3] For example, in the Greater Logic, the Philosophy of Right, and the Lectures on ancient philosophy, Plato's ethical dialogues are repeatedly presented as attempts to counter the legitimacy of particular subjective views, motives and actions on the grounds that they must threaten the harmony (or justice) of the *kallipolis*' true ethical life.

Hegel contends that this struggle is reflected at the level of philosophic method in highly ambivalent treatments, especially by Plato and Aristotle, of the logical principles of non-contradiction and *tertium non datur*. For Hegel, the validity of these principles is in question precisely when the intelligibility of speculative concepts of reason is at stake, for example self-knowing consciousness, self-determining will, or the universal singularity of the ego. While violations of the formal logical principles are explicitly repudiated in Eleatic and classical philosophy, the possibility that their application may be appropriate to some contents of consciousness though not to others surfaces repeatedly in Plato's and Aristotle's texts—mostly, however, only to be rejected.

Hegel maintains that with respect to method, Plato and Aristotle often share with their criticized predecessors more than they are willing—or able—to concede. He goes so far as to maintain, for instance, that despite Plato's criticism of pre-Socratics' arguments he never truly overcomes the '*original* natural intuition'[4] that characterizes pre-Socratic thinking.

Hegel uses the expression 'natural intuition' in several occasions when characterizing ancient philosophic thought in a general way. The phrase does not always carry a straightforward pejorative connotation. In the Doctrine of Being (Greater Logic) he praises Anaxagoras as the first thinker to have intuited the implicitly speculative truth that *nous* is the principle of all there is. Without consciously developing this intuition to its conceptual (ultimately speculative-idealistic) consequences, Anaxagoras still provides a perspective (an 'intellectual view:' see below) on the universe that forms the core of all subsequent philosophic inquiry. The Anaxagorean *nous* contains the intuition that the subject-matter of thought cannot be mere being in-itself devoid of thought and, *vice versa*, that thought cannot consist of mere forms or symbolic marks of a subject-matter that has no essential connection with it. In Hegel's terms, the meaning implicit in this intuition is that while the Concept is the thought-determination of all being, being is the necessary form of existence of the Concept.

> [Anaxagoras] laid thereby the foundation for an intellectual view of the universe whose pure form must be *the logic*. This view is not concerned with a thinking *about something* that for itself would be a foundation extrinsic to thinking, nor with forms that would provide mere *signs* of the truth; rather, the necessary forms and own determinations of thinking are the content and the highest truth itself (*GW* 21, 34/Miller 50).[5]

Parmenides' 'one' and Heraclitus' 'becoming,'[6] Hegel continues, rest upon the same productive intuition. So does the Pythagoreans' 'number,' the universal element. To Pythagoras, 'number' appears best suited to function as an 'ontological middle' of sorts between a merely sensible and a merely intelligible dimension of the world's essence. But despite the sophisticated nature of this intuition, the Pythagoreans' choice is only 'the latest stage of that incompleteness [of thinking] by which the universal is apprehended as encumbered with the sensible.'[7] Being the birthplace of philosophic self-knowledge, the philosophy of the pre-Socratics can only find expression in a language suitable to the intuitive phase of self-knowing, namely the language of representation. In its choice of argumentative and expository forms, pre-

Socratic philosophy expresses the bold and impetuous 'childhood of philosophizing.'[8]

Hegel does not maintain, of course, that Plato and Aristotle merely reproduce the intuitive insights and the representational language of their predecessors. Thales' water, Anaximander's *apeiron,* Empedocles' elements or Democritus' atoms and void are being grasped in the classical era as general representations standing for concepts of objectivity. By uncovering the conceptual core of those particular representations, Plato and Aristotle do indeed inaugurate thought's discovery of its own universality in the manifold particularity of its objects. With this turn of consciousness begins philosophy proper as self-apprehension of thinking.

Lest Hegel's historical conception of such 'turns of consciousness' be misunderstood, it must be noted that his understanding of the conditions under which Plato's and Aristotle's work became possible is quite 'materialistic.' This can be appreciated by noting the passage from Aristotle's *Metaphysics* that Hegel chooses in the 1831 preface to the Greater Logic to illustrate the new conditions of spirit in the classical period: 'It was when almost all the necessities of life and the things that make for comfort and recreation were present, that such knowledge began to be sought.'[9] Still, for all its social and economic foundations (or perhaps because of these) this revolution is for Hegel nothing short of an 'infinite progress'[10] of thought in history.

Despite the praise, however, Hegel insists that even the philosophers of the classical age never cast off entirely the representational nature of their philosophizing, which displays throughout, he says, the 'substantial' character of 'immediate' forms of knowledge. Comparing his own work with Plato's, for instance, Hegel stresses the greater simplicity and abstractness of classical theorizing and of its subject-matter. The tale is told, he writes in the 1831 preface, that Plato revised his books on the state seven times. Hegel, whose work is a product of the modern world and must accordingly deal with 'a deeper principle, a more difficult subject-matter and a richer and broader material'[11] wishes that he could have revised his books seventy-seven times. The relative simplicity of the ethical life and body politic in Plato's world finds expression in the relative immediacy and abstractness of Plato's political thought.

As for dialectics, be it understood as philosophical method or objective structure of the world, Hegel comments repeatedly on Plato's 'poor' grasp of it even in those texts—such as the lectures on Plato's philosophy—in which he praises the *eide* as embodying the first speculative insight into the unity of thought and being. Plato's explicit appreciation of the power and value of dialectic does not reflect the implicit workings of dialectic in the principles of his philosophy. What goes under the name of 'dialectic' in the dialogues, Hegel alleges, is mostly a subjective strategy to either bring opponents' claims to collapse—under the weight of their own lightness, as it were—or to expose their vacuity in some other way. On occasion, dialectic is portrayed in Plato's works as a subjective irrational zeal aimed at destroying what he holds to be universal and permanent. In Plato's work, we read in the introduction to the Greater Logic,

> dialectic is commonly regarded as an extrinsic and negative activity allegedly not belonging to the matter in question, having its ground in the mere futility of a subjective mania to unsettle and dissolve for oneself the stable and true, or at least leading to nothing but the futility of the object treated dialectically (*GW* 21, 40/Miller 56).[12]

Even in his more positive evaluations and uses of dialectic, Plato understands it as a mere method of argumentation, essentially arbitrary, 'extrinsic' or 'subjective' in that it does not reflect the structure of objectivity.

Hegel returns to the topic of the abstract and one-sided character of the ancients' grasp of dialectic in the Greater Logic's Doctrine of the Concept. The context is the elucidation of the dialectical structure of the concept of reason *par excellence*, that is, thinking or the ego. In the same way in which the principle of self-determining subjectivity emerges occasionally in Plato's political philosophy only to be ultimately suppressed, so the notion of self-thinking thought surfaces in Plato's metaphysics only to be denounced as foolishness, self-defeating outrage or unsubstantiated subjective opinion.[13] On occasion, Hegel characterizes this aspect of Plato's thought as a lingering Parmenideanism.

Eleatic thought (and, with qualifications, its Platonic and Aristotelian renditions) is for Hegel a fundamentally abstract, non-self-reflexive mode of metaphysical thought. In the lectures on ancient philosophy he characterizes the latter and its persisting influence through medieval and modern metaphysics with these words:

> In this manner of ratiocination we see a dialectic that can be called metaphysical ratiocination. The principle of identity underlies it: 'the

nothing equals nothing, it neither passes over into being nor *vice versa*; thus, nothing can arise from sameness.' The being . . . of the Eleatic school is . . . this sinking into the pit of the identity of the understanding. This most ancient manner of argumentation is still valid to the present day, e.g. in the so-called proofs of the unity of God (*W* 18, 299).[14]

The prototype of 'metaphysical ratiocination' is of course Parmenides' proposition 'it is' (often rendered, if inaccurately, as 'the one is')[15] but in Hegel's view Plato's understanding of it falls in the same category. Plato takes the concept of being expressed by the copula in its 'immediate' sense, namely as referring to external reality. This interpretation suppresses, rather than exposing, the speculative core of the statement (a core independent of Parmenides' own self-understanding). In declaring the 'one' to be necessarily and unequivocally bound up with existence to the exclusion of everything else, Hegel comments in the Doctrine of Being,[16] Parmenides' proposition refers not to the external, but to the internal unity of the world. The proposition refers to the unity that thinking itself is. What Plato cannot grasp, according to this interpretation, is that the utterance 'the one is' (or 'it is') adumbrates the speculative truth that would find its first modern expression in the Cartesian *cogito, sum*.[17]

In the *Encyclopaedia*'s Philosophy of Spirit Hegel criticizes along the same lines Plato's non-dialectical understanding of *physis*. The 'in-itself subjectivity' of nature, he writes, seems to elude Plato entirely. The latter shows no interest in the conceptual structure of natural objects in general or, more specifically, in the continuity between organic self-development, the natural soul's self-gathering (described in Hegel's Anthropology),[18] consciousness's self-relation (Phenomenology),[19] and spirit's self-knowing (Psychology).[20] Plato's difficulties become nearly insurmountable wherever he treats of the most subjective of natural bodies, namely that of a person. His philosophy cannot unlock the mystery of the dialectical identity of soul and living body because it ultimately does not advance beyond a rigid dualism of the categories 'something' and 'other'[21] to attain the concept of their dialectical unity.[22] In order to grasp the speculative idea that the Concept is the truth of actuality (for example, that the soul is the concept or truth of the living body)[23] pre-modern thinkers would have to renounce the expectation that truth be 'something tangible'[24] that is, that it belongs to the domain of externality. The grasp of the Idea fares no better, in Hegel's opinion, in the neo-Platonic appropriations of the *eide*, which

Plato at least had identified with the eminently real. This the Neoplatonists took to mean that the ideas enjoy a higher and separate existence in God's mind: the 'tangibility,' Hegel comments, 'is for example even dragged into the Platonic ideas . . . as if they were just as much as existing things, though in another world or region.'[25]

Grasping Plato's ideas in a genuinely speculative manner—something Hegel is not even willing to attribute to Plato himself—would yield the realization that they mean neither more nor less than the concepts of the objects cognized through them:

> The Platonic idea is nothing other than the universal or, more precisely, the concept of the object; only in its concept does something have actuality; to the extent that it is different from its concept it ceases to be actual and is a nullity; the dimension of tangibility and sensuous self-externality belongs to this null aspect (*GW* 21, 34/Miller 50).[26]

But the relevant aspect of ancient philosophers' struggle against the immanent dialectic of actuality is that the conflict has strong ethical and political connotations. At times, dialectic is tolerated as an innocuous instance of foolishness, but in contexts where fundamental concerns of human life and political existence are at stake, dialectic is denounced as reckless speculation aimed at the perturbation of established truths and at the justification of vice and corruption. This, Hegel remarks in the concluding chapter of the Greater Logic, is 'a view that emerges in Socrates' dialectic against that of the Sophists, and a wrath which, conversely, itself cost Socrates his life.'[27]

Despite the fact that Hegel's overall judgment on Greek philosophy's ability to account for speculative objects of reason is a negative one, his assessment of philosophic methods in ancient philosophy appears to be more differentiated. While for example an ancient philosopher may explicitly repudiate self-contradictory propositions as meaningless, he may at the same time employ such propositions directly or indirectly in the discussion of complex enough states of affairs—even if only with the intent to deny the latter's existence. The Eleatic Zeno's paradoxes of motion are a case in point.

Hegel's commentary on the paradoxes in the Lectures on ancient philosophy well illustrates his conception of the successive sublation of philosophic methods and principles in the history of philosophy. For all its limitations, Zeno's ingenuous recognition of the contradictions inherent in the concept of physical motion amounts for Hegel to a recognition of the peculiar nature of speculative objects of reason. As such, Zeno's insight is fully sublated in modern philosophy, including Hegel's own.

The leap from analyzing a philosopher's theory of locomotion to attributing to it speculative import may seem incongruous. Hegel anticipates this objection by explaining that Zeno's focus on locomotion (and not, for example, on 'freedom' or on 'consciousness of self') exemplifies precisely that historical necessity by which spirit's self-knowing always starts out from abstract exteriority in its journey towards increasingly concrete inwardness: 'The reason that dialectic first fell upon motion is precisely that dialectic itself is this motion or motion itself is the dialectic of all that is. The thing, as moving,[28] has its dialectic itself in it,[29] and motion is this: to become an other to oneself, to sublate oneself.'[30]

For Hegel, the fact that a recognition of dialectics begins historically with an investigation into the nature of locomotion simply instantiates the general law of the history of philosophy he has expounded in the 1820 Introduction to these lectures: when philosophic, that is, self-reflexive thinking steps onto the stage of history, it directs its gaze at first outwardly. Cosmos, chaos, atoms, boundlessness, matter, the elements or physical motion are its explicit topics. But this externality soon reveals itself to be part of an inward-bound investigation: 'the outward going of the philosophical Idea . . . is not . . . a becoming other but likewise a going-into-itself.'[31]

In addition to his discussion in the Lectures, Hegel refers to Zeno's arguments in both the Greater and Lesser Logic as radical novelties in the ancient understanding of the relation between being and thinking. In the following, I focus mainly, though not exclusively, on the paradox of the moving arrow ('the Arrow') as paradigmatic of Zeno's method and its Hegelian interpretation.

In view of the fact that Zeno's own formulation of the paradoxes is unknown,[32] and in order to fully appreciate Hegel's stance on the Arrow, it will be necessary to focus at first on Aristotle's treatment, which is at once (literally: in one and the same paragraph) a rendition and a criticism of Zenonian thinking (section 6.1 below: Potential and actual motion). Moreover, since Hegel's conception of contradiction grows out of his critical examinations of Kant's treatment of antinomy, contradiction and contrariety, and since Kant himself has words of high praise for Zeno in the Antinomy of Pure Reason, an account of Kant's appraisal of the Eleatic philosopher's accomplishments (section 6.2: Pure motion) is equally necessary for a full appreciation of Hegel's own (section 6.3: Contradiction in motion).

6.1 Potential and actual motion: Aristotle

The various versions of the Arrow that have reached us can be fairly boiled down to any argument equivalent to the following:

[Premise 1:] Motion is changing of place.[33]
[P2:] Any object occupies at any moment only one place (equal to it).
[P3:] But an object in motion ought at any moment both be and not be in the same place (or: it ought to move in the place it occupies and in a place it does not occupy).
[P4:] The latter expresses a contradictory state of affairs.
[Conclusion:] Thus, motion cannot exist (or: Thus, nothing moves).

At first, the argument appears to be providing the simple logical analysis of a physical phenomenon. The analysis, however, leads to the dramatic and improbable consequence of denying the existence of the phenomenon altogether, as if Zeno's main intent were to shock his audience by proving that phenomenal reality must be rejected for the sake of logical purity (that is, absence of contradiction). Indeed many commentators, from ancient to contemporary, have taken this to be the central meaning of the paradox and have constructed their answers or 'solutions' accordingly. Among the ancients, Diogenes the Cynic is the first who, by the ironic character of his 'refutation,' shows perhaps an awareness that the issues raised in the argument reach further than confirming a hiatus between the requirements of formal logic and the ways of the natural world. Instead of attacking Zeno's premises or constructing a counterargument, Diogenes is said to have contradicted the conclusion performatively, namely by getting up and walking away.[34] But the Cynic's gesture, Hegel remarks in the Greater Logic, is only the palpable sign of the impotence of ancient philosophy *vis-à-vis* the insuppressible dialectic of *Wirklichkeit*. Diogenes' use of '*sensuous consciousness*' as falsification of a reasoning that yields uncommonsensical results is a 'vulgar refutation that . . . must be left to its own devices.'[35]

(i) A continuum of continuity and discreteness

Aristotle's criticism of the Arrow in the *Physics* focuses at first upon its premises. He does not call into question the inference from premises to conclusion. He seems to consider the argument, in other words, valid but unsound. To summarize the strategy that will be shown in more detail below, Aristotle's first move consists of attacking Zeno's premises as allegedly containing a specific, namely atomistic, theory of space and time. In these ill-conceived presuppositions, he maintains, space is thought to be a paradoxical composite of a-dimensional points, and time a composite of duration-less moments. It is easy to see how from such assumptions could follow an internally contradictory description of motion and, thus, the denial of its existence. Further steps in Aristotle's anti-Zenonian argument show, however, that he does not ultimately refute the thesis of the inherent contradiction of the concept of motion, except in the sense that he carries the contradiction onto a different ontological level, namely that of the contradictory determinations of the *dynamis* and *energeia* (or also *entelecheia,* as in the crucial passage 263 b 5) of objects of thought.

Hegel is critical of Aristotle's (half-hearted, as we will see) refutation. The originality of Hegel's reading of the paradox consists, first, in drawing attention to an unstated premise of the argument: [P5] 'States of affairs expressed by self-contradictory propositions cannot exist.' Second, Hegel shows that by tacitly accepting this premise Zeno's conclusion follows whether space and time are being conceived atomistically or holistically. The contradictory description of locomotion [P3] follows validly from both sets of assumptions. 'Zeno's dialectic of matter,' Hegel writes, 'has not been refuted to the present day.'[36]

Aristotle's most condensed assessments of the Arrow are found in the sixth book of the *Physics,* chapter 9: 'Zeno's reasoning, however, is fallacious, when he says that if everything when it occupies an equal space is at rest, and if that which is in locomotion is always in a now, the flying arrow is therefore motionless. This is false: for time is not composed of indivisible nows any more than any other magnitude is.'[37] And: 'The third [paradox] is that already given above, to the effect that the flying arrow is at rest, which result follows from the assumption that time is composed of moments: if this assumption is not granted, the conclusion will not follow.'[38]

In these passages, Aristotle's refutation is based on rejecting an atomistic conception of space and time. He first attributes such a conception to Zeno, then refutes it and goes on to repudiate the whole argument as resting upon false premises.

The *Physics* contains a treatment of all four Zenonian paradoxes. Given that our present goal is a critical elucidation of philosophic methods and our focus is on the Arrow, it will suffice to consider passages directly relevant to the latter. Aristotle refutes the atomistic hypothesis by two arguments that are supposed to work in concomitance. The first aims at proving that the alleged 'indivisibles' (*adiairetoi*) making up space and time cannot be continuous, the second, that they cannot be (contiguously) successive. First: the hypothesized indivisibles of space and time cannot be continuous because while 'things [are] continuous if their extremities are one,'[39] to have extremities is to be divisible into parts—which is precisely what is excluded by the atomistic assumption. Second: space and time cannot even be composed of successive indivisibles or else (as is the case e.g. for the series of natural numbers) there would be 'nothing of their own kind intermediate between them.'[40] But we cannot think of the space between two points on a line except as being a length composed of points, nor of the time between two moments except as being an interval composed of moments. Thus, points and moments can be neither continuous nor successive. But if such indivisibles can be neither continuous nor successive, then they are not the constitutive elements of space and time.

This discussion appears to convey Aristotle's awareness of an intrinsically paradoxical nature of space and time. Even without challenging the legitimacy of dichotomizing 'divisibility' and 'indivisibility' as exclusive alternatives, Aristotle recognizes that the problems intrinsic to the notions of space and time *as instances of infinity* remain: 'Nor can there be anything of any other kind between [points or instants], for it would be either indivisible or divisible, and if it is divisible, divisible either into indivisibles or into divisibles that are always divisible, in which case it [the something of another kind] is continuous.'[41]

Similarly, even if one allows for motion and rest to be mutually exclusive states of bodies, the paradox of motion would continue to arise. Bodies would rest in each part of the continuum while moving through the whole: 'If[42] everything must be either at rest or in motion . . . it follows that a thing can be at the same time continuously at rest and in motion: for . . . it is in motion over the whole ABC and at rest in any part (and consequently in the whole).'[43]

Thus, Zeno's absurd consequence arises either from the arrow's having to traverse discrete points of space during discrete instants of time without being able to be anywhere in between, or from the arrow's motion having to consist of states of rest.[44]

One might think that the situation would be different if Zeno had presupposed space and time as absolutely continuous. In this case, objects moving in space and time could be thought of as moving at all times and everywhere (or in every position) in their trajectory. At the very least, the paradox of the arrow would not arise. As Hegel points out, however, not much would be won by way of such a 'resolution.' There are actually two other Zenonian paradoxes, the so-called Dichotomy and Achilles that, though not based on atomistic assumptions about space and time, yield the same conclusion as the Arrow. Here is Aristotle's summary of both:

> The first [Dichotomy] asserts the non-existence of motion on the ground that that which is in locomotion must arrive at the half-way stage before it arrives at the goal. . . . The second is the so-called Achilles, and it amounts to this, that in a race the quickest runner can never overtake the slowest, since the pursuer must first reach the point whence the pursued started, so that the slower must always hold a lead. This argument is in principle the same as that which depends on bisection, though it differs from it in that the spaces with which we have successively to deal are not divided into halves. The result of the argument is that the slower is not overtaken (*Physics* 239 b).

By means of these paradoxes, Zeno demonstrates that a body in motion, having to move through infinitely divisible places, will never reach its goal or, rather, it will not move at all.

(ii) An intuition of infinitesimal motion

Faced with this new set of paradoxes arising from non-atomistic presuppositions, Aristotle attempts a solution at first by distinguishing kinds of infinity, namely infinite division or extension vs. infinite divisibility or intension.[45] True enough, an infinitely extended continuum cannot be traversed in a finite time.[46] This, however, does not apply to traversing a limited continuum whose infinite parts are not actual but potential (not divided but divisible). Thus, Aristotle's discussion moves (in the eighth book) into entirely new territory. The contradictory nature of locomotion must now be resolved by thinking of space and time in the metaphysical perspective of the actuality and potentiality of the real. Space and time, he explains, cannot be considered as actually divided but rather only as potentially divisible *ad infinitum*. At first, he appears confident that raising the problem onto this level will serve to destroy Zeno's inference. Instead of getting rid of the paradox, however, this move seems to draw Aristotle much closer to Zeno's thesis than was to be expected at the beginning of the discussion:

> Therefore to the question whether it is possible to pass through an infinite number of units either in a time or in a length[47] we must reply that in a sense it is and in a sense it is not. If the units are actual, it is not possible; if they are potential, it is possible . . . for

> though it is accidental[48] to the line to be an infinite number of half-distances, essence is other than being [*he d'ousia estin etera kai to einai*]. It is also plain that unless we hold that the point of time that divides earlier from later always belongs only to the later . . . we shall be involved in the consequence that the same thing at the same moment is and is not, and that a thing is not at the moment when it has become (*Physics* 263 b).

Thus, Aristotle maintains that infinite divisibility constitutes the potency, not the actuality of space and time. The potential infinite divisibility of space and time is, then, not an appropriate foundation for analyzing the actual event of motion. Still, the contradiction seems to reappear under the guise of an opposition between the potentiality and actuality of space, time, and thus motion. Implicit in Aristotle's rejection of the actuality of indivisible points and instants is, perhaps, an insight into the notion of infinitesimal interval. He has anticipated this notion in the fourth book, chapter 13, with regards to time: 'The now . . . is a limit of time [*to de nun . . . peras chronou estin*].'[49] He has argued for this conception in book six, chapter 3: if we think of *to nun* properly, that is, not as part of a longer interval (as in 'the "present" day') but in and by itself, as what divides past from future (or connects them),[50] we will have to define it as the uttermost (*eschatos*) time of both past and future, that is, as the last limit of the past and the first limit of the future: 'it is, we maintain, a limit of both [*amphoin einai peras*].'[51] These passages at the very least suggest that already for Aristotle the notion of limit can contain simultaneously the predicates of indivisibility and extension. In spatial terms, the limit must be thought of as an indivisible stretch, in temporal terms, as an indivisible interval. In such stretches and intervals the arrow may then be said to move without contradiction.

The notions of 'indivisible stretch' and 'indivisible interval,' however, are far from pellucid, at least from the perspective of Aristotle's hitherto Zeno-criticism.[52] If it is contradictory to think of duration-less moments constituting time (as Aristotle maintains), it seems equally contradictory to think of time intervals that are not even potentially divisible. For the same reason, the self-contradictory character of a-dimensional points constituting lines seems hardly overcome by the introduction of indivisible stretches.

Aristotle's strategies for disproving Zeno's inference seem to have entered a dead end. On the one hand, the attack on the Arrow's alleged atomism leaves a different set of paradoxes unscathed. Indeed, the hypothetical replacement of atomism with holism in the premises of the Arrow is no hindrance to concluding again that physical motion is illusory. On the other hand, the distinction between actuality and potentiality only shifts the contradiction onto a different level. It now becomes a contradiction between the potential discreteness and actual continuity of space and time.

There is an additional perplexity involved in accepting Aristotle's offered 'solution.' If the atomistic hypothesis is essential to the Arrow, then the Zenonian conclusion is actually too weak. If anything were at every duration-less instant in an a-dimensional point, then, rather than at rest, it would be neither in motion nor at rest. Aristotle himself recognizes this at several junctures in book six. If considered at a single moment, he writes for example at 239 b,[53] a body will not even be at rest: 'for at a now it is not possible for anything to be either in motion or at rest.' Aristotle, however, is apparently unwilling to grant that his own reasoning is simply a stronger version of Zeno's insight into the paradox that motion is.

In conclusion, it seems that Zeno's conception of locomotion as inherently self-contradictory is in principle independent of atomistic or non-atomistic conceptions he may or may not have embraced regarding space and time. The real bone of contention in the discussion surrounding the paradoxes seems rather to lie buried in their enthematic character, that is, in the hidden premise: 'States of affairs expressed by self-contradictory propositions cannot exist.'

6.2 Pure motion: Kant

Kant's sympathetic appraisal of Zeno's thinking anticipates Hegel's overall positive assessment of the Eleatic philosopher's contribution to the history of philosophy.

In the Antinomy of Pure Reason[54] we find a brief treatment of a number of arguments ascribed to Zeno by Plato, but Kant discusses in depth the metaphysical idea of motion in the chapter on Phoronomy of the *Metaphysical Foundations of Natural Science* (1786).[55] In the following, Kant's conception of pure motion as outlined in the *Metaphysical Foundations* will be treated first. After this follows a discussion of those aspects of the antinomies of pure reason that have direct relevance to Zeno's problem.

(i) Motion in the Phoronomy

The reflections on the nature of motion contained in the Phoronomy presuppose the Kantian distinction between objects of a possible experience and objects of which there may be only ideas. In this Kantian text, the distinction does not only concern 'objects' in the sense familiar to the physicist and the metaphysician, but applies to space as well. Since mobility can only be experienced through sensible intuition (it is not one of the *a priori* categories of the understanding, Kant notes in the last Observation of Explanation 1), then both a body in motion and the space in which it is experienced—that is, the matter and form of motion—must be perceivable. Kant calls this perceivable space 'material,' 'relative'[56] or 'empirical.'[57] Further, since matter in the Phoronomy is defined as 'the movable in space,'[58] even material space must be movable in (another) space: 'A movable space . . . presupposes in turn an other wider material space . . . and so forth into infinity.'[59]

Accordingly, an object moving with a determinate velocity[60] in its material space may move with a different velocity or be altogether unmoved relative to any other wider material space. The Observation that follows is of immediate relevance to the topic being considered here: 'All motion that is an object of experience is merely relative.'[61] To assume, instead, that objects (including material spaces) must ultimately move in one fixed space amounts to investing an ideal entity with ontological status. A fixed or absolute space is not an object of experience, but only a thought that 'means nothing but each and every other relative space.'[62] In other words, the concept of absolute space is merely a representation of the infinite regress of material spaces in which each given, experienced motion takes place. To lend that concept actual existence 'means to mistake the *logical universality* . . . for a *physical universality* . . . and to misunderstand reason in its idea.'[63]

If we take Zeno's moving arrow to stand for a generic object of experience, then this Explanation 1 of the Phoronomy lays to rest at least the *tertium non datur* hypothesis imputed (perhaps correctly) by Aristotle to Zeno: 'everything must be either at rest or in motion.'[64] To the contrary, the arrow can be described as being in both conditions at once, provided one does not privilege one material space over others as frames of reference.

In his next Explanation 2, Kant cautions against identifying motion with change of place. Unless we reduce our concept of 'body' to that of 'point' (the latter's motion requiring indeed a change of position in space)[65] material bodies can very well be in motion without changing place, witness circular motions, fermentation[66] and so forth. The most general definition of a body's motion, therefore, is not simply 'change of place' (as assumed by Zeno) but rather '*change* of its *external relations* to a given space.'[67] It must be noticed that for Kant, because of the relative character of motion *vis-à-vis* diverse material spaces (established in Explanation 1) the narrower definition 'change of place' does not even apply unconditionally to locomotion.

Since our present focus on the paradoxical character of motion is instrumental to grasping the ancient understanding of the contradiction inherent in concepts akin to that of self-relating subjectivity, it is worthwhile calling to mind here that not only Zeno but Plato himself appears to find motions that do not involve change of place quite intractable. Despite his recognition that locomotion differs from other kinds of movement, Plato's recurrent strategy is to reduce other motions to composites of (absolute) rest and change of place, that is, to reduce them ultimately to separable forms of locomotion (which he considers free of contradiction). The underlying aim of his complex but often inconclusive discussions of this topic is actually to prove that notions of subjectivity such as that of *enkrateia heautou* (control of self) are senseless expressions better to be replaced with conceptions of the interaction of different 'parts,' one exercising and the other(s) suffering mastership.

Plato's reductionist strategy may be briefly illustrated by an exchange between Socrates and Glaucon in the fourth book of the *Politeia*.[68] While they are discussing the unity and tri-partition of the soul, Socrates and Glaucon agree on the principle that one and the same thing (an individual soul, for example, or a single part of it) can neither do nor suffer opposite deeds at one and the same time and in one and the same respect.[69] As an illustration of wrong reasoning in such matters, Socrates brings up the example of spinning tops revolving around a fixed axis. He claims that it would be logically inappropriate for someone, no matter how 'amusing and [. . .] sophisticated' (a Sophist, in other words) to describe such objects as simultaneously resting and moving. The only acceptable description of spinning tops would be one that separates center from periphery. These being distinct parts of the object, they may be thought of without contradiction as finding themselves in opposite states: the center, resting, the periphery, moving. Motion revolving around a central axis is also discussed in the same terms in the dialogue *Parmenides*—this time, however, in order to deny the 'one' any possibility of its being in motion, on account of its lacking parts:

> [I]f the one moved spatially, it would surely either spin in a circle . . . or change from one place to another. . . . [I]f it spins in a circle, it must be poised on its middle and have other parts of itself that move round the middle. But how will a thing that has nothing to do with

> middle or parts manage to be moved in a circle round its middle? (*Parmenides* 138 c–d).

In the *Politeia*, at any rate, Plato is emphatic about the inadmissibility of contradictions in rational discourse, and yet he appears also conscious of powerful undercurrents against this conviction:

> [Socrates:] No such statement will disturb us, then, or make us believe that the same thing can be, do, or undergo opposites, at the same time, in the same respect, and in relation to the same thing. [Glaucon:] They won't make me believe it, at least. [Socrates:] Nevertheless, in order to avoid going through all these objections . . . let's assume that our hypothesis is correct . . . If it should ever be shown to be incorrect, all the consequences we've drawn from it will also be invalidated (*Politeia* 436e–437).

This reasoning is eventually used to support the claim that the definition of the soul (and then that of the city) as a unity of different and even opposite functions does not contain contradiction. This is how Socrates characterizes in the *Politeia* the unintelligibility of a genuine unity of opposites with regards to the expression 'control of self':

> Moderation is surely a kind of order, the mastery of certain kinds of pleasures and desires. People indicate as much when they use the phrase 'self-control' and other similar phrases. I don't know just what they mean by them. . . . Yet isn't the expression 'self-control' ridiculous? The stronger self that does the controlling is the same as the weaker self that gets controlled, so that only one person is referred to in all such expressions. . . . The expression is apparently trying to indicate that, in the soul of that very person, there is a better part and a worse one and that, whenever the naturally better part is in control of the worse, this is expressed by saying that the person is self-controlled or master of itself (*Politeia* 430 e–431).

We may now return to Kant's analysis of the 'extrinsic' dialectic of the motion of physical bodies. After reminding us that all motion is defined by two parameters: velocity and direction, Kant proceeds to define rest as a positive attribute of bodies, rather than as mere lack of motion: 'Rest is the permanent presence (*praesentia perdurabilis*) in the same place; permanent is what exists through a time, that is, what lasts' (Explanation 3).[70] As is the case with all other necessary attributes, also motion or rest will belong to bodies at every instant and place of their existence.

Kant proceeds to illustrate the three principles just established, namely: first, that motion and rest are relative to material spaces; second, that motion and changing of place are not identical; and third, that rest is enduring presence in one place. The illustration is carried out through two thought-experiments: a body's uniform oscillation[71] and the vertical throw of a body. The first exemplifies the ideal motion of an ideal body not subject to gravity (the example does not involve the swinging motion of a suspended body). The second exemplifies the motion of a physical body subject to the force of gravity.

In the first example, the fact that the total time of one oscillation (with uniform velocity) is equal to the sum of the times employed in each direction indicates that at the point of return the body cannot be at rest—or else the time of its enduring presence there (its *praesentia perdurabilis*) would increase the total time of oscillation. At the point in question, the body behaves exactly as if it were continuing with uniform velocity along a straight line, never losing (nor acquiring) velocity and thus never resting at any one point. *Ergo*, even at the point of return the body must be in motion. 'A body in motion is for one instant in each point of the line it runs through. The question is whether it is therein at rest or in motion. Without doubt, one will say the latter, as it is present in this point only insofar as it moves.'[72] On the other hand, at the point of return the oscillating body has either no direction or diametrically opposed directions at once: it is both still leaving and already returning to the start, which seems to indicate a paradoxical state of directionless motion (not entirely unlike that of Zeno's arrow at each point of its trajectory).

In the second of Kant's examples, a vertical throw involves the pull of gravity. This implies that the body's velocity is not uniform. The body will reach the point of return after losing its upward motion (due to the infinite decrease of its acceleration) and before acquiring its downward one. In between these two, the body must be said to be at rest: 'and so I ask whether the body could be considered moved or resting in B. Without doubt one will say: resting.'[73] On the other hand, after reaching the peak of its trajectory the body will not lose motion entirely: it will simply continue at uniform velocity (because now uninfluenced by gravity) through infinitesimal spaces for an infinitesimal time (because of the immediately renewed onset of gravity).

Both illustrations make us aware that by assuming that rest and motion are contradictory states of matter we may never step out of

Zeno's conundrum (though we may of course, following Diogenes, reject his conclusion pragmatically—that is, dogmatically).

These two analogous but contrasting thought-experiments highlight the conceptual difference between uniform and accelerated velocity: in the first case, no velocity is ever lost, thus excluding the object's enduring presence (not its presence *tout court*!) at any point of its path—even at the one point where intuition would expect it to rest. In the second case, the gradual neutralization of acceleration through the opposing force of gravity causes the body to eventually reach a velocity whose 'degree is smaller than any specifiable velocity,'[74] a moment in which it travels uniformly through 'a space . . . smaller than any specifiable space.'[75] Since no external force acts upon it, the movement of the body at this point is in principle not available to experience and thus the *experienced* body will be absolutely unmoved. Thus the illustrations show, according to Kant, that a body can be in a permanent 'state' without being 'static:' motion is also a state, but one of *kinesis* and not *hexis*. 'To be in a *permanent state* and to *endure therein* . . . are two different concepts.'[76]

Through the combination of (a) the idea that motion is change of a body relative to given spaces and (b) the idea of a body not subject to any forces, Kant has shown how inertial motion is conceptually different but experientially indistinguishable from rest.

There are numerous problems in this text that cannot be discussed here.[77] The one result of Kant's reflections that is immediately relevant to our topic is that rest and motion are not contradictory attributes of material bodies. Rest is not simply absence of motion.[78] Rest is a kind of motion. Thus, the concept of a body's presence in one place does not imply that of the body's forfeiture of motion in that same place.

Kant's reflections ought not be read, of course, as an exegesis of Zeno's understanding of motion but merely as preliminaries to a possible modern defense of it. Among other differences, Kant's reasoning rests on the programmatic distinctions of thought from representation and of conceptualization from experience, that are alien to pre-Socratic philosophy. The psychological fact that we cannot imagine nor experience movement in a point, motion without direction, or infinitesimal space and time, is a ground of rejection of the existence of motion for the ancient though not for the modern thinker. Furthermore, while Zeno infers from the apparently self-contradictory nature of motion that everything rests, Kant's reflections warrant the opposite conclusion: nothing ever rests, but what appears to be rest is inertial motion.

On one important issue, however, Kant endorses Zeno's reasoning explicitly: even if motion and rest are not contradictories, Zeno is still right in barring the simultaneous attribution of both to the same object *in the same respect*. Because of the relativity of motion discussed in Explanation 1, even for Kant the condition of 'sameness of respect' must remain unfulfilled: bodies can neither be *experienced* nor can they be *thought* as moving and resting in the same respect, but only as moving and resting simultaneously with respect to different material spaces encapsulating them.

(ii) Motion in the Antinomy

The seemingly contradictory but truly contrary nature of opposing predicates is the main theme underlying Kant's discussion, in the Antinomy of Pure Reason, of three further arguments ascribed to Zeno by Plato. Kant paraphrases them as follows: first, a proof that the universe (or god) is neither finite nor infinite; second, a proof to the effect that the universe is neither in motion nor at rest; and finally, a third argument according to which the universe can be neither like nor unlike all other things.[79] In general, Kant thinks that Plato's reconstruction of Zenonian arguments is overly simplistic, making the target of his criticism appear rather as a straw man: '*Zeno* the *Eleatic*, a subtle dialectician, was already severely censured by Plato as a wanton sophist who, to show his art, would seek to prove some proposition through convincing arguments and then immediately to overthrow the same proposition through other arguments just as strong.'[80]

Kant defends Zeno against Plato's accusations. While the statement that the universe is neither in motion nor at rest (to choose only the second issue) may seem at first unintelligible, it can be shown to express a truth of reason. Inasmuch as the universe means all there is (*das Weltall*), neither being-in-motion nor being-at-rest applies to it. Thus, with regard to this object, motion and rest are merely contraries: 'if by the word *god* he understood the universe, then he must of course say that neither is it persistingly present in its place (at rest) nor does it alter its place (move), because all places are only in the universe, hence *this* universe itself is in *no place*.'[81]

Kant identifies the difference between contrary and contradictory relations as one between dialectical and analytical opposition:

> Permit me to call such an antithesis *dialectical*, but that of contradiction *analytical opposition*.[82] Thus of two judgments dialectically opposed to one another both could be false for the reason that the

> one does not merely contradict the other, but says something more than is required for a contradiction.[83]

In the Zenonian arguments discussed by Kant, the object of reference is (unbeknownst to Zeno, of course) a world beyond the possibility of experience, that is, the object of an idea of pure reason. From the first and second antinomies Kant derives the seeming rationality of *denying* that two dialectically antithetic features can be predicated of an object of reason. From the third and fourth antinomies he derives the seeming rationality of simultaneously *attributing* dialectically antithetic predicates to such an object.[84]

Whether we focus on the arguments of the Phoronomy or on those of the Transcendental Dialectic, they do explain Kant's qualified acceptance of Zeno's arguments. His own solution to the paradoxical character of ideas of reason is of course profoundly different from Zeno's solution of the paradoxes of motion. Kant can rely on the highly sophisticated perspectivism, not available to Zeno, afforded by the distinction of what can be *known* in experience and what must be *thought* beyond possible experience.

With respect to the 'external' topic of objects in motion, Kant's own overcoming of Zeno's problem ultimately parallels Aristotle's two-pronged judgment on the Dichotomy and Achilles: to the question whether motion is possible or not 'we must reply that in a sense it is and in a sense it is not.'[85] This is the philosophical approach that Hegel would call the philosophy of the 'insofar,' that is, an external reflection now connecting and now separating opposites by *'Insofars, Sides and Aspects'*[86] and unwilling to take reality by its roots: 'The usual tenderness for things, whose only concern is that they do not contradict themselves, forgets here as in other cases that in this way the contradiction is not resolved but merely shifted to somewhere else, into the subjective or external reflection in general.'[87]

6.3 Contradiction in motion:[88] Hegel

Like Kant before him, Hegel takes seriously the intelligibility of Zeno's contradictory description of motion. At the onset of his Zeno lecture he praises the Eleatic philosopher as the proper 'initiator of dialectic.'[89] For an assessment of the lecture's main claims it will be useful to recall some aspects of Hegel's treatment of the logical categories of identity and difference from the doctrines of Being and of Essence.

(i) Motion, grasped

The first move in Hegel's lecture is devoted to eliminating any naïve understanding of the philosophic significance of the Zenonian paradoxes. Their conclusions on the alleged inexistence of motion are to be understood, not as claiming the unreality of locomotion—a hopelessly irrelevant claim, as any Cynic will very simply show[90]—but rather as proof of the inherently contradictory character of the concept of motion.[91] While other Eleatic philosophers used *kinesis* to denote particular kinds of motions, Zeno instead 'spoke of and argued against motion as such or pure motion.'[92] In this sense, Zeno's thinking marks a progress over Parmenides' and Xenophanes': the objects of his reflection are 'concepts and thoughts'[93] rather than representations of natural phenomena or of other subject-matter. Zeno's main achievement does not lie in having crafted what could be termed a negative version of the ontological argument: since the concept of motion entails contradiction, no real motion may exist. Philosophers like Thales, Zeno or Socrates have often been targets of ridicule for allegedly being so aloof as to ignore or deny hard facts. Hegel (himself an occasional target) puts the meaning of Zeno's thought into proper perspective:

> Aristotle maintains that Zeno denied motion because it contains an inner contradiction. This is not to be taken to mean that motion is not at all. . . . There is no question that movement, this phenomenon, exists; motion has as much sensuous certainty as the fact that there are elephants. It did not even occur to Zeno to deny motion in this sense. The question is rather about its truth; motion, however, is untrue because it is contradiction. By this he meant to say that no true being[94] belongs to it (*W* 18, 305).[95]

Diogenes' performative 'refutation' symbolizes all commonsense responses to philosophy. Hegel wants first of all to clear our path from the primitivism of such pragmatist metaphysics: 'one must not make do with sensuous certainty, but must grasp.'[96] Diogenes' deed relies on the prejudice that truth lies in the object and thought need only adequate itself to the latter in order to find truth. If the Cynic's action is intended as refutation of the argument, however, it is a self-defeating one: the contradiction is now not only spoken of, but performed, while its explanation remains as obscure as before.

What Zeno's arguments demonstrate, then, is not a delusion of our senses but a conceptual contradiction. Trivially enough, whatever is perceived is real to perception. Only thought draws a distinction between 'true' and 'false' perceptions or between 'true' and 'false' reality.[97] According to Hegel, what distinguishes Zeno's contribution to the history of philosophy is his attempt, not to deny the universally experienced (*bekannt*) phenomenon of motion but to account for its conceptual structure (*Erkenntnis*).

The lecture's second move consists of tracing motion's contradiction to its roots in the concepts of space and time. The main presupposition of Dichotomy and Achilles is the continuous nature of space and time. But the concept of continuity (as Aristotle himself has shown in *Physics* 231 b 10) contains the moment of infinite discreteness. The line (the geometrical representative of continuity), for example, is continuous not because it lacks parts, or else it would lack dimension. The line is continuous because its parts are potentially infinite. Thus, it is precisely on account of their continuity that space, time and motion are potentially divisible *ad infinitum*. An infinitely divisible continuum consists of infinitely shrinking parts or, as geometricians call them, points. 'Point' and 'line,' on the other hand, are defined in contradictory terms:

> For us there is no contradiction in the representation of the point . . . or the now being posited as a continuity, a length (day, year); but their concept is self-contradicting. Selfsameness, continuity, is absolute connection, annihilation of all difference, of all *negativum*, of being-for-self; the point, instead, is the pure being-for-self, the absolute self-differentiating and sublating of all sameness and connection with what is other (*W* 18, 307).[98]

Accordingly, it may be said that Dichotomy and Achilles contain the historically first formulation of Hegel's 'spurious infinite,'[99] a conception in which infinity is understood now under the guise of absolute continuity and now under that of absolute discreteness. This is the infinite 'that is the contradiction as displayed in the sphere of being.'[100]

As for the Arrow, if it indeed presupposes the atomistic nature of space and time as collections of 'heres' and 'nows,' it shows, inversely, how discreteness develops into continuity. Every one of the flying arrow's positions is nothing but a place identical to the arrow, and every instant of its flight is the instant in which it exists. Only quantity, not quality, plays a role in the identification of the points and instants of the arrow's trajectory. Thus, every point (or place) is identical to all other points (or places), every instant to all other instants. If mere quantities are identical, however, there is nothing to keep them from collapsing into one. The atomistic whole is truly the absolute continuum.

Hegel's reasoning here is based on the analysis of 'atomism' (understood as theoretical supposition or metaphysical prejudice) delivered in the Logic. In the section marking the transition from the category of quality to that of quantity in the Lesser Logic (§ 98) Hegel explains the logical identity of 'attraction' and 'repulsion' (that is, the sense in which they are one and the same force) largely in the same terms used in the lecture on Zeno to explain 'continuity' and 'discreteness.' In a whole considered only quantitatively, the many 'ones' are thought as being connected (attraction) through only one type of relation, and that is the negation of any connection to all others (repulsion). In the ensuing Remark and Additions he comments that to think in atomistic terms is, therefore, to obliterate internal differentiation (qualitative determination) from the objects of thought: 'quantity is nothing but sublated quality.'[101] The first consequence of the elimination of qualitative criteria in discernment is that only objects' external relations can be considered—whereby thinking becomes mere 'external reflection.' But if no internal differentiation is discernible and every object is simply one, then all objects will have only one and the same determinacy, consisting of their in-difference to all others. This is why the objects of atomistic thinking must all be the same. This elimination of internal difference, whose result Hegel calls 'absolute indifference,' characterizes all reasoning in the exclusive terms of continuity, discreteness, number, quantum, degree, ratio, or measure.

(ii) Contradiction, subjective and objective

The same argument is developed with more detail in the Greater Logic's Doctrine of Being. In the chapter on Quantity, Hegel comments that while the pure notion of quantity means absolute continuity and not an aggregate of *quanta* (a sum of magnitudes), it always contains the '*real possibility* of the one,'[102] that is, it contains its divisibility into *quanta* as its moment. In the thought of quantity, in other words, we think first of all of continuity; but while continuity means reiteration of the same, quantity is sameness of many (namely of its ones or *quanta*), not trivial self-sameness of one. Thus, the first determination of quantity in general is to be a unity of continuity and discreteness. *Vice versa*, while the notion of *quantum* (or magnitude) means the fundamental, discrete unit of quantity, it also contains the moment of continuity—or else it could not produce continuity by being reiterated. In the first Remark of this chapter Hegel criticizes atomistic reasoning in terms that may actually equally well be directed against some of Aristotle's arguments against Zeno's alleged atomism—such as the argument that, in order to guarantee continuity, points and instants must either have overlapping extremities or nothing of their own kind in-between one another (cf. above, 6.1 i).[103] This reasoning, Hegel claims, presupposes exactly the conflation of 'continuity' and 'composition' that it intends to criticize. It ignores that actual continuity and potential discreteness as such are not contradictories. The single points of a line contain the continuity represented by the line as much as the line contains the discreteness represented by its points:

> For a-conceptual *representative thinking*, continuity easily becomes *composition*. . . . But with regard to the One it has been shown that . . . continuity is not external but rather belongs to it and is grounded in its essence. This *externality* of continuity for the ones is, in general, that to which atomism clings and the relinquishing of which presents such a difficulty for representational thinking (*GW* 21, 178/Miller 188).[104]

As modern examples of non-atomistic conceptions of quantity, Hegel quotes Spinoza and Leibniz. Spinoza writes that 'in the imagination' (that is, when conceived '*abstracte sive superficialiter*') quantity is found to be 'finite, divisible and composed of parts;' 'in the intellect' instead (that is, when conceived as substance, '*quod difficillime fit*'), quantity is found to be 'infinite, one [*unica*] and indivisible.'[105] To this, Hegel adds Leibniz's laconic statement: 'It is not at all improbable that matter and quantity are really the same.'[106] Indeed, Hegel concurs, 'matter' denotes the external existence of the pure thought determination called 'quantity.' Other examples of quantity thus conceived are space, time, light or even the 'I.' All of these exemplify pure quantity in that they consist of the 'continuous *self-production* of their unit,'[107] that is, they are instances of the *continuous* reproduction of *discrete* quanta. Space is continuous reiteration of different but identical places; time, of different but identical instants. The 'I' continuously reproduces itself by identifying with an unending stream of sensations, perceptions, and representations while distinguishing itself from them. Each of these instances of pure quantity must be described as an identity-in-difference. Thus it is that we do not have perceptions of them, only concepts. Beyond its Parmenidean formulations in terms of 'self-same heres' and 'self-same nows,' the deeper meaning of Zeno's reasoning lies in having articulated the concept of an objective identity-in-difference.

Zeno, Plato, Aristotle or Kant all dare to think the contradiction and yet they all find it unacceptable. Whether they refer to incompatible actions, to incompatible statements, or to the incompatibility between predicates and certain kinds of objects, their goal is to overcome the contradiction by proving it illusory. The arrow merely *seems* to be in flight; the soul, to harbor contradictory appetites; the state, to hold antagonistic interests; space-time, to be continuous and yet discrete; objects of reason, to admit of antithetic predicates. The solution is deemed to lie in changing the subject's perspective: premises must be revised, assumptions dropped, distinctions introduced, causes and remedies must be sought for the 'inevitable, though not unsolvable, illusion.'[108] These are, in Hegel's view, subjective solutions, never definitive (as Kant himself recognizes) and thus no genuine solutions at all.

Breaking with this tradition, Hegel claims that contradiction itself, together with its solution, lies in the essence of the object and not in alleged shortcomings of the subject's perspective. In the case of Zeno's subject-matter, this means that sensuous motion is the manifestation of an '*existent* [*daseiende*] contradiction itself.'[109] Precisely the fact of the arrow's being in one place at one time and not being in that same place at the same time is the reason why the arrow moves. This contradiction is not unacceptable to thinking as much as it is untenable in reality. It is not the onlooker's perspective, but the essence of what motion is, that is, its concept, that is contradictory. Universal motion is the result of the intrinsic contradictoriness of all reality:

> External, sensuous motion itself is its [contradiction's] external existence [Dasein]. Something moves only, not because it is here in this now and there in another now, but rather because in one and the same now it is here and not here, or because it simultaneously is and is not in this here.[110]

(iii) A Parmenidean beyond Parmenides

We may now return to Hegel's specific assessment of Zeno in the Lectures. He claims that there is intrinsic in the Eleatic's understanding of locomotion an intuition of the dialectic of continuity and discreteness. Paraphrasing Aristotle's rendition of the Arrow, Hegel writes:

> [Zeno] says, 'the flying arrow rests' for the reason that 'what is in motion is always in the self-same now' and the self-same here, that is, in the 'undistinguishable' (*en to nun, kata to ison*); it is here, and here, and here . . . this, however, we don't call motion but rest . . . In the here, now as such lies no difference. . . . True objective difference does not arise in such sensuous relations, but only in the spiritual (*W* 18, 314–15).[111]

Zeno's significance lies precisely in having shown that, when continuity is assumed, discreteness turns out to be its moment, and that when discreteness is presupposed, continuity results. Zeno's philosophical insight is, thus, an original one. It is not at all a repetition of Parmenidean theses through different formulations, as Socrates maintains in Plato's *Parmenides*:

> I see, Parmenides, said Socrates, that Zeno's intention is to associate himself with you by means of his treatise no less intimately than by his personal attachment. In a way, his book states the same position as your own; only by varying the form he tries to delude us into thinking that his thesis is a different one. You assert . . . unity; he asserts no plurality. . . . Your arguments seem to have nothing in common, though really they come to very much the same thing (*Parmenides* 128 a-b).

Contrary to Plato, Hegel considers Zeno's thought as inaugurating a new stage in the philosophic understanding of being and *logos*. Parmenides had demonstrated that being is one and immutable on the grounds that its opposite cannot be. He had used the apparent falsehood contained in the thought of non-being in order to establish the exclusive truth of being. Hegel objects to the method of developing an antithesis *ad absurdum* in order to prove the corresponding thesis. A *reductio*, he argues, is a merely formal and negative procedure that does not prove anything affirmative.[112] After all, by applying the same method in the Antinomy of Pure Reason, Kant is able to show that the world is being rationally conceived as both limited and unlimited, discrete and continuous, determined by natural necessity and by freedom, dependent and independent from an absolute being. Zeno's arguments (including the paradoxes) go well beyond Parmenides' *reductio*: 'The false must not be presented as false because the opposite is true, but by itself. We find this rational insight awakening in Zeno.'[113] The Arrow, for example, does not prove motion's un-truth by starting out from the truth of rest. It actually assumes the existence of motion in its premises and fights 'the war in enemy's country'[114] by showing motion to be un-true on account of its own inner contradiction.

In Hegel's view, the impossibility of describing a phenomenon in non-contradictory terms is not a sufficient reason for denying the phenomenon's existence. The missing premise of the Arrow, namely that contradictory states of affairs do not exist, is a dogma of ratiocination, not a necessary principle of reason. The Arrow's proper conclusion, thus, appears to be quite different from the one stated by Zeno and debated by his commentators. The appropriate conclusion appears to be that motion is the expression of contradiction in the realm of experience: 'One has to grant the ancient dialecticians the contradictions that they point out in motion, but from granting this does not follow that therefore there is no motion, but much rather that motion is the *existent* [*daseiende*] contradiction itself.'[115]

As mentioned in the beginning of this chapter, Hegel calls the dialectic displayed by the ancients 'negative,' 'subjective' or 'external.' This dialectic either questions only one side of an issue and concludes by dogmatically upholding the other side, or, as is the case with some Sophists, keeps questioning alternately both sides in an oscillating pattern, remaining undecided and indifferent toward any one alternative. The first kind leads to dogmatism (as often in Plato), the second issues in relativism (the philosophy of the 'insofar' foreshadowed in Aristotle). Though Zeno himself cannot be said to have overcome subjective dialectic, his arguments at the very least signal the awareness that rational objects of reflection may contain a 'positive,' 'objective' or 'inward' dialectic of their own. These are intelligible objects that contain opposing characteristics and whose adequate description will necessarily imply self-contradictory propositions.

Going beyond the logic of motion, Hegel famously argues for the intrinsic contradictoriness of the very concept of 'object' as 'thing' in the Logic's Doctrine of Essence. In the chapter on the category of existence he analyzes the meaning of the latter when attributed to 'matters' or also 'appearances' (as opposed to its attribution to so-called things-in-themselves). The argument (that need here only be recalled, not reconstructed) opens with an analysis of 'The Thing and its Properties' and concludes with the 'Dissolution of the Thing.' The dissolution takes place because of the internal contradictions of the concept of 'thing' as a uniform whole of differing properties. The Remark concluding the chapter contains an intense attack against mechanistic explanations of the unity *cum* multiplicity of physical objects. For example, the assumption of the 'porosity of matters' deludes common sense into believing that it has found a solution to the paradox of many matters' simultaneous presence in one and the same perceived object. This illusion arises by replacing the idea of the unity of objects and their properties with that of the 'interpenetration' of different 'porous matters' (in much the same way in which atomism replaces continuity with composition), thus substituting figurative for speculative thinking. In this way, the understanding explains away the contradictory thought of a genuine unity of different matters as simultaneous differences within that unity:

> The usual subterfuge by which *representation* keeps away the *contradiction* of the *independent* subsistence of the *many* matters *in One*, or their reciprocal *indifference* in their *interpenetration*, relies, as is well known, on the *smallness* of parts and pores. Where difference-in-itself, contradiction and the negation of negation occur, in general where *conceptual grasp* is required, representation falls back to external, *quantitative* difference. . . . But the concept of the thing is [such] that in the *this* the one matter finds itself where the other one is, and the penetrating [matter] is also penetrated in the same point. . . . This is contradictory; but the thing is nothing other than this very contradiction; that is why it is appearance (*GW* 11, 338–9/Miller 497).[116]

Hegel's conception of 'the appearances' as manifestation of the inherent contradiction of thing-hood parallels his conception of motion as manifestation of the inherent contradiction of spatial-temporal objects. In Zeno's thought, dialectic makes its first appearance as objective structure of the object of reflection. This embodies a dialectic that is 'not a movement only of our insight, but demonstrated from the essence of the subject-matter, that is, from the pure concept of the content.'[117] If we set aside normative metaphysical prejudices about how the world ought to be (for example, that it must be free of contradiction) we will discover that the very notion of a moving object requires it to be, at every instant, both in a place and not in that same place, and to subsist in every place both at one instant and not at that same instant. This is an adequate description of motion and remains so whether we assume that space and time are continuous, composed of discrete entities, or consisting of indivisible stretches and intervals. There is still, of course, a strong Parmenidean element in Zeno's reasoning. It is the assumption that the self-contradictory character of any subject-matter has the power to nullify it. Zeno suspends his judgment at the very moment in which he attains a speculative insight (an 'immanent contemplation,' Hegel says[118]) into the logic of his subject. It is essential to all Eleatic philosophy to declare a subject-matter inexistent as soon as its inner contradiction emerges.[119]

Hegel's interest in following the development of 'external' or 'subjective' dialectic all the way to this dead end is of course neither purely nor primarily epistemological. In the lectures on Leucippus and Democritus he comments that while the first historical focus of atomism was on nature, modernity has adopted its principles for theorizing the sphere of *Geist*: 'For Leucippus and Democritus the determinacy [of the 'one'] . . . remained physical; but it also emerges in the spiritual. In the sphere of the will, the view may be expressed that in the state the single will, as atom, is the absolute. Such are the more recent theories of the state, and they have even practical effects.'[120]

The lasting influence of atomistic thought on the political philosophies of modernity, in particular on contractarianism, is recalled also in the *Encyclopaedia*'s Doctrine of Being:

> In modern times, the atomistic view has become even more important in the *political* [realm] than in the physical. According to this view, the will as such of the *single individuals* is the principle of the state; the element of attraction is the particularity of needs, of inclinations; and the universal, the state itself, is the external relationship of the contract (*E* § 98 Remark).[121]

The logical core of Democritus' *atomos* or Aristotle's *adiairetos* is the thought determination of being-one or absolute singularity. This notion does not denote a determinate quantum of matter, but the mere concept of quantum in general. Hegel expressly rejects Aristotle's interpretation of Leucippus' atoms as being invisible 'owing to the minuteness of their bulk.'[122] Atoms are imperceptible, Hegel objects, simply because 'the one cannot be seen, it is an abstraction of thought.'[123] In modern philosophy, the same abstraction has been extended to human beings, citizens or private *bourgeois*. The building blocks of the body politic are now called 'individuals.' But for the same reason that 'atom' does not denote an empirical determinacy of matter, 'individual' does not denote a natural creature.

Hegel views Zeno's paradoxes as playing in the history of ancient philosophy a role similar to that played by Kant's antinomies in the history of modern philosophy.[124] While acknowledging the dialectical nature of reason, Kant fails to recognize that antitheses do not arise only in the attribution of opposite predicates to objects of reason, but are rather already implicit in the concepts of the objects themselves. Hegel writes:

> The profounder insight into the antinomial or . . . dialectical nature of reason demonstrates . . . any concept to be the unity of opposed moments. . . . Becoming, *Dasein* etcetera and any other concept could thus provide its particular antinomy. . . . Further, Kant did not take the antinomy to be in the concepts themselves but in the already *concrete* form of cosmological determinations. In order to have the antinomy in pure form . . . the thought determinations must not be

> taken in their application ... but must be considered purely for themselves (*GW* 21, 180/Miller 191).[125]

After recognizing the inherently contradictory character of motion as unity of multiplicity, Zeno withdrew all being from it, and thus all truth from its cognition. The Eleatic tenet that only what is simply and absolutely one can exist and be known is equivalent, so Hegel, to Kant's conception of knowledge of appearances: 'It is by and large the same principle: "The content of consciousness is only an appearance, not anything true".'[126]

Hegel's idea of an objective dialectic allowing for the real existence and sublation of contradiction is meant to overcome this last refuge of skepticism. It aims, in other words, at producing affirmative results from the negative, dialectical disintegration of concepts initiated in antiquity by Zeno's radical mind. The ultimate affirmative result of the unfolding of this dialectic through the history of spirit and its reflection in philosophy is the modern discovery and grasp of individual universal subjectivity, that is, the Concept's grasp of itself as subject-object: a creature of natural necessity whose nature is freedom.

Notes

1 A Philosophy of the History of Philosophy

1. The intricate editorial history of the lectures and introductions is told in E. Moldenhauer and K. M. Michel eds, *G.W.F. Hegel. Werke in zwanzig Baenden* (Frankfurt: Suhrkamp, 1969–79), vol. 20, pp. 520 ff. This work is cited in the following as *W* followed by volume and page or section [§] number.
2. I borrow the expression 'theory of the history of philosophy' from K. Duesing, *Hegel und die Geschichte der Philosophie. Ontologie und Dialektik in Antike und Neuzeit* (Darmstadt: Wissenschaftliche Buchgesellschaft,1983), p. 7.
3. 'Die Geschichte der Philosophie muss selbst philosophisch seyn' (*GW* 18, 39). The textual basis for the analysis that follows is the critical edition: W. Jaeschke ed., *G.W.F. Hegel. Vorlesungsmanuskripte II (1816–1831), Gesammelte Werke* vol. 18 (Hamburg: Meiner, 1995). This edition is cited throughout as *GW* followed by volume and page number. The translations are my own but I consult throughout the 1892–6 edition by E.S. Haldane and F.H. Simson, *Hegel's Lectures on the History of Philosophy* (New York: The Humanities Press, 1974) as well as the translation of the Heidelberg and Berlin introductions by T.M. Knox and A.V. Miller, *G.W.F. Hegel. Introduction to the Lectures on the History of Philosophy* (Oxford: Clarendon Press, 1985).
4. 'Dass das, was der Geist seinem Begriffe nach oder *an sich* ist, auch im Dasein und fuer sich sei (somit Person, des Eigentums faehig sei, Sittlichkeit, Religion habe)—diese Idee ist selbst sein Begriff (als *causa sui*, d.i. als freie Ursache, ist er solches, *cuius natura non potest concipi nisi existens*; Spinoza, Ethik I, Def. I). In eben diesem Begriffe . . . liegt die Moeglichkeit des Gegensatzes zwischen dem, was er nur *an sich* und nicht auch *fuer sich* ist . . . und hierin die *Moeglichkeit der Entaeusserung der Persoenlichkeit.*' In the following, all references to the 1821 *Philosophy of Right* (*Grundlinien der Philosophie des Rechts oder Naturrecht und Staatswissenschaft im Grundrisse*) are to *W* 7 followed by section number and 'Remark' or 'Addition.' The translations are mine but I consult throughout T.M. Knox ed. and trans., *Hegel's Philosophy of Right* (Oxford: Oxford University Press, 1952) and A.W. Wood ed., H.B. Nisbet trans., *Hegel. Elements of the Philosophy of Right* (Cambridge: Cambridge University Press, 1991).
5. 'Nach dieser Idee behaupte ich nun, dass die Aufeinanderfolge der Systeme der Philosophie in der *Geschichte dieselbe* ist, als die *Aufeinanderfolge in der* logischen *Ableitung* der Begriffsbestimmungen der Idee.'
6. 'Das Denken . . . ist zu dem . . . Anfange der Wissenschaft zurueck zu weisen, welchen Parmenides gemacht hat, der sein Vorstellen . . . zu dem *reinen Gedanken*, dem Seyn als solchen, gelaeurtert und erhoben . . . hat.—Was das *Erste* in der *Wissenschaft* ist, hat sich muessen *geschichtlich* als das *Erste* zeigen. Und das Eleatische *Eine* oder *Seyn* haben wir fuer das Erste des Wissens vom Gedanken anzusehen' (*GW* 21, 75–6/Miller 88). The genitive

case in the last phrase ('the first knowing of thought') is intentionally ambivalent: according to Hegel, pure being is the first cognition *about* thought as much as *by* thought. In the following, all references to the *Science of Logic* ('Greater Logic') are to *GW* 21 (Doctrine of Being, 2nd edn, 1832), *GW* 11 (Doctrine of Essence, 1813) and *GW* 12 (Doctrine of the Concept, 1816). The translations are mine. For ease of reference, the citations include the corresponding pages of A.V. Miller trans., *Hegel's Science of Logic* (New York: Humanities Press, 1969) (cited as Miller followed by page number).

7. Aristotle, *De Anima* 430 a 5. Unless otherwise noted, all quotations of this work are from the translation by R.D. Hicks, *De Anima* (New York: Prometheus Books, 1991). In this instance, in order to respect the internal consistency of this passage, I modify Hicks' translation of *autos de noetos* ('the mind itself') with 'thought itself.' On the other hand, Hicks' translation of *theoretike* with 'speculative' is fully justified in this context: first, because both words are equally rooted in the language of optics; second, because the particular point that Aristotle is making is that the ultimate subject matter of the treatise is self-reflective thought.
8. 'So ist der Anfang der Philosophie, die in allen folgenden Entwicklungen gegenwaertige und sich erhaltende Grundlage, das seinen weitern Bestimmungen durchaus immanent Bleibende' (*GW* 21, 58).
9. *GW* 18, 37.
10. '. . . auf dem Standpunkt, den Menschen . . . nach *einer Existenz* . . . zu nehmen, die seinem Begriffe nicht angemessen ist' (*W* 7, § 57 Remark).
11. 'Die Sklaverei faellt . . . in eine Welt, wo noch ein Unrecht Recht ist' (*W* 7 § 57 Addition).
12. *GW* 18, 43.
13. '*Die Wahrheit aber ist Eine,*—dieses unueberwindliche Gefuehl oder Glauben hat der Instinct der Vernunft . . . [d]ass die Wahrheit nur eine ist . . . darin folgt schon der Instinct des Denkens' (*GW* 18, 43 and 45).
14. See below, Chapter 3, 3.1.
15. *GW* 18, 46.
16. *GW* 18, 47–8.
17. 'Es ist hierin dass sich die Vernunfterkenntnis von der blossen Verstandeserkenntnis unterscheidet, und es ist das Geschaeft des Philosophirens gegen den Verstand zu zeigen, dass das Wahre, die Idee nicht in leeren Allgemeinheiten besteht, sondern in einem Allgemeinen, das in sich selbst das Besondere, das Bestimmte ist' (*GW* 18, 45).
18. All references to the *Encyclopaedia of Philosophical Sciences* are to the 1830 edition (cited as *E* followed by section [§] number). With few exceptions noted explicitly, I make use of the following translation of the *Encyclopaedia* Logic ('Lesser Logic'): T.F. Geraets, W.A. Suchting, H.S. Harris, eds and trans, *G.W.F. Hegel. The Encyclopaedia Logic (with the Zusaetze)* (Indianapolis: Hackett, 1991). I note expressly my occasional disagreements with this translation, based on the German text in *GW* 20 and, for the Additions, *W* 8.
19. 'Der *Begriff* als solcher enthaelt die Momente der *Allgemeinheit,* . . . der *Besonderheit,* . . . und der *Einzelnheit,* als der Reflexion in sich der Bestimmtheiten der Allgemeinheit und Besonderheit, welche negative Einheit mit sich das *an und fuer sich bestimmte* und zugleich mit sich identische oder allgemeine ist' (*E* § 163).

20. The distinction between concepts (and objects) of reason and concepts (and objects) of the understanding is discussed below, Chapter 2, 2.4.
21. The translations of the *Phenomenology of Spirit* (1807) are my own. The textual basis is *GW* 9. I have consulted throughout A.V. Miller's *Hegel's Phenomenology of Spirit* (Oxford: Oxford University Press, 1977). For ease of reference, the citations are given as *GW* 9, page number/Miller with page number.
22. 'Nennen wir *Begriff*, die Bewegung des Wissens, den *Gegenstand* aber, das Wissen als ruhige Einheit, oder als Ich, so sehen wir, dass nicht nur fuer uns, sondern fuer das Wissen selbst, der Gegenstand dem Begriffe entspricht.—Oder auf die andere Weise, den *Begriff* das genannt, was der Gegenstand *ansich* ist, den Gegenstand aber das, was er als *Gegenstand*, oder *fuer ein* anderes ist, so erhellt, dass das Ansichseyn, und das fuer ein anderes seyn dasselbe ist.'
23. Nonstandard analytic philosophy of logic shares many of Hegel's views on the meaningfulness and viability of contradictions. See for example the numerous outstanding contributions of G. Priest on this subject, such as his *In Contradiction: a Study of the Transconsistent* (Dordrecht: Martinus Nijhof, 1987); the two historical introductions to *Paraconsistent Logic. Essays on the Inconsistent* (edited with R. Routley and J. Norman, Muenchen: Philosophia Verlag, 1989); and 'What's so bad about contradictions?' *The Journal of Philosophy*, 95 no. 8 (1998) 410–26.
24. 'Die Geschichte des Geistes ist seine *Tat*, denn er ist nur, was er tut' (*W* 7 § 343). The complete passage is quoted in the closing of the present chapter.
25. '[D]ie Lebendigkeit des Geistes . . . ist Trieb, geht ueber in den Hunger und Durst nach Wahrheit, nach Erkenntnis derselben, dringt nach Befriedigung dieses Triebs'. '[D]as Wahre [hat] den Trieb . . . sich zu *entwickeln*. Nur das Lebendige, das Geistige bewegt, ruehrt sich in sich, entwickelt sich. Die Idee ist so, concret an sich und sich entwickelnd, ein organisches System, eine Totalitaet welche ein *Reichtum von Stuffen und Momenten in sich enthaelt.*'
26. For the logic of urge or *Trieb* see Hegel's analysis of 'Life' in the Doctrine of the Concept from the Greater Logic (*GW* 12, 179 ff./Miller 761 ff.).
27. 'Das Fortgehen des Begriffs ist nicht mehr Uebergehen noch Scheinen in Anderes, sondern *Entwicklung*, indem das Unterschiedene unmittelbar zugleich als das Identische mit einander und mit dem Ganzen gesetzt, die Bestimmtheit als ein freies Seyn des ganzen Begriffes ist' (*E* § 161).
28. Two excellent and concise discussions of Hegel's uses of *Unterschied* and *Differenz* in the Logic are in Geraets/Suchting/Harris, *The Encyclopaedia Logic*, pp. xxiii–xxiv, and M. Inwood, *A Hegel Dictionary* (Oxford: Blackwell, 1998), pp. 131–3.
29. '[D]ass die philosophisch erkannte Wahrheit im Elemente des Gedankens, in der Form der Allgemeinheit ist, . . . es ist diss unserer gewoehnlichen Vorstellung gelaeuffig. Aber dass das Allgemeine selbst in sich seine Bestimmung enthalte, . . . hier faengt ein eigentlich philosophischer Satz an—hier tritt darum das noch nicht philosophisch erkennende Bewusstseyn zurueck, und sagt es *verstehe* diss nicht.'
30. 'Ich ist der Inhalt der Beziehung, und das Beziehen selbst' (*GW* 9, 103/Miller 104). The complete passage is quoted in this chapter, 1.1 (ii).
31. *E* § 163.

32. 'Sollte das Absolute durch das Werkzeug uns nur ueberhaupt naeher gebracht werden, . . . wie etwa durch die Leimruthe der Vogel, so wuerde es wohl, wenn es nicht an und fuer sich schon bey uns waere . . . dieser List spotten . . . Oder wenn die Prueffung des Erkennens, das wir als ein *Medium* uns vorstellen, uns das Gesetz seiner Strahlenbrechung kennen lehrt, so nuetzt es ebenso nichts, sie im Resultate abzuziehen; denn nicht das Brechen des Strahls, sondern der Strahl selbst, wodurch die Wahrheit uns beruehrt, ist das Erkennen.'
33. 'Weil . . . diese Darstellung nur das erscheinende Wissen zum Gegenstande hat, so . . . kann [sie] . . . als der Weg des natuerlichen Bewusstseyns, das zum wahren Wissen dringt, genommen werden; oder als der Weg der Seele, welche die Reihe ihrer Gestaltungen, als durch ihre Natur ihr vorgesteckter Stationen durchwandert, dass sie sich zum Geiste laeutere . . . Das natuerliche Bewusstseyn wird sich erweisen, nur Begriff des Wissens, oder nicht reales Wissen zu seyn.' This point that Hegel makes in the *Phenomenology* has been often ignored in twentieth-century commentaries, despite Hegel's insistence that natural consciousness *per se* 'loses its truth on this path [to philosophy] [verliert auf diesem Wege seine Wahrheit]' (*GW* 9, 56/Miller 49). Phenomenological knowing is *not*, for Hegel, knowledge of the true.
34. *GW* 9, 55/Miller 49.
35. The use of the English expression 'to realize' for 'to become aware of' is the closest psychological counterpart to the speculative meaning of Hegel's 'self-realization' (or 'self-actualization') of consciousness.
36. 'Ich ist der Inhalt der Beziehung, und das Beziehen selbst; es ist selbst gegen ein anderes, und greifft zugleich ueber diss andre ueber, das fuer es ebenso nur es selbst ist' (*GW* 9,103/Miller 104).
37. 'Ferner geht diese Entwicklung nicht nach Aussen als in die Aeusserlichkeit, sondern das Auseinandergehen der Entwicklung ist eben so ein Gehen nach Innen; . . . Indem das Hinausgehen der philosophischen Idee in ihrer Entwicklung nicht . . . ein Werden zu einem Andern sondern ebenso ein Insich-hineingehen, ein sich in [sich] Vertieffen ist, so macht das Fortschreiten die vorher allgemeine, unbestimmtere Idee in sich *bestimmter*.'
38. For an overview of the role of Hegel's *Erinnerung* in thought's general economy, both in logical and psychological perspective, see the recent contribution by A. Nuzzo, 'Thinking and Recollecting. Logic and Psychology in Hegel's Philosophy,' forthcoming in G. Gigliotti (ed.), *La memoria* (Napoli: Bibliopolis/Vrin, 2005).
39. '. . . durch die vollstaendige Erfahrung ihrer selbst zur Kenntnis desjenigen gelangt, was sie an sich selbst ist' (*GW* 9, 55/Miller 49).
40. The text of Hegel's Anthropology is in *GW* 20. The Additions are in *W* 10. Unless stated otherwise, I quote from the English translation by M.J. Petry, *Hegel's Philosophy of Subjective Spirit*, vols 1–3 (Boston: Reidel, 1978).
41. Petry (§ 412) translates 'Soul which posits its being over against itself,' but Hegel uses the verb in the past tense: *entgegengesetzt hat*. Indeed, the soul's process of positing its own content as an other from itself must be concluded for it to cease to be mere soul and to begin its journey as consciousness. The logic underlying this process is explained in the Greater Logic, Doctrine of Being, Chapter 1,C: the truth of becoming is not just

that being and nothing are permanently passing into one another, but that each has always already done so (*GW* 21, 69/Miller 82–3).

42. '*An sich* hat die Materie keine Wahrheit in der Seele; als fuersichseyende scheidet diese sich von ihrem unmittelbaren Seyn, und stellt sich dasselbe als Leiblichkeit gegenueber . . . Die Seele, die ihr Seyn sich entgegengesetzt, es aufgehoben und als das ihrige bestimmt hat, hat die Bedeutung der *Seele*, der *Unmittelbarkeit* des Geistes, verloren. Die wirkliche Seele . . . ist an sich die fuer sich seyende *Idealitaet* ihrer Bestimmtheiten, in ihrer Aeusserlichkeit *erinnert* in sich und unendliche Beziehung auf sich' (*E* § 412).
43. See above, 1.1.
44. 'Die Philosophie ist nun fuer sich das Erkennen dieser Entwicklung, und ist als begreiffendes Denken selbst diese denkende Entwicklung. Je weiter diese Entwicklung gediehen, desto vollkommner ist die Philosophie.'
45. On this traditional use of 'history' in English, French and German philosophy see D. Perinetti, 'Philosophical Reflection on History', in K. Haakonssen (ed.), *The Cambridge History of Eighteenth-Century Philosophy* (Cambridge: Cambridge University Press, 2004).
46. *Geschichte* derives from *geschehen*, whose core meaning in its Old High German form (*scehanto*) is 'to turn [out] suddenly.' Over time, the latter acquired the connotation of the unexpected, new event (*Ereignis*) and finally that of *Werden*, becoming in general.
47. Such an a-historical or even anti-historical approach seems to me to be embodied in J.R. Searle's *The Mystery of Consciousness* (New York: New York Review of Books, 1997). The subject matter is here introduced with remarks about the 'mistakes and errors' of 'our religious and philosophical tradition,' errors that are said to 'plague' contemporary mind theory. The latter, we are told, would be better off without the 'obsolete categories'(p. xii) of the said tradition. Of course Searle's own thesis—'consciousness is a natural, biological phenomenon. It is as much part of our biological life as digestion, growth, or photosynthesis' (p. xiii)—is at least as traditional as the eighteenth- and nineteenth-century theories of J.O. de la Mettrie, P.-J. Cabanis, C. Vogt or E. Du Bois-Reymond. This peculiar lack of interest in predecessors of one's own perspective appears also in D. Dennett's approach to what he calls 'the mind (or brain)' in *The Intentional Stance* (Cambridge: MIT Press, 1997, p. 123). Despite assurances that his theory is a strictly philosophical one, Dennett's sparse references to the theories and controversies on mind in Western philosophy before the twentieth century are oddly selective. In *The Mind's I* (with D.R. Hofstadter, New York: Bantam, 1982), for example, he leaps from a sketch of Locke's ('and many subsequent thinkers') conception of conscious mind as 'transparent to itself,' to Freud, here characterized as the initiator of a theory of 'the existence of *un*conscious mental processes' (*ibid.* pp. 11–12). This approach neglects, among others, Leibniz's rebuttal of Locke, his theory of *pétites perceptions* (*Nouveaux essais sur l'entendement humain*, 1765), of the degrees of life in the monad (*Monadologie*, 1720) and of the difference of perception from apperception (*Principes de la nature et de la grace fondés en raison*, 1718); it ignores apperception's central role in Kant's theory of mind; it overlooks Hegel's differentiation between conscious and unconscious thinking (*Philosophy of Spirit*, Anthropology, *E* § 398) and implicit and explicit soul

content (*E* §§ 402–3); finally, in mentioning Freud it disregards the latter's extensive debt to Nietzsche on this subject. Similarly, Dennett's references to Cartesian dualism in *Consciousness Explained* (New York: Little, Brown and Co., 1991) ignore Descartes' repeated stress on the non-ontological character of his conception of persons as composites, on his deriving the notions of mind and body-substances from that of their unity, and on body and soul as *substances incomplètes vs.* their unity in the human being as *substance complète* (see the Sixth Meditation, but also his correspondence with Elizabeth and Régius and his replies to Arnauld). Thus, there are more 'somewhat distinct ancestries worth noting' (*Consciousness Explained*, p. 44) than Dennett actually notices. Th. Nagel offers a cultural explanation for this approach to philosophic investigation. In *Other Minds* (New York: Oxford University Press, 1995) he claims that in Anglo-American analytic philosophy 'philosophers don't have to know much about history or anything about literature, but they are expected to know some science, to have at least an amateur's grasp of the contributions of Newton, Maxwell, Darwin, Einstein, Heisenberg, Cantor, Goedel, and Turing . . . all of which provide data for philosophical reflection' (p. 7). If this is so, one cannot help wondering why in the said tradition Plato, Aristotle, Spinoza, Leibniz, Kant or Hegel are not seen as providing at least as good 'data for philosophical reflection' as Maxwell or Goedel do.

48. '. . . das STUDIUM *der Geschichte der Philosophie* [ist] *Studium der Philosophie* selbst,—wie es denn nicht anders seyn kann' (*GW* 18, 50).
49. *GW* 18, 52. The full passage is quoted below, 1.2 (i).
50. 'Ich behaupte, dass wenn man die *Grundbegriffe* der in der Geschichte der Philosophie erschienenen Systeme rein dessen entkleidet, was ihre aeusserliche Gestaltung, ihre Anwendung auf das Besondere, und dergleichen betrift, so erhaelt man die verschiedenen Stuffen der Bestimmung der Idee selbst in ihrem logischen Begriffe' (*GW* 18, 49–50). For an exhaustive explication and critical assessment of this thesis and its metaphysical presuppositions see K. Duesing, *Hegel und die Geschichte der Philosophie. Ontologie und Dialektik in Antike und Neuzeit* (Darmstadt: Wissenschaftliche Buchgesellschaft, 1983.)
51. On the margin of this passage in the manuscript, Hegel notes: 'only because of this do I bother to deal with it, to lecture on it' (*GW* 18, 51)—that is, on the history of philosophy.
52. In 1820, Hegel is referring to the 1817 text of the *Encyclopaedia*. All citations in the following refer to the corresponding sections in the 1830 edition. In the latter, the metaphysics of time is developed in *E* §§ 254–9.
53. In particular, *GW* 9, 428 ff./Miller 486 ff.
54. See *E* §§ 254–6.
55. See *E* §§ 257–9.
56. In particular, *E* §§ 391–402.
57. See *E* §§ 392–5.
58. See *E* §§ 396–8.
59. The most in-depth treatment of the logical identity of soul and living body in Hegel is, in my view, M. Wolff's book-length commentary on § 389 of the 1830 *Encyclopaedia*: M. Wolff, *Das Koerper-Seele Problem. Kommentar zu Hegel, Enzyklopaedie (1830), § 389* (Frankfurt: Klostermann, 1992).

60. 'Der Geist ist die existierende Wahrheit der Materie, dass die Materie selbst keine Wahrheit hat' (*E* § 389 Remark).
61. See *E* §§ 399–403.
62. Habituation is described in *E* §§ 409–10.
63. 'Das Ich ist der durch die Naturseele schlagende und ihre Natuerlichkeit verzehrende *Blitz*' (*E* § 412 Addition).
64. 'Es ist oben ueber das Wesen des Geistes angefuehrt worden, dass sein Seyn seine That ist . . . Naeher ist seine That die, *sich zu wissen*. Ich bin, unmittelbar, aber bin ich so nur als lebendiger Organismus; als Geist bin ich nur, insofern ich mich weiss. *Gnothi seauton, wisse dich* . . . ist das absolute Gebot, welches die Natur des Geistes ausdrueckt.'
65. 'Diss *Daseyn* und damit in der Zeit seyn, ist ein Moment nicht nur des einzelnen Bewusstseyns ueberhaupt, das als solches wesentlich endlich ist, sondern auch der Entwicklung der philosophischen Idee im Elemente des Denkens. Denn die Idee in ihrer Ruhe gedacht, ist wohl zeitlos . . . Aber die Idee ist als concret, als Einheit unterschiedener . . . wesentlich nicht Ruhe . . . sondern als Unterscheidung in sich . . . tritt sie . . . in die Aeusserlichkeit im Element des Denkens, und so erscheint im Denken die reine Philosophie als eine in der Zeit fortschreitende Existenz.'
66. 'In der Wirklichkeit ist nun die wissende Substanz frueher da, als die Form oder Begriffsgestalt derselben' (*GW* 9, 428/Miller 486).
67. '[Der Geist] . . . ist an sich die Bewegung, die das Erkennen ist—die Verwandlung jenes *Ansichs* in das *Fuersich*, der *Substanz* in das *Subject*, des Gegenstands des *Bewusstseyns* in Gegenstand des *Selbstbewusstseyns*, d.h. in ebensosehr aufgehobnen Gegenstand, oder in den *Begriff*' (*GW* 9, 429/Miller 488).
68. 'In dem *Begriffe*, der sich als Begriff weiss, treten hiemit die *Momente* frueher auf, als das *erfuellte Ganze*, dessen Werden die Bewegung jener Momente ist. In dem *Bewusstseyn* dagegen ist das Ganze, aber unbegriffne, frueher als die Momente.'
69. '. . . um ihren [der Philosophie] Fortgang als Entwicklung der Idee zu erkennen, muss man freylich *die Erkenntnis der Idee* schon mitbringen' (*GW* 18, 50).
70. 'Als der *Gedanke* der Welt erscheint sie erst in der Zeit, nachdem die Wirklichkeit ihren Bildungsprozess vollendet und sich fertig gemacht hat. Dies, was der Begriff lehrt, zeigt notwendig ebenso die Geschichte, dass erst in der Reife der Wirklichkeit das Ideale dem Realen gegenueber erscheint und jenes sich dieselbe Welt, in ihrer Substanz erfasst, in Gestalt eines intellektuellen Reichs erbaut.'
71. Knox, *Philosophy of Right*, paraphrases *sich fertig gemacht hat* with 'is already there cut and dried' (p.12), Nisbet, *Elements*, with 'has attained its completed state' (p. 23).
72. *E* §§ 575–7.
73. *E* § 574.
74. 'Um noch ueber das *Belehren*, wie die Welt sein soll, ein Wort zu sagen, so kommt dazu ohnehin die Philosophie immer zu spaet' (*W* 7, pp. 27–8).
75. See *GW* 9, 103/Miller 104.
76. 'Die Geschichte des Geistes is seine *Tat*, denn er ist nur, was er tut, und seine Tat ist, sich, und zwar hier als Geist, zum Gegenstande seines Bewusstseins

zu machen, sich fuer sich selbst auslegend zu erfassen. Dies Erfassen ist sein Sein und Prinzip, und die *Vollendung* eines Erfassens ist zugleich seine Entaeusserung und sein Uebergang.' See also *GW* 18, 52, quoted above.

2 The Experience of Thought

1. Geraets/Suchting/Harris translate *begreifendes Erkennen* with 'conceptually comprehensive cognition.'
2. *E* §§ 1–18.
3. The contemporary ellipsis seems appropriate in translating the male relative pronoun *er* in contexts in which it refers to *Mensch* and not to *Mann*. In these contexts, we have to assume (by the principle of charity, but also by the lights of logic) that the German author is using the male pronoun because the reference is to a grammatically male substantive, not to a substantive that refers to male referents.
4. 'Indem nur dem Menschen Religion, Recht und Sittlichkeit zukommt, und zwar nur deswegen, weil er denkendes Wesen ist, so ist in dem Religioesen, Rechtlichen und Sittlichen,—es sey Gefuehl und Glauben oder Vorstellung,—das *Denken* ueberhaupt nicht unthaetig gewesen; die Thaetigkeit und die Productionen desselben sind darin *gegenwaertig* und *enthalten*' (*E* § 2 Remark).
5. *E* § 2 Remark.
6. *De Anima* 432 a 1–2.
7. *Das Denken* as distinguished from *der Gedanke*, thought.
8. Geraets/Suchting/Harris: 'conceptually comprehensive cognition.'
9. Geraets/Suchting/Harris: 'human import of consciousness.'
10. Instead of *Einbildung*, Hegel uses here *Phantasie*, the German equivalent of Aristotle's image-producing function of the soul, *phantasia*.
11. See *E* § 3.
12. 'Vorstellungen ueberhaupt koennen als *Metaphern* der Gedanken und Begriffe angesehen werden' (*E* § 3 Remark).
13. 'Das Prinzip der *Erfahrung* enthaelt die unendlich wichtige Bestimmung, dass fuer das Annehmen und Fuerwahrhalten eines Inhalts der Mensch selbst *dabei seyn* muesse' (*E* § 7 Remark).
14. '. . . dass er [der Mensch] solchen Inhalt mit *der Gewissheit seiner selbst* in Einigkeit und vereinigt finde' (*E* § 7 Remark).
15. See I. Kant, *Critique of Pure Reason*, second edition (1787), (cited in the following as *CPR* B) B 1: 'But though all our cognition commences *with* experience, yet it does not on that account all arise *from* experience.' Unless otherwise specified, I use the translation by P. Guyer and A.W. Wood (Cambridge: Cambridge University Press, 1998).
16. *E* § 2.
17. 'Aber umgekehrt wird sie [die spekulative Philosophie] ebenso behaupten: "nihil est in sensu, quod non fuerit in intellectu",—in dem ganz allgemeinen Sinne, dass der *nous* und in tieferer Bestimmung *der Geist* die Ursache der Welt ist, und in dem naehern (s. § 2), dass das rechtliche, sittliche, religioese Gefuehl ein Gefuehl und damit eine Erfahrung von solchem Inhalte ist, der seine Wurzel und seinen Sitz nur im Denken hat.'

18. The nature of this circularity is discussed below, 2.2.
19. In particular (as indicated in Chapter 1, n. 47) Hegel is very much indebted to Leibniz's distinction between perceived and apperceived sensations and to his daring psychological conception of consciousness's unconscious *petites perceptions*.
20. See *GW* 9, 66/Miller 61. The full quote is given below.
21. 'Vergleichen wir das Verhaeltnis, in welchem das *Wissen* und der *Gegenstand* zuerst auftrat, mit dem Verhaeltnisse derselben, wie sie in diesem Resultate zu stehen kommen, so hat es sich umgekehrt. Der Gegenstand . . . ist nun das unwesentliche der sinnlichen Gewissheit . . . , sondern sie ist itzt in dem entgegengesetzten, nemlich in dem Wissen . . . vorhanden. Ihre Wahrheit ist in dem Gegenstande, als *meinem* Gegenstande, oder im *Meynen*, er ist, weil *Ich* von ihm weiss.' Miller's translation of *Meynen* with 'being mine' (Miller 61), as if it were a reiteration of the preceding adjectival *'mein(em)'*, is all the more surprising as his translation of *Meynen* in the title of this chapter is entirely accurate: 'Sense-Certainty: Or the "This" and "Meaning"' (Miller 58).
22. *E* § 2 Remark. *Nachdenken* ('after-thinking') is the term preferred by Hegel to refer to common as distinguished from speculative reflection (*Reflexion*). *Nachdenken* includes psychological reflection, instrumental reasoning and ratiocination in general.
23. *E* § 2 Remark. One aim of Hegel's criticism here is of course Kant's tenet 'thoughts without content are empty, intuitions without concepts are blind' (*CPR* B 75). The presuppositions and consequences of this Kantian principle are discussed below, 2.3 (i).
24. *E* § 412 Addition. See Chapter 1 n. 63.
25. See *E* § 3. Hegel's criticism of these assumptions is often praised as overcoming the problems raised by Kant's dualism of intuitions and concepts. Without wanting to deny that Kant's theory of knowledge is in some serious sense dualistic, still it must be stressed that, in contrast to much of classical empiricism, the German idealist tradition including Kant always comprises in its notion of experience (*Erfahrung*) a non-sensible dimension. Against the background of this tradition, Hegel is not discovering new land here, except for a shift of emphasis. In the idealist tradition, *Erfahrung* never refers to a multiplicity of sensations, but always requires a non-sensible principle of their unification—a principle, to paraphrase David Hume, that can bundle them into *Erfahrung* to begin with. An interesting discussion of this matter in contemporary terms, couched as a dilemma between framing human cognition in a 'space of reasons' *versus* a 'space of nature' can be found in J. McDowell, *Mind and World* (Cambridge: Harvard University Press, 1996). A detailed study of Hegel's concept of experience (centered on 'perception') compared with the empiricist notion is K.R. Westphal, *Hegel, Hume und die Identitaet wahrnehmbarer Dinge* (Frankfurt: Vittorio Klostermann, 1998).
26. 'Der wahrhafte *Inhalt* unseres Bewusstseyns [wird] in dem Uebersetzen desselben in die Form des Gedankens und Begriffs *erhalten*, ja erst in sein eigenthuemliches Licht gesetzt' (*E* § 5).
27. This is J.A. Smith's translation in J. Barnes, ed., *The Complete Works of Aristotle*, vol. 1 (Princeton University Press: Princeton, 1984).

28. This is R.D. Hicks' translation.
29. See *De Anima* 412 a 20–5.
30. See n. 23 above and section 2.3 (i) below.
31. *CPR* B 74.
32. For the distinction between *Historie* and *Geschichte* see Chapter 1, 1.1 (iii).
33. Even this aspect of Hegel's theory of cognition is adumbrated in Aristotle, namely in his discussion of the different respects in which actuality can be said to be prior to potentiality: see for example *Metaphysics* IX, 1050 a.
34. 'Womit muss der Anfang der Wissenschaft gemacht werden?' (*GW* 21, 55/Miller 67).
35. See *E* § 2: 'At first and in general, philosophy can be determined as *thinking consideration* of objects.'
36. '. . . ihr [der Philosophie] Inhalt [ist] kein anderer . . . , als der im Gebiete des lebendigen Geistes urspruenglich hervorgebrachte und sich hervorbringende, zur *Welt*, aeussern und innern Welt des Bewusstseyns gemachte Gehalt, . . . ihr Inhalt [ist] die *Wirklichkeit*. Das naechste Bewusstseyn dieses Inhalts nennen wir *Erfahrung*' (*E* § 6).
37. '[Es ist] fuer den hoechsten Endzweck der Wissenschaft anzusehen . . . , durch die Erkenntnis dieser Uebereinstimmung, die Versoehnung der selbstbewussten Vernunft mit der *seyenden* Vernunft, mit der Wirklichkeit hervorzubringen' (*E* § 6). This is the general framework for Hegel's discussion of what contemporary philosophy calls the problem of 'externalism vs. coherentism'. Theoretical thought's adequacy with *experienced* actuality is the 'external proof of a philosophy's truth' (*ibidem*) but it must be complemented with philosophy's 'internal proof,' i.e. the coherence of its principles in a system. An exemplary discussion of this aspect of Hegel's epistemology is K.R. Westphal's 'Is Hegel's *Phenomenology* Relevant to Contemporary Epistemology?' in *The Bulletin of the Hegel Society of Great Britain* 41/42(2000): 43–85.
38. Not, as too often translated, 'absolute knowledge.' *Absolutes Wissen* is not synonymous with *absolute Erkenntnis*, an expression which, as far as I am aware, is not used by Hegel.
39. See *E* §§ 556–63.
40. See *E* §§ 564–70.
41. 'Diese Wissenschaft ist . . . die Einheit der Kunst und Religion . . . zum *selbstbewussten Denken* erhoben . . . Dies Wissen ist damit der denkend erkannte *Begriff* der Kunst und Religion' (*E* § 572).
42. *E* § 6 Remark.
43. See for example R. B. Brandom, *Tales of the Mighty Dead. Historical Essays in the Metaphysics of Intentionality* (Cambridge: Harvard University Press, 2002). Brandom maintains that Hegel's view of what it means to be rational is to be a 'concept user,' which in turn implies 'being subject to . . . conceptual norms' (p. 12). These norms are supposed to regulate acceptable linguistic behaviors in any given 'linguistic community' (p. 31). Hegel's merit *vis-à-vis* his predecessors would consist in having introduced in the explanation of conceptuality the (Sellarsian) dimension of a normative practice of 'giving and asking for reasons' (p. 9). This interpretation looks like a promis-

ing program for an empirical inquiry into the formation and use of particular concepts in specific linguistic systems—an enterprise that never occurred to Hegel to undertake.

44. See T. Pinkard, 'Hegel's *Phenomenology* and *Logic*: an Overview', in K. Ameriks, ed., *The Cambridge Companion to German Idealism* (Cambridge: Cambridge University Press, 2000), 161–79. Like Brandom (see n. 43), also Pinkard recurs to Sellars' conception in order to re-interpret Hegel's absolute Idea as 'normative whole of the "space of reasons".'
45. See *W* 7 §§ 71–4.
46. On the Platonic and Neo-Platonist dimensions of Hegel's metaphysics of 'the true' see the work of J.-L. Vieillard-Baron and that of K. Duesing. For Vieillard-Baron, see *Platon et l'Idealisme Allemand 1770–1830* (Paris: Beauchesnes, 1979), especially section four: 'Interpretation et assimilation de Platon dans le système hegelien.' For Duesing, see his *Hegel und die Geschichte der Philosophie* (1983), in particular Chapter 2 on Hegel's speculative interpretation of Greek thought; and his *Hegel e l'antichità classica*, S. Giammusso, ed. (Napoli: La Città del Sole, 2001), especially Chapters 1 and 2 on Hegel's interpretation of Plato's ontology.
47. An earlier version of this section was presented (with the title 'Wie aus dem Begriff des Ich dessen Realitaet vernuenftig auszuklauben sei [How the reality of the ego may be rationally extracted from its concept]' to the XXIV Conference of the International Hegel Society, F. Schiller-University, Jena, 30 August 2002.
48. See *E* § 62.
49. '. . . einen Gegenstand *begreifen* heisst insofern nichts als ihn in der Form eines *Bedingten* und *Vermittelten* fassen . . . In [Jacobi's] Polemik wird das Erkennen nur als Erkennen des Endlichen aufgefasst, als das denkende Fortgehen durch Reihen von *Bedingtem* zu *Bedingtem* . . . Erklaeren und Begreifen heisst hiernach, etwas als *vermittelt* durch ein *Anderes* aufzuzeigen; somit ist aller Inhalt nur ein *besonderer, abhaengiger* und *endlicher*.'
50. See *E* § 63 Remark.
51. *GW* 12, 173/Miller 755.
52. This double meaning of *Verstandesbegriffe* in Hegel makes the term entirely dependent upon its context. This is one source for some confusion in the literature regarding the meaning of this class of concepts. Some light is shed on this in section 2.4 (i) below.
53. *E* § 64.
54. F.H. Jacobi, *Ueber die Lehre des Spinoza* (1785). *Werke*. K. Hammacher and W. Jaeschke eds (Hamburg: Meiner, 1998), vol. 1:1, p. 116.
55. *E* § 64 Remark.
56. See Aristotle, *Metaphysics* XII, 1074 b 30–5: 'Therefore it must be itself that thought thinks . . . and its thinking is a thinking on thinking.'
57. *E* § 2. The full quote has been given in the introduction to this chapter.
58. This has been discussed above in 2.2.
59. *CPR* B 377.
60. *CPR* B 377.
61. *CPR* B 74.
62. *CPR* B 75–6.

63. I. Kant, *Logik*, § 1. In: *Kants Gesammelte Schriften* vol. IX (Berlin: De Gruyter, 1923) (cited in the following as *Logik*).
64. *CPR* B 14–18.
65. *CPR* B 37–40 (Transcendental Aesthetic).
66. *CPR* B 129–36 (Transcendental Logic).
67. *CPR* B 377.
68. I. Kant, *Logik* § 1.
69. *CPR* B 40. See also B 33 and B 377.
70. *CPR* B 33. I am modifying slightly the Guyer/Wood translation.
71. See *E* § 62 cited above, as well as *E* § 25 and § 28 Addition.
72. *CPR* B 39.
73. One may further compare the already cited passages *CPR* B 33 and B 377 with B 74.
74. *CPR* B 74.
75. See *CPR* B 34.
76. *CPR* B 34–5.
77. *CPR* B 35.
78. *CPR* B 34.
79. One can object that there is no inconsistency in stating that empirical-sensible intuition could be mediated in its genesis while being present to the mind immediately. This important objection cannot be taken into due consideration here except to remark that Hegel's criticism is aimed also at the crass separation between genesis and nature of cognitive modes.
80. G.W.F. Hegel, *Glauben und Wissen* (1802), *GW* 4. For an English translation, see W. Cerf and H.S. Harris, *Faith & Knowledge* (Albany: SUNY Press, 1977).
81. *CPR* B 15.
82. *CPR* B 130.
83. *CPR* B 132.
84. *CPR* B 132.
85. See *GW* 4, 327.
86. '. . . die hoechste Idee . . . als eine leere Gruebeley und einen unnatuerlichen blossen Schulwitz, aus Begriffen eine Realitaet heraus zu klauben' (*GW* 4, 325). Kant's remark is in the Transcendental Dialectic under the section heading 'On the impossibility of a cosmological proof of God's existence,' but he is there referring to the previous section 'On the impossibility of an ontological proof of God's existence': 'It was entirely unnatural, and a mere novelty of scholastic wit, to want to take an idea contrived quite arbitrarily and extract from it the existence of the corresponding object itself' (*CPR* B 631).
87. *CPR* B 74.
88. Kant's 'metaphysical ideas' are god, freedom and immortality.
89. I replace the imperative 'ought not' in Geraets/Suchting/Harris with 'do allegedly not' for Hegel's '*nicht . . . sollten*.' In this passage, *sollen* simply indicates indirect speech.
90. *E* § 64 Remark, discussed above in section 2.3 (i).
91. ". . . das Bewusstsein unterscheidet nemlich, aber ein solches, das fuer es sogleich ein nicht unterschiedenes ist" (*GW* 9, 103/Miller 104).
92. I replace 'imagine' in Geraets/Suchting/Harris with 'represent' for Hegel's *vorstellen*.

93. *E* § 42 Addition 2.
94. *CPR* B 399.
95. *CPR* B 132.
96. Kant himself writes that the '"I think" ... serves to distinguish ... two kinds of objects ... *I*, as thinking, am an object of inner sense, and am called "soul." That which is an object of outer sense is called "body"' (*CPR* B 400).
97. *CPR* B 1.
98. *E* § 8.
99. *CPR* B 14.
100. *E* § 28.
101. *E* § 41.
102. *E* § 40.
103. G.W. Leibniz, *New Essays on Human Understanding* (1704), P. Remnant and J. Bennett, eds (Cambridge: Cambridge University Press, 1982), p. 53.
104. G.W. Leibniz, *Principes de la nature et de la grace fondés en raison* (1714), § 13. A. Robinet, ed. (Paris: Presses Universitaires, 1954).
105. *E* § 402 Addition.
106. See *Metaphysics* IX, 1047 a–1048 b.
107. *W* 7 § 27.
108. Hegel hardly ever uses this term. He founds it redundant (see for example *GW* 12, 173/Miller 755) because once empirical notions and transcendental categories have been classified as determinations of the understanding, 'concept' *per se* is left for the domain of reason. But Hegel's own terminology is less than consistent in this case. I will use the expression 'concept of reason' to signify the second of the meanings of 'concept' in Hegel's philosophy delineated here.
109. Cf. Aristotle's *Metaphysics* IX, 1050 a.
110. This is a reference to the four aspects of thinking explicated in the preceding §§ 20–3: (a) as one of the subjective faculties (next to sensibility, intuition, and so on) thought results in the abstract (classificatory) grasp of its object. (b) As reflection, it yields a concept of the essence (or truth) of its object and (c) it results in the consciousness that the object is mediated by thinking. (d) As this consciousness, thought is grasp of the object as mediated by the ego, or cognition of the 'thinking subject.'
111. *E* § 28 Addition.
112. Contemporary genetics considers an organism's mature stage to be in principle present, as 'in-formation' (internal idea), in its genetic make up. This is the biological counterpart of the conception of development that Hegel, following Aristotle, explains in terms of self-actualizing potency.
113. See above, section 2.1.
114. See *E* § 24 Addition 1: 'But "to be animal," the kind considered as the universal, pertains to the determinate animal and constitutes its determinate essentiality.'
115. *K. Marx. Early Political Writings*, J. O'Malley and R.A. Davis, eds (Cambridge: Cambridge University Press, 1994), pp. 123–4 ('German Ideology').
116. I follow the customary use of the capital letter in the English translation of *der Begriff*.

3 Conceptualizing Thought

1. *E* § 24 Addition 2.
2. E § 24.
3. Contemporary Hegel literature occasionally ignores Hegel's insistence that his logic is a metaphysics or *prima philosophia*. This attitude works to the detriment of one's ability to gain an intellectual entry into his system. R. Brandom, for example ('Some Pragmatist Themes in Hegel's Idealism', in *European Journal of Philosophy* 7:2, 1999) castigates Kant and Hegel for 'devoting relatively too much time to developing . . . their (in the transcendental sense [*sic*]) logical apparatus, and . . . too little time to applying it to the use of ground-level concepts.' This idea is surprising only until one realizes that for Brandom 'ground-level concepts' are concepts with empirical referents, not logical or metaphysical categories. Though Hegel's many versions and re-workings of the *Science of Logic* are admittedly voluminous and intimidating, the Logic is certainly neither a transcendental apparatus (Hegel's repeated arguments against transcendental justification speak for themselves) nor an instrument to be 'applied' to empirical concepts (or to anything else). Both in intention and execution, Hegel's Logic consists precisely of the analysis of the most 'ground-level' concepts there are (and of course the same must be said of the *Critique of Pure Reason*).
4. This title is suppressed in the 1830 Logic of the *Encyclopaedia*.
5. See above, Chapter 2, 2.2.
6. *De Anima* 402 a 10.
7. *De Anima* 429 a 13–430 a 5. This passage is also discussed in Chapter 1 above, n. 7.
8. 'Ich beschraenke mich hier auf eine Bemerkung, die fuer das Auffassen der hier entwickelten Begriffe dienen kann . . . Der Begriff, insofern er zu einer solchen *Existenz* gediehen ist, welche selbst frey ist, ist nichts anderes als *Ich* oder das reine Selbstbewusstseyn. Ich *habe* wohl Begriffe, das heisst bestimmte Begriffe; aber Ich ist der reine Begriff selbst, der als Begriff zum *Daseyn* gekommen ist.'
9. Influential contemporary interpretations, for example, A. Wood's outstanding *Hegel's Ethical Thought* (Cambridge: Cambridge University Press, 1990), differ significantly from my reading of the role of logic and metaphysics in Hegel's philosophy of the person. On the one hand, Wood admits 'we cannot understand Hegel's social and political concerns without reference to his speculative metaphysics' (p. 6). On the other hand, Wood also argues: 'Hegel's treatment of metaphysical issues is best viewed as an attempt to interpret these issues as an expression of cultural and existential concerns' (*ibidem*). Thus, it is not clear whether Hegel's metaphysics is a foundation or a disguise of his *Realphilosophie*. Possibly, one reason for this ambiguity lies in Wood's assumption that the Logic is a prolegomenon and not the foundation of the system. However, even apart from Hegel's explicit statements in this regard, it seems reasonable to consider the Logic as foundational: for example, by showing how the concept of mind relates to that of will, the Logic makes intelligible the historical movement of consciousness into self-consciousness and self-will—while this history would not even be detected without identifying that logic. Thus, the *Realphiloso-*

phie does indeed include a treatment of 'the self-conception of modern human beings' (Wood p. 5) but is not narrowly about 'the social and spiritual predicament of modern Western European culture' (*ibidem*). The real development is for Hegel inherently universal because it rests upon a logical foundation.

10. *E* § 161 Addition.
11. See *E* § 83 and *E* § 24 Addition 2.
12. See *E* §§ 84 and 161 Addition.
13. See *E* §§ 112 and 161 Addition.
14. This has been discussed above in Chapter 1, 1.1 (i).
15. 'Die vorhergehenden logischen Bestimmungen, die Bestimmungen des Seyns und Wesens, sind ... nur *bestimmte* Begriffe, Begriffe an sich oder, was dasselbe ist, *fuer uns*, indem das *Andere*, in das jede Bestimmung *uebergeht* oder in welchem sie *scheint* ..., nicht als *Besonderes*, noch ihr Drittes als *Einzelnes* oder *Subject* bestimmt, nicht die Identitaet der Bestimmung in ihrer entgegengesetzten, ihre Freiheit *gesetzt* ist, weil sie nicht *Allgemeinheit* ist.'
16. See *E* § 182.
17. 'Nehmen wir z.B. den *Schluss* (nicht in der Bedeutung der alten, formellen Logik, sondern in seiner Wahrheit) ... Diese Form des Schliessens ist eine allgemeine Form aller Dinge. Alle Dinge sind besondere, die sich als ein Allgemeines mit dem Einzelnen zusammenschliessen' (*E* § 24 Addition 2).
18. 'Nehmen wir das Tiersein vom Hunde weg, so waere nicht zu sagen, was er sei' (*E* § 24 Addition 1).
19. 'Der vernuenftige Schluss dagegen ist, dass das Subject durch die Vermittlung *sich mit sich selbst* zusammenschliesst. So ist es erst Subject' (*E* § 182).
20. *E* § 162 Remark.
21. On the term *Historie* used here by Hegel see above, Chapter 1, 1.1 (iii).
22. I have modified slightly the translation by Geraets/Suchting/Harris.
23. See also Chapter 1, 1.1 (iii) and n. 38.
24. 'Das *zweyte* Negative, das Negative des Negativen, zu dem wir gekommen, ist jenes Aufheben des Widerspruches, aber ist sowenig als der Widerspruch ein *Thun einer aeusserlichen Reflexion*, sondern das *innerste, objectivste Moment* des Lebens und Geistes, wodurch ein *Subject, Person, Freyes* ist.'
25. For Aristotle's conception of substance as sub-ject of predications see *Metaphysics* VII 1028 b-1029a; for the material counterpart of *hypokeimenon* as *hule* (matter), see *Physics* I, 190 a-b.
26. *Metaphysics* XII 1073 a 5.
27. *Metaphysics* XII 1072 b 20–5.
28. *E* § 158.
29. See *E* § 162 (quoted above) and the more detailed discussion of *E* § 163 below, 3.2 (iii).
30. See Plato, *Phaedo* 65 c: 'And indeed the soul reasons best when none of these senses troubles it, neither hearing nor sight, nor pain nor pleasure, but when it is most by itself ... in its search for reality.' This is G.M.A. Grube's translation in J.M. Cooper, ed., *Plato. Complete Works* (Indianapolis: Hackett, 1997).
31. '[D]er Begriff als solcher laesst sich nicht mit den Haenden greifen, und ueberhaupt muss uns, wenn es sich um den Begriff handelt, Hoeren und Sehen vergangen sein' (*E* § 160 Addition).

32. *E* § 162 Remark. The full passage has been quoted above.
33. *E* § 162 Remark.
34. *E* § 24 Addition 2.
35. For the conflation of 'particular' and 'singular' in English texts and its origins in medieval nominalism see H.S. Harris's and T.F. Geraets's Introduction to Harris/Geraets/Suchting (1991), p. xix. For a general clarification of Hegel's use of this terminology see the entry 'universal particular and individual' in M. Inwood (1992).
36. For example, in the Introduction to the Philosophy of Spirit (*E* § 377) and in the *Lectures on the Philosophy of History* (*W* 12) discussed below. On Hegel's evaluation and interpretation of *gnothy seauton* see in particular: A. Peperzak, *Selbsterkenntnis des Absoluten: Grundlinien der Hegelschen Philosophie des Geistes* (Stuttgart: Fromman-Holzboog, 1987); and B. Tuschling, 'Die Idee in Hegel's Philosophie des Subjektiven Geistes' in F. Hespe and B. Tuschling, eds, *Psychologie und Anthropologie oder Philosophie des Geistes* (Stuttgart: Fromman-Holzboog, 1991).
37. '. . . der Mensch *ueberhaupt* soll sich selbst erkennen' (*W* 12, 272) (see n. 39).
38. G.W.F. Hegel, *Vorlesungen ueber die Philosophie der Geschichte, W* 12.
39. 'Aber diese alte Loesung durch Oedipus, der sich so als Wissender zeigt, ist mit ungeheurer Unwissenheit verknuepft ueber das, was er selbst tut. Der Aufgang geistiger Klarheit in dem alten Koenigshause ist noch mit Greueln aus Unwissenheit gepaart, und diese erste Herrschaft der Koenige muss sich erst, um zu wahrem Wissen und sittlicher Klarheit zu werden, durch buergerliche Gesetze und politische Freiheit gestalten.'
40. *E* § 160 Addition.
41. *E* § 161 Addition.
42. For an instantiation of this interpretation by Hegel, see my discussion of his reading of Plato's *Parmenides* in Chapter 4.
43. *E* §§ 79–83 ('More Precise Conception and Division of the *Logic*').
44. *E* § 79.
45. *E* § 83.
46. 'Der Begriff ist das *Freie*, als die *fuer sie seiende substantielle Macht*, und ist *Totalitaet*, indem *jedes* der Momente *das Ganze* ist, das *er* ist, und als ungetrennte Einheit mit ihm gesetzt ist; so ist er in seiner Identitaet mit sich das *an und fuer sich Bestimmte*.'
47. See *E* § 91 Addition: '*Daseyn* as existing determinacy . . . [is] what one means by *reality*. . . . In this same sense the body can also be called the reality of the soul, this right the reality of freedom or, more generally, the world the reality of the divine concept.' See also *W* 7 § 1 Addition: 'The concept and its existence are two sides, distinct and united, like soul and body [Leib]. The body is the same life as the soul. . . . And so the reality [Dasein] of the concept is its body [Koerper]. . . . The unity of reality and the concept, of body and soul, is the Idea. . . . The Idea of right is freedom, and in order to be truly comprehended, the Idea must be recognizable in its concept and in the latter's reality.' (My translations.)
48. 'Die *Gestaltung*, welche sich der Begriff in seiner Verwirklichung gibt' (*W* 7 §1 Remark).
49. The concept of *Persoenlichkeit* (that I translate with 'personhood' to avoid the psychologism associated with 'personality') must of course be distin-

guished from the Latin *persona* and its English cognates 'personification,' 'impersonation' or (psychological) 'personality,' all of which lack the self-determinative connotation under discussion.

50. 'Die Goetter der Alten wurden zwar gleichfalls als persoenlich betrachtet; die Persoenlichkeit eines Zeus, eines Apoll usw. ist indes nicht eine wirkliche, sondern nur eine vorgestellte, oder, anders ausgedrueckt, es sind diese Goetter bloss Personifikationen, die als solche sich nicht *selbst wissen*, sondern nur *gewusst werden*' (*E* § 147 Addition).
51. *E* § 162 Remark.
52. *E* § 160. The full quotation has been given above.
53. *E* § 163 Addition 1. This is discussed more in depth in 5.3(ii), n. 65.
54. *W* 7 § 124 Remark.
55. *W* 7 § 206 Remark.
56. See also the Remark to § 185: 'The principle of the *independent, in itself infinite, personhood* of the individual, that is, of subjective freedom . . . does not come into its own in that merely substantial form of actual spirit,' that is, in Plato's state. This is discussed in more detail below, Chapter 5, 5.3 (i).
57. For example, in *E* § 91 Addition: 'The basis of all determinacy is negation (*omnis determinatio est negatio*, as Spinoza says).'
58. Contradiction in motion is discussed below, Chapter 6.
59. *GW* 9, 103/Miller 104. See Chapter 2, n. 91.
60. 'Der *Begriff* als solcher enthaelt die Momente der *Allgemeinheit*, als freier Gleichheit mit sich selbst in ihrer Bestimmtheit,—-der *Besonderheit*, der Bestimmtheit, in welcher das Allgemeine ungetruebt sich selbst gleich bleibt, und der *Einzelheit*, als der Reflexion-in-sich der Bestimmtheiten der Allgemeinheit und Besonderheit, welche negative Einheit mit sich das *an und fuer sich Bestimmte* und zugleich mit sich identische oder allgemeine ist' (*E* § 163).
61. See *E* §164: 'the determinations of reflection are *supposed* to be grasped and to be valid each on its own, separately from the one opposed to it; but . . . in the Concept their *identity* is *posited*.'
62. *GW* 9, 66/Miller 62.
63. A conflation of 'universal' and 'common'/'general' with regards to the conception of the ego seems to underlie Allen Wood's Hegel interpretation (1990): 'Hegel [insists that] one "moment" of the will, that which enables me to apply the word "I" to myself at all, is the moment of "universality," in which I identify myself with what is common to all beings capable of calling themselves "I"' (p. 18). Though I disagree with this interpretation, I recognize its consistency with Wood's overall approach to Hegel's *Realphilosophie*, according to which the latter may (or must) be made sense of independently of the Logic.
64. 'Nun aber ist das Allgemeine des Begriffs nicht bloss ein Gemeinschaftliches, welchem gegenueber das Besondere seinen Bestand fuer sich hat, sondern vielmehr das sich selbst Besondernde (Spezifizierende) und in seinem Anderen . . . bei sich selbst Bleibende. Es ist von der groessten Wichtigkeit sowohl fuer das Erkennen als auch fuer unser praktisches Verhalten, dass das bloss Gemeinschaftliche nicht mit dem wahrhaft Allgemeinen, dem Universellen, verwechselt wird.'
65. *GW* 12, 17.

66. 'Nennen wir *Begriff*, die Bewegung des Wissens, *den Gegenstand* aber, das Wissen als ruhige Einheit, oder als Ich, so sehen wir, dass nicht nur fuer uns, sondern fuer das Wissen selbst, der Gegenstand dem Begriffe entspricht.—Oder auf die andere Weise, den *Begriff* das genannt, was der Gegenstand *ansich* ist, den Gegenstand aber das, was er . . . *fuer ein* anderes ist, so erhellt, dass das Ansichseyn, und das fuer ein anderes seyn dasselbe ist . . . Ich ist der Inhalt der Beziehung, und das Beziehen selbst.'
67. 'Die Natur, Momente und Bewegung dieses Wissens hat sich also so ergeben, dass es das reine *Fuersichseyn* des Selbstbewusstseyns ist; es ist Ich, das *dieses* und kein anderes *Ich* und das ebenso unmittelbar *vermittelt* oder aufgehobenes *allgemeines* Ich ist' (*GW* 9, 428/Miller 486).
68. *E* § 164 Remark.
69. The example is from the Addition to *E* § 156.
70. *E* § 163 Remark.
71. 'Das *Wirkliche*, weil es nur erst *an sich* oder *unmittelbar* die *Einheit* des Wesens und der Existenz ist, *kann* es wirken; die Einzelheit des Begriffes aber, ist schlechthin das *Wirkende*, und zwar auch nicht mehr wie die *Ursache* mit dem Scheine, ein Anderes zu wirken, sondern das Wirkende *seiner selbst*.'
72. *E* § 163 Remark.
73. *E* §163 Addition 1.
74. *E* § 163 Addition 1. See also above, 3.2 (i) and below, 5.3 (ii).
75. See for example *W* 7 §§ 2 Remark, 21 Remark, 48 and Remark, 57 Remark and Addition.
76. Aristotle, *Politics*, Book I, chapter 4, 1254 a 15. I have modified slightly B. Jowett's translation of this passage (in J. Barnes's edition) in order to do justice to the text, that insists on the slave's humanity: '*anthropon on* ([despite] being human)' is repeated twice in this passage, but has found no place in Jowett's translation.
77. J.-J. Rousseau, *Du contrat social; ou, principes du droit politique* (1762), in *Oeuvres complètes de Jean-Jacques Rousseau* (Dijon: Gallimard, 1964), vol III. The two quotes are from Book One, chapters 1 and 4, respectively. The translation is by D. Cress, *J.-J. Rousseau. The Basic Political Writings* (Indianapolis: Hackett, 1987).
78. *W* 7 § 57. The passage is quoted in full in 5.3 (ii).
79. 'Diese fruehere unwahre Erscheinung betrifft den Geist, welcher nur erst auf dem Standpunkte seines Bewusstseins ist; die Dialektik des Begriffs und des nur erst unmittelbaren Bewusstseins der Freiheit bewirkt daselbst den *Kampf des Anerkennens* und das Verhaeltnis der *Herrenschaft* und der *Knechtschaft*' (*W* 7 § 57 Remark).
80. '. . . dass der Mensch an und fuer sich nicht zur Sklaverei bestimmt sei, . . . dies findet allein in der Erkenntnis statt, dass die Idee der Freiheit wahrhaft nur als *der Staat* ist" (*W* 7 § 57 Remark).

4 Hegel's Reading of Plato's *Parmenides*

1. *GW* 4, 207.
2. See above, Chapter 2, 2.4 (i).
3. The Hegelian equivalence of 'finitude' and 'bad infinity' with lack of self-reflexivity, and of 'genuine infinity' with self-reflexivity, that I take for

granted here, is concisely explained and criticized by M. Inwood (1992): 'The bad infinite is expressed by a straight line . . . the true infinite by a circle. . . . He applies this idea [of true infinity] to any relatively self-contained reciprocal or circular structure . . . [for example,] the spirit or self-consciousness that is not limited by its other, but at home (*bei sich*) in it; and logic itself, in which thought has itself as its object' (p. 141).

4. See K. Duesing (2001), Chapter 2.
5. 'Zeiten . . . worin . . . der Parmenides des Plato, wohl das groesste Kunstwerk der alten *Dialektik*, fuer die wahre Enthuellung und den *positiven Ausdruck des goettlichen Lebens* gehalten wurde, und sogar bey vieler Truebheit dessen, was die *Ekstase* erzeugte, diese missverstandne Ekstase in der That nichts anderes als *der reine Begriff* seyn sollte'.
6. For the Greater Logic, see *GW* 11 (Doctrine of Essence), 311–12/Miller 466; *GW* 12 (Doctrine of the Concept), 241–4/Miller 830–2. For the Lesser Logic, see *E* §§ 92 Addition, 95 Remark, 96 Addition, 121 Addition, 142 Addition, and 214.
7. See *W* 19, Part One: History of Greek Philosophy.
8. It has been shown convincingly that Hegel's interpretation (even if considered a projection) is not equivalent to that of the Neoplatonists. See for example K. Duesing's argument in (1983). It cannot be my task here to clarify the distinction between the Neoplatonic and the Hegelian Plato-interpretation, so I presuppose this difference in what follows.
9. The complete quote (from *GW* 18, 49) has been given in Chapter 1.
10. H. Diels/W. Kranz, *Die Fragmente der Vorsokratiker* (Dublin/Zuerich: Weidmann, 1966), vol. I, pp. 227–45.
11. See above, Chapter 2, 2.4 (i).
12. As far as I have been able to determine, one other exception is the contemporary Italian translator E. Pegone. See below, n. 55.
13. *GW* 18, 48.
14. See for example the very influential study by H.F. Cherniss, 'Parmenides and the "Parmenides" of Plato,' *The American Journal of Philology*, 53 no. 2 (1932) 122–38.
15. Plato, *Parmenides* 137 b. Quotations from the dialogue are taken mostly from the M.L. Gill/P. Ryan translation in J.M. Cooper (1997). I have noted the places in which I had to modify this translation after comparison with the Greek text in the Burnet edition: J. Burnet, ed., *Platonis Opera* (Oxford, Clarendon Press, 1900–7), t. 3.
16. To understand Plato's notion that ideas have the 'most real' existence one must recall that for him a 'real being' (*ontos on*) is only what cannot have become, i.e. it cannot have a history of less or nil reality. This real being is then precisely what can be known with full clarity, that is, by thought itself without mingling of opinion and sensation. For Plato's own characterization of the ideas see in particular *Phaedo* 65 d–e and *Parmenides* 135 b–c. For his thesis that the ideas do exist separately, see *Politeia* 508 c and *Timaeus* 52 a–c. For the notion that ideas are the causes of sensible things, see for example *Phaedo* 100 b–101 c.
17. B. de Spinoza, *Ethica ordine geometrico demonstrata* (1677), Part I: Concerning God, Definition 1: 'Per causam sui intelligo id cuius essentia involvit existentiam sive id cuius natura non potest concipi nisi existens.' In: *Opera*, C. Gebhardt ed. (Heidelberg: C. Winter, 1925) vol. 2.

18. *Parmenides* 126 a–137 b.
19. 137 b–166 c.
20. 129 b.
21. 129 b.
22. 129 d.
23. 129 a.
24. 136 b.
25. In the *Sophistes*, the dialogue dedicated to the discussion of the ideas' relations among themselves, Plato singles out Existence, Sameness, Difference, Motion and Rest as being the most fundamental ideas and calls them 'highest kinds', *megista gene* (at 254 d).
26. *Parmenides* 129 d–e.
27. 131 a–e.
28. 132 a–b.
29. 132 b.
30. Or 'results from thoughts': *ek noematon . . . einai.*
31. *Parmenides* 132 c.
32. 135 e.
33. Though I follow the gist of Gill/Ryan's translation (J. Cooper 1997), I have modified this passage. The justification for these changes is given in the following.
34. For this concise reconstruction of the gist of the *Parmenides'* part two (as for much enlightenment on the most puzzling aspects of the dialogue) I am indebted to K. Duesing (2001).
35. *Parmenides* 137 d.
36. 137 e.
37. 138 a.
38. 138 b–139 b.
39. 139 a–e.
40. 139 e–140 d.
41. 140 b–141 d.
42. 166 c.
43. My analysis is based on the following selection: H. Cherniss, 'Parmenides and the "Parmenides" of Plato,' *American Journal of Philology*, 53/2 (1932). P. Friedlaender, *Platon*, 3 vols. Berlin: de Gruyter, 1954. A.E. Taylor, *Plato. The Man and His Work*. New York: Meridian, 1956. J.-L. Vieillard-Baron, *Platon et l'idealisme allemand (1770–1830)*, Paris: Beauchesne, 1979. R.-P. Haegler, *Platons 'Parmenides'*, Berlin: W. De Gruyter, 1983. K. Duesing (1983) and (2001). F. von Kutschera, *Platons Parmenides*, Berlin: De Gruyter, 1995.
44. This is the translation in B. Jowett, ed. and trans., *Plato. Dialogues* (Oxford: Clarendon Press, 1953) vol. 2. Jowett's reading has been followed almost uniformly up to and including Gill/Ryan's translation in J. Cooper (1997).
45. In F. MacDonald Cornford, *Plato and Parmenides. Parmenides' Way of Truth and Plato's Parmenides* (New York: Humanities Press, 1939) p. 108.
46. F. Schleiermacher's and E. Pegone's translations are being discussed below.
47. The first edition of Ficinus' *Platonis Opera Omnia* dates from 1484. I have been able to consult the 1491 edition (see next endnote). Despite close resemblance, the correspondence of modern translations to Ficino's Latin is only partial. Among other things, as I argue below, Ficino's *(sup)positio* is

not semantically equivalent to 'supposition,' 'assumption' or 'hypothesis' in their subjective modern acceptation.

48. The wording in the 1491 edition is the following: 'Unde igitur incipiemus? quidve primum supponemus? an vultis, postquam negotiosum ludum ingressi sumus, a me ipso meaque suppositione in primis exordiar, de ipso uno supponens, sive unum sit, sive non, quid accidat?' (M. Ficinus, *Platonis opera omnia*, ed. de Venetiis per Bernardinum de Choris et Simonem de Luero, 1491).
49. M. Ficinus, *Platonis opera omnia* (Biponti: ex typographia Societatis, 1787).
50. For an exact reconstruction of the fascinating history of the editions of Ficino's translation see J. Hankins, 'Some Remarks on the History and Character of Ficino's Translation of Plato' in G.C. Garfagnini, ed., *Marsilio Ficino e il ritorno di Platone* (Firenze: Leo Olschki Editore, 1986) vol. 1.
51. F. Schleiermacher, *Platons Werke* (Berlin: G. Reimer, 1855–62; first edition 1804–7) vols 1–6.
52. '. . . by taking the one itself as ground' (. . . *indem ich das Eins selbst zugrunde lege*).'
53. A. Diès, *Platon. Oeuvres complètes* (Paris: Les Belles Lettres, 1923) t. 8, p. 71.
54. Interestingly, H.G. Liddell and R. Scott's augmented *Greek–English Lexicon* (Oxford: Clarendon Press, 1996) does not provide even one instance of *emautou* as 'my' or 'mine,' but renders it exclusively as 'of me,' 'of myself' or, impersonally, 'of oneself'. The *Lexicon* gives as example Plato's *Charmides* at 155 d: '*ouket'en emautou en*' ('I no more was master of myself').
55. Pegone's translation of the *Parmenides* is in E.V. Maltese ed., *Platone. Tutte le Opere* (Roma: Newton & Compton, 1997) vol. 2, p. 167.
56. For *hen esti* see *Parmenides* 128 d and 137 b; for *peri tou henos* see 137 b. The expression *to hen* recurs too often to cite.
57. Diels-Kranz 28 B 8.
58. For example, the subject of the threefold predication discussed here is merely a relative clause: '*hos estin*,' the 'that it is' (Diels-Kranz 28 B 8, 2).
59. Haegler (1983) can find only one instance of *eon* accompanied by the determinate article, namely Diels-Kranz 28 B 4. But there are actually a few more: 28 B 6, and 28 B 8 30 and 35.
60. *Parmenides* 128 a: '*hen phes einai to pan*'.
61. 128 d; Gill and Ryan translate *ei hen esti* ('if one is') with 'if it is one' but, to justify the addition of the pronoun 'it,' they must recur to a note that makes 'the all' into the subject of the phrase: 'i.e., the all (cf. 128 a 8–b 1).'
62. Haegler (1983) p. 105.
63. See *Timaeus* 92 a, *Laws* 682 c, *Politikos* 289 a and 308 a.
64. Even in Plato: see *Protagoras* 313 a.
65. See *Timaeus* 26 a and 53 d, *Laws* 812 a, and *Phaedo* 101 d.
66. The closest the Latin *suppositio* comes to the English '(pre)supposition' is in its plural use indicating 'circumstances.' The farthest is its juridical denotation of '(fraudulent) substitution' (for example, the *suppositio* of a legitimate with an illegitimate son).
67. For the Greater Logic, see *GW* 21, 53 ff./Miller 67 ff., and *GW* 11, 241 ff./Miller 389 ff.
68. *GW* 11, 258 ff./Miller 408 ff.
69. *GW* 11, 291 ff./Miller 444 ff.

70. *GW* 12, 14/Miller 580.
71. An in-depth analysis of Parmenides' poem is beyond the scope of this study, but it should be mentioned that a version of the identity of being and thinking may well be already foreshadowed in the poet's words at Diels-Kranz 28 B 3: 'the same it is to think and also to be' (*to gar auto noein estin te kai einai*).
72. *Parmenides* 139 c–e.
73. *GW* 12, 17/Miller 583.
74. Diels-Kranz 28 B 8, 30.
75. *Parmenides* 139 c.
76. 139 d–e.
77. 139 e.
78. This is argued similarly in other dialogues both preceding and following the *Parmenides*: see for example *Politeia* 436 b and *Sophistes* 230 b, 263 b.
79. *GW* 12,15/Miller 582.

5 Greek Moral Vocabulary: 'Shame is the greatest compulsion'

1. Demosthenes, *First Philippic* 10, quoted in K.J. Dover (1974) p. 228. The full quotation is: 'In my view, shame at what has been done is the greatest compulsion upon free men.' 'Free men' is specified in contrast to 'slaves,' for whom the greatest compulsion is fear of bodily punishment.
2. '... die Verwandlung jenes *Ansichs* in das *Fuersich*, der *Substanz* in *das Subject*, des Gegenstands des *Bewusstseyns* in Gegenstand des *Selbstbewusstseyns*, d.h. in ... aufgehobnen Gegenstand, oder in den *Begriff*' (*GW* 9, 429/Miller 488).
3. The full passage has been discussed in Chapter 3, 3.2 (iii).
4. Allan Bloom's commentary on relevant passages in the *Politeia* (A. Bloom, *The Republic of Plato*, New York: Basic Books, 1968), is illuminating. On the one hand, Bloom thinks that the theory of the correspondence of individual soul and single city is fundamental for Socrates to argue convincingly that it is advantageous to virtuous individuals to devote their lives to a virtuous city (p. 344). On the other hand, Bloom states explicitly that there is no satisfactory justification for this all-important parallelism in the *Politeia*. He writes: 'A city, like a man, desires wealth, needs food, and deliberates. But a city cannot reproduce or philosophize; all forms of *eros* are cut off from it. In this sense a city cannot be properly compared to a man' (p. 376).
5. Quotations from the *Politeia*, *Apology*, *Crito* and *Laws* are from J.M. Cooper (1997). *Politeia* is translated by G.M.A. Grube with revisions by C.D.C. Reeve; *Apology* and *Crito* are also translated by Grube, *Laws* by T.J. Saunders.
6. 'die selbstaendige Entwicklung der Besonderheit' (*W* 7 § 185 Remark).
7. 'Recht der subjektiven *Freiheit*' (*W* 7 § 124 Remark).
8. The Logic's chapter on the Idea treats the necessary correspondence of cognitive and ethical developments of consciousness. In the *Encyclopaedia* Logic, the internal transition of the Idea from theoretical cognition (knowl-

edge) of the true to practical cognition (will) of the good is presented concisely in § 232 and Addition.

9. As for the history of applied science and technology, Hegel classifies scientific-technological landmarks as a subcategory of economic ones. See for example § 198 of the *Philosophy of Right* (*W* 7): 'Further, the abstraction of the activity of production makes working ever more *mechanical* thus finally enabling it to have man step aside and to install the *machine* in his place [Die Abstraktion des Produzierens macht das Arbeiten ferner immer mehr *mechanisch* und damit am Ende faehig, dass der Mensch davon wegtreten und an seine Stelle die *Maschine* eintreten lassen kann.]'
10. Both Knox and Nisbet render *Sittlichkeit* with 'ethical life.' I prefer the abstract 'ethicality.' Despite its awkwardness, this word stresses the generic connotation of Hegel's term. After all, we do translate *Moralitaet* with 'morality' and not with 'the moral life,' unless we intend to denote a particular form of morality: the moral life of someone.
11. See Abstract Right, part 3: 'Wrong' (*W* 7 §§ 82–104).
12. For a concise and comprehensive treatment of the uses of *Unterschied* and *Differenz* by Hegel see Inwood (1992), pp. 131–2.
13. 'Der wichtigste Punkt fuer die Natur des Geistes ist das Verhaeltnis nicht nur dessen, was er *an sich* ist, zu dem, was er *wirklich* ist, sondern dessen, als *was er sich weiss*; dieses Sichwissen ist darum, weil er wesentlich Bewusstsein, Grundbestimmung seiner *Wirklichkeit*.'
14. Compare this passage with Aristotle, *De Anima* 402 a 1–10: 'Cognition is . . . a thing of beauty and worth, and this is true of one cognition more than another . . . [W]e may with good reason claim a high place for the inquiry concerning the soul.'
15. 'Die Erkenntnis des Geistes ist die konkreteste, darum hoechste und schwerste. *Erkenne dich selbst*, dies absolute Gebot, hat weder an sich noch da, wo es geschichtlich als ausgesprochen vorkommt, die Bedeutung nur einer *Selbsterkenntnis* nach den *partikulaeren* Faehigkeiten, Charakter, Neigungen und Schwaechen des Individuums, sondern die Bedeutung der Erkenntnis des Wahrhaften des Menschen wie des Wahrhaften an und fuer sich,—des *Wesens* selbst als Geistes.'
16. *De Anima* 426 b 20–9.
17. Among the many outstanding studies of the role of 'shame' in Greek culture from philosophical, psychological and anthropological perspectives, only a few can be named: C.E. von Erffa, '*Aidos* und verwandte Begriffe in ihrer Entwicklung von Homer bis Demokrit,' *Philologus*, Supplementband XXX, 2 (1937); J.G. Peristiany ed., *Honour and Shame. The Values of Mediterranean Society* (Chicago: University of Chicago Press, 1966); J.K. Campbell, 'The Greek Hero,' in J.G. Peristiany/J. Pitt-Rivers eds, *Honor and Grace in Anthropology* (Cambridge: Cambridge University Press, 1992); D.L. Cairns, *Aidos. The Psychology and Ethics of Honour and Shame in Ancient Greek Literature* (Oxford: Clarendon Press, 1993); B. Williams, *Shame and Necessity* (Berkeley: University of California Press, 1993). A concise and forceful treatment of ancient shame and its relation to modern popular conceptions and self-deceptions is to be found in Dover (1974), in particular Chapter 5, pp. 226–42. Dover makes a strong argument, backed by textual and circum-

stantial evidence, for the lack of success of Plato's efforts to distinguish fear of external consequences from feelings of guilt. On the other hand, he stresses that these conceptions typical of antiquity are alive and well in contemporary ethical life.

18. Dover (1974) p. 37.
19. *Crito* 52 a.
20. *Apology* 28 c.
21. *Apology* 28 b 9–c.
22. *Apology* 28 d.
23. *Aischuno* means literally 'I disfigure' or 'I make ugly,' and is therefore used as a metaphor for 'I dishonor.' The passive form *aischunomai* is then used (repeatedly in the *Iliad* and *Odyssey*) to mean 'I am dishonored,' 'I feel shame.'
24. Achilles' speech is in the *Iliad*'s book 18, verses 97–110.
25. Dover (1974) p. 18.
26. One such noticeable exception may be a case pointed out by Dover. In Euripides' *Phoenisse*, Antigone contradicts her father's traditional views regarding the ethical quality of the lives of unmarried and childless women in a way that might suggest that a distinction is being made between social role playing and moral subjectivity: '[Oedipus:] It is disgraceful [*aischros*] for a daughter to go into exile with a blind father. [Antigone:] Not if she is right-thinking [*sophronein*], father; it is honorable [*gennaios*]' (Dover 1994, p. 240–1).
27. Dover (1974) p. 242.
28. Dover (1974) p. 223.
29. Socrates' references to the demonic voice are discussed further in the next section.
30. See I. Kant, *Beantwortung der Frage: Was ist Aufklaerung*? (1784). *Kants gesammelte Schriften*, vol. 8, p. 35.
31. In particular, *Politeia* 476 a–480 a.
32. *Crito* 47 b–c.
33. Grube (in Cooper 1997) translates 'Do you not think that Socrates would appear to be an unseemly kind of person?' There is, however, no mention of 'persons' in Plato's text: that to which unseemliness is predicated is the action of Socrates, not Socrates himself.
34. *Crito* 54 d.
35. *'tauta . . . ego doko akouein'*.
36. *'en emoi haute he eche touton ton logon bombei'*.
37. See above, Chapter 3, 3.2 (iii).
38. Knox translates *am tiefsten verletzte* with 'he did fatal injury.' But the injury perpetrated by Plato against that principle could not be called fatal by Hegel, given his thesis that first the feudal-Christian and then the modern world developed from that principle. H.B. Nisbet's translation is more accurate: 'inflicted the gravest damage.'
39. 'Im Verlaufe der folgenden Abhandlung habe ich bemerkt, dass . . . im Bewusstsein des in sie [die griechische Sittlichkeit] einbrechenden tieferen Prinzips, das an ihr unmittelbar nur als eine noch unbefriedigte Sehnsucht und damit nur als Verderben erscheinen konnte, *Platon* . . . Hilfe dagegen hat suchen muessen . . . durch welche er jenes Verderben zu gewaeltigen

sich ausdachte, und wodurch er ihren tieferen Trieb, die freie unendliche Persoenlichkeit, gerade am tiefsten verletzte.'

40. For the absolute idealist, the contradiction giving rise to epochal revolutions is that between dormant but increasingly active 'principles' of a social formation and the established, dominant form of its self-understanding. For the historical materialists who followed, the contradiction internal to epochal modes of production became that between relations and modes of production.
41. 'Form des Geistes, in einer untergeordneteren, abstrakteren [Form] existierend' (*E* § 404 Remark).
42. The uses of 'spirit,' 'consciousness,' 'mind' and more rarely 'soul' are sometimes conflated in the literature. In Hegel's system, however, their use is quite consistent. *Geist* is the genus, embracing subjective and objective spirit. Both include distinguishable, though of course not separable forms. In subjective spirit, the object of the phenomenology is consciousness, of psychology, mind, and of anthropology, soul.
43. 'In diesem Teil werden wir die Seele, weil sie hier auf dem Standpunkt ihrer Entzweiung mit sich selber erscheint, im Zustande ihrer *Krankheit* zu betrachten haben. Es herrscht in dieser Sphaere ein Widerspruch der Freiheit und Unfreiheit der Seele; denn die Seele ist einerseits noch an ihre Substantialitaet gefesselt . . . waehrend sie andererseits schon sich von ihrer Substanz, von ihrer Natuerlichkeit zu trennen beginnt, und sich somit auf die Mittelstufe zwischen ihrem unmittelbaren Naturleben und dem objektiven, freien Bewusstsein erhebt.'
44. *W* 7 p. 26.
45. See *E* § 2, where philosophy is defined as '*thinking consideration* of objects.'
46. *W* 7 p. 26.
47. *E* § 6 Remark.
48. *W* 7 p. 24.
49. 'Diese einfachen Saetze haben manchen Auffallend geschienen . . . aber . . . [es] ist so viel Bildung vorauszusetzen, dass man wisse, . . . dass ueberhapt das Daseyn zum Teil *Erscheinung* und nur zum Teil Wirklichkeit ist' (*E* § 6 Remark). In the English-speaking context, Knox's rendition of *gegenwaertige Welt* in the passage quoted above with 'world as it is' may have helped establish the pertinacious view that Hegel advocates acquiescence to the *status quo*, whatever it may be.
50. '[S]elbst die *Platonische* Republik, welche als das Sprichwort eines *leeren Ideals* gilt, [hat] wesentlich nichts aufgefasst . . . als die Natur der Griechischen Sittlichkeit' (*W* 7 p. 24).
51. Literally, soundness of mind: *to sophronein*.
52. *E* § 114. The full passage is given below.
53. 'Es ist in ihr [der Sphaere des Wesens] alles so gesetzt, dass es sich auf sich bezieht und dass zugleich darueber hinausgegangen ist,—als ein *Sein der Reflexion*, ein Sein, in dem ein Anderes scheint und das in einem Anderen scheint.—Sie ist daher auch die Sphaere des *gesetzten Widerspruches*' (*E* § 114).
54. See in particular: A. Fuks, 'Plato and the social question: the problem of poverty and riches in the *Republic*,' *Ancient Society* 8 (1977), 49–83. M.H. Jameson, 'Agriculture and Slavery in Classical Athens,' in *Classical Journal*

73 (1977–8), 122–45. G.E.M. de Ste. Croix, *The Class Struggle in the Ancient Greek World* (Ithaca, Cornell U.P., 1981). De Ste Croix (p. 70) refers approvingly to Fuks' talk of Plato's 'obsessive conviction' that 'the tense political atmosphere and acute civil strife of his day were the direct consequence of increasing contrasts between wealth and poverty. In particular Plato realized that an oligarchy . . . will actually be two cities, one of the poor and the other of the rich, "always plotting against each other" (551 d).'

55. De Ste. Croix (1981) p. 42.
56. *Politeia* 414 c–d.
57. This can only be done, of course, by reserving the phenomenon of slavery for a related, but separate analysis. In a discussion of Plato's theory of the *polis*, this is a legitimate move, as Plato dedicates little more than passing remarks to the existence of slaves and their function as a group, and does not include them in the social hierarchy at all.
58. Indeed, the two may be intimately connected. But I will not follow up on the question of whether they share the same ground, as I am presently interested only in Hegel's reading of Greek *Wirklichkeit*.
59. '[Das Prinzip] der *selbstaendigen in sich unendlichen Persoenlichkeit* des Einzelnen, der subjektiven Freiheit' (*W* 7 § 185 Remark).
60. 'Recht der subjektiven *Freiheit*' (*W* 7 § 124 Remark).
61. '[D]as Prinzip der Persoenlichkeit ist die Allgemeinheit' (*E* § 163 Addition 1).
62. 'Nun aber ist das Allgemeine des Begriffs nicht bloss ein Gemeinschaftliches, welchem gegenueber das Besondere seinen Bestand fuer sich hat, sondern vielmehr das sich selbst Besondernde (Spezifizierende) und in seinem Anderen . . . bei sich selbst Bleibende . . . Das Allgemeine in seiner wahren und umfassenden Bedeutung ist uebrigens ein Gedanke, von welchem gesagt werden muss, dass es Jahrtausende gekostet hat, bevor derselbe in das Bewusstsein der Menschen getreten . . . ist.'
63. 'Die sonst so hochgebildeten Griechen haben weder Gott in seiner wahrhaften Allgemeinheit gewusst noch auch den Menschen. . . . So bestand denn auch fuer die Griechen zwischen ihnen selbst und den Barbaren eine absolute Kluft, und der Mensch als solcher war noch nicht anerkannt in seinem unendlichen Werte und seiner unendlichen Berechtigung' (*E* § 163 Addition 1). This has been discussed above, 3.3.2 (iii).
64. The most famous discussion is of course that of Aristotle, *Politics*, first book, chapter 4 and third book, chapter 6.
65. If *Sache* (in *selbstlose Sache*) is read as *Ding*, Hegel's characterization of the ancient conception of the slave as 'thing devoid of self' must appear as an oversimplification. The same happens if 'devoid of self' is taken to mean altogether 'soulless.' Hegel is of course perfectly aware that, even for the ancients, slaves are living human beings. His point is that they are not persons. In the first book of the *Politics* (at 1253 b 1 ff.) Aristotle distinguishes explicitly between *poietika organa*, means of production proper, and *praktika organa*, means for the support and improvement of life. The latter are living and have souls, and the slave is defined precisely as such an *empsychon organon*. But the slave's *psyche* is only a natural soul, not also an ego equivalent to that of the master. Hegel's use of *Sache* here instead of *Ding* is therefore justified, as Inwood (1992, p. 288 ff.) explains: the German

Sache is a more forceful antonym of *Person* than is *Ding*, a generic term for all kinds of existences.

66. 'Was dem Sklaven fehlt, das ist die Anerkennung seiner Persoenlichkeit; das Prinzip der Persoenlichkeit aber ist die Allgemeinheit. Der Herr betrachtet den Sklaven nicht als Person, sondern als selbstlose Sache, und der Sklave gilt nicht selbst als Ich, sondern der Herr ist sein Ich' (*E* § 163 Addition 1).
67. The lectures at issue here are those of the year 1825–6. I quote this passage in the translation by T.M. Knox and A.V. Miller, *G.W.F. Hegel. Introduction to the Lectures on the History of Philosophy* (Oxford: Clarendon Press, 1985), p. 75. I have replaced 'law' with 'right' for Hegel's *Recht*.
68. *W* 7 §§ 54–8.
69. 'Die behauptete Berechtigung der *Sklaverei*' (*W* 7 § 57 Remark).
70. 'die Behauptung des absoluten Unrechts' (*W* 7 § 57 Remark).
71. Aristotle, *Politics*, 1254 a 15.
72. J.-J. Rousseau (1762). D.A. Cress ed. (1987) p. 141.
73. 'Der Mensch ist nach der *unmittelbaren* Existenz an ihm selbst ein Natuerliches, seinem Begriffe Aeusseres; erst durch die *Ausbildung* seines eigenen Koerpers und Geistes, *wesentlich* dadurch, dass *sein Selbstbewusstsein sich als freies erfasst*, nimmt er sich in Besitz und wird das Eigentum seiner selbst und gegen andere. Dieses Besitznehmen ist . . . dies, das, was er seinem Begriffe nach (als eine *Moeglichkeit* . . .) ist, in die *Wirklichkeit* zu setzen.'
74. '*Existenz* . . . die seinem Begriffe nicht angemessen ist' (*W* 7 § 57 Remark).
75. '*organon pro organon*' (Aristotle, *Politics* 1253 b 30).
76. 'Diese fruehere unwahre Erscheinung betrifft den Geist, welcher nur erst auf dem Standpunkte seines Bewusstseins ist' (*W* 7 § 57 Remark).
77. 'Die Dialektik des Begriffs und des nur erst unmittelbaren Bewusstseins der Freiheit bewirkt daselbst den *Kampf des Anerkennens* und das Verhaeltnis der *Herrenschaft* und der *Knechtschaft* . . . Dass aber der objektive Geist, der Inhalt des Rechts, nicht selbst wieder nur in seinem subjektiven Begriffe und damit, dass dies, dass der Mensch and und fuer sich nicht zur Sklaverei bestimmt sei, nicht wieder als ein blosses Sollen aufgefasst werde, dies findet allein in der Erkenntnis statt, dass die Idee der Freiheit wahrhaft nur als *der Staat* ist.'
78. 'Die Idee des *Platonischen* Staats enthaelt das Unrecht gegen die Person, des Privateigentums unfaehig zu sein, als allgemeines Prinzip. Die Vorstellung von einer . . . Verbruederung der Menschen mit *Gemeinschaft der Gueter* und der Verbannung des privateigentuemlichen Prinzips kann sich der Gesinnung leicht darbeiten, welche die Natur der Freiheit des Geistes und des Rechts verkennt.'
79. *W* 7 p. 18. Regarding Hegel's bitter sentiments toward the mathematician and philosopher Fries one may want to look also at his introduction to the first edition (1812) of the Doctrine of Being (*GW* 11, pp. 23–4).
80. Knox (1952), p. 322. Nisbet's (1991) comments on this passage (p. 407) are largely the same as Knox's.
81. See *Laws* 739 c–e.
82. *Politeia* 434 c.
83. For textual examples see Dover (1974) p. 170 ff. and the works cited there: V. Ehrenberg, *The People of Aristophanes* (New York: Barnes & Noble, 1974)

and F. Egerman, *Vom attischen Menschenbild* (Munich, Kommissionsverlag Filser, 1952).

84. See *W* 7 § 121 Addition.
85. *W* 7 § 120.
86. The self-condemnation of Oedipus following his entirely unintentional incestual act can of course be considered the literary paradigm of ancient moral feelings about, and understanding of, individual agency in its moral dimension. Today's documented phenomena of persistent guilt feelings in victims of incestual abuse show that the perceptive side of our 'ancient' psyche can survive even the most radical revolutions in thought.
87. 'das *Recht* des *Subjekts*, in der Handlung seine *Befriedigung* zu finden' (*W* 7 § 121).
88. 'Beduerfnissen, Neigungen, Leidenschaften, Meinungen, Einfaellen usf.' (*W* 7 § 123).
89. 'Glueckseligkeit als Zustand fuer das ganze Leben, stellt Totalitaet des Genusses auf. Diese ist etwas Allgemeines und eine Regel fuer die einzelnen Genuesse, . . . die Begierde zu Hemmen, allgemeinen Massstab vor Augen zu haben' (*W* 18, 186–7).
90. 'In der Glueckseligkeit . . . [ist] die Form der Allgemeinheit . . . schon, aber das Allgemeine tritt auch noch nicht fuer sich heraus. . . . Der Mensch als denkend geht nicht bloss auf den gegenwaertigen Genuss, sondern auch auf die Mittel fuer den kuenftigen. . . . Diese erbauliche Geschichte charakterisiert ganz den Standpunkt der Reflexion damaliger Zeit.'
91. *W* 7 § 123 Remark.
92. 'Das Recht der *Besonderheit* des Subjekts, sich befriedigt zu finden, oder, was dasselbe ist, das Recht der *subjektiven Freiheit* macht den Wende- und Mittelpunkt in dem Unterschiede des *Altertums* und der *modernen* Zeit' (*W* 7 § 124 Remark).
93. Knox (1967) p. 339.
94. 'Wahl des Standes' (*W* 7 § 185 Remark).
95. *Politeia* 563 c–d.
96. Also referred to as 'particularity for itself' (*Besonderheit fuer sich*) (*W* 7 § 185).
97. *W* 7 § 183.
98. 'Die buergerliche Gesellschaft bietet in diesen Gegensaetzen und ihrer Verwicklung das Schauspiel ebenso der Ausschweifung, des Elends und des beiden gemeinschaftlichen physischen und sittlichen Verderbens dar' (*W* 7 § 185).
99. This and the next two examples are taken from Dover (1974) p. 20.
100. Dover (1974) notes appropriately that this fragment, lacking any context, may as well have been meant sarcastically. The expression 'well [*alethes*] educated' may have read 'guileless,' *euethes*. Still, even in this interpretation the fragment testifies to the recognition of particular and highly unusual conceptions of the good.
101. 'Diese Staaten . . . konnten die Entzweiung [ihrer Sittlichkeit] . . . und die unendliche Reflexion des Selbstbewusstseins in sich nicht aushalten und erlagen dieser Reflexion, wie sie sich hervorzutun anfing, der Gesinnung und dann der Wirklichkeit nach' (*W* 7 § 185 Remark).
102. *W* 7 § 206 Remark.
103. *W* 7 § 299 Remark.

104. 'die Zuteilung der Individuen zu den Staenden [ist] der *blossen* Geburt . . . ueberlassen' (*W* 7 § 206 Remark).
105. 'Fortschritt im Bewusstsein der Freiheit' (*W* 12 p. 32).
106. 'So in die Organisation des Ganzen nicht aufgenommen und in ihm nicht versoehnt, zeigt sich deswegen die subjektive Besonderheit . . . als Feindseliges, als Verderben der gesellschaftlichen Ordnung' (*W* 7 § 206 Remark).
107. 'Die selbstaendige Entwicklung der Besonderheit . . . ist das Moment, welches sich in den alten Staaten als das hereinbrechende Sittenverderben und der letzte Grund des Untergangs derselben zeigt' (*W* 7 § 185 Remark). The 'decline' of ancient social orders refers of course to their loss of supremacy on the world-historical stage—not to their utter disappearance, as the twenty-first century world stage distinctly shows.
108. 'die Angel . . . , um welche die bevorstehende Umwaelzung der Welt sich gedreht hat' (*W* 7 p. 24).
109. See *W* 7 124 Remark.
110. *W* 7 § 299.
111. '*Platon* laesst in seinem Staate die Individuen den besonderen Staenden durch die Oberen zuteilen und ihnen ihre *besonderen* Leistungen auflegen . . . ; in der Feudalmonarchie hatten Vasallen ebenso unbestimmte Dienste, aber auch in ihrer *Besonderheit* . . . In diesen Verhaeltnissen mangelt das Prinzip der *subjektiven Freiheit*, dass das substantielle Tun des Individuums . . . durch seinen *besonderen Willen* vermittelt sei,—ein Recht, das allein durch die Forderung der Leistungen in der Form des allgemeinen Wertes moeglich . . . ist'. This concept is illustrated further in the Addition to this § 299.
112. For Hegel's determination of the nature of money see *W* 7 § 63 Addition.
113. 'Der selbstsuechtige Zweck in seiner Verwirklichung, so durch die Allgemeinheit bedingt, begruendet ein System allseitiger Abhaengigkeit' (*W* 7 § 183).
114. See *W* 7 § 185 Addition: 'If Plato's state wanted to exclude particularity, it could not be helped, since such help would contradict the infinite right of the Idea to let particularity be free [Wenn der Platonische Staat die Besonderheit ausschliessen wollte, so ist damit nicht zu Helfen, denn solche Hilfe wuerde dem unendlichen Rechte der Idee widersprechen, die Besonderheit frei zu lassen].'
115. *W* 7 § 154.
116. For Hegel's use of 'concrete' as a synthesis of differences that have grown together, and of 'abstract' as indicating homogenization and reduction, see Chapter 3, 3.1.
117. 'In den Staaten des klassischen Altertums findet sich allerdings schon die Allgemeinheit vor, aber die Partikularitaet war noch nicht losgebunden und freigelassen. . . . Das Wesen des neuen Staates ist, dass das Allgemeine verbunden sei mit der vollen Freiheit der Besonderheit und dem Wohlergehen der Individuen, . . . der Besonderheit, die ihr Recht behalten muss.'

6 Dialectic Matters: Starting Out with Simple Motion

1. 'Die selbstaendige Entwicklung der Besonderheit' (*W* 7 § 185 Remark).
2. 'Freie unendliche Persoenlichkeit' (*W* 7, Preface p. 24).

3. 'Die Nagel . . . , um welche die [damals] bervorstehende Umwaelzung der Welt sich gedreht hat' (*W* 7, Preface p. 24).
4. '*Urspruengliche* natuerliche Anschauung' (*W* 7 §185 Remark).
5. '[Anaxagoras] hat damit den Grund zu einer Intellektualansicht des Universums gelegt, deren reine Gestalt *die Logik* sein muss. Es ist in ihr nicht um ein Denken *ueber Etwas*, das fuer sich ausser dem Denken zugrundelaege, zu tun, um Formen, welche blosse *Merkmale* der Wahrheit abgeben sollten; sondern die notwendigen Formen und eigenen Bestimmungen des Denkens sind der Inhalt und die hoechste Wahrheit selbst.'
6. For Hegel's remarks on the contrast and common ground of Parmenides and Heraclitus in the Doctrine of Being see *GW* 21, 73 ff./Miller 83 ff. For his detailed interpretation and assessment of both philosophers, which is not my task here, one must turn to the *Lectures on the History of Philosophy* (*W* 18), Chapter 1, C. ('The Eleatic School') and D. ('Philosophy of Heraclitus').
7. 'die letzte Stufe der Unvollkommenheit . . . , das Allgemeine mit Sinnlichem behaftet zu fassen' (*GW* 21, 204/Miller 213).
8. 'Kindheit des Philosophierens' (*GW* 21, 321/Miller 324). As for intuitive modes of cognition in modern philosophy, Hegel analyzes these at length in the Lesser Logic, §§ 61–78 ('Third Position of Thought Towards Objectivity'). The paradox of all intuitionistic cognitivism, whether ancient or modern, lies in the fact that while intuition is defined by the immediacy of its relation to the object, cognition is defined as the process of mediation *par excellence* between knowing subject and known object. On the relation and difference of speculative knowing and mystical intuition see *E* § 82 Addition, discussed in Chapter 2, 2.3 (i).
9. Aristotle, *Metaphysics* 982 b 20.
10. 'unendlicher Fortschritt' (*GW* 21, 12/Miller 33).
11. 'ein tieferes Prinzip, einen schwereren Gegenstand und ein Material von reicherem Umfang' (*GW* 21, 20/Miller 42).
12. 'Gewoehnlich sieht man [in Plato's Werk] die Dialektik fuer ein aeusserliches und negatives Tun an, das nicht der Sache selbst angehoere, in blosser Eitelkeit als einer subjektiven Sucht, sich das Feste und Wahre in Schwanken zu setzen und aufzuloesen, seinen Grund habe oder wenigstens zu Nichts fuehre als zur Eitelkeit des dialektisch behandelten Gegenstandes.'
13. See *GW* 12, 243/Miller 832.
14. 'Wir sehen in dieser Weise des Raesonnements eine Dialektik, die man metaphysisches Raesonnement nennen kann. Das Prinzip der Identitaet liegt dem zugrunde: "Das Nichts ist gleich Nichts, geht nicht ins Sein ueber, noch umgekehrt; aus Gleichem kann daher nichts entstehen." Das Sein . . . der eleatischen Schule ist . . . dieses Versenken in den Abgrund der Verstandesidentitaet. Diese aelteste Weise der Argumentation ist noch immer, bis auf den heutigen Tag, gueltig, z.B. in den sogenannten Beweisen von der Einheit Gottes.'
15. For the exegetical problems related to Parmenides' 'one' see Chapter 4 above, in particular 4.2.
16. See, in particular, *GW* 21, 87–8/Miller 93.
17. For Hegel's own formulation of the speculative content of the *cogito*-argument see *E* § 64, Remark, discussed above in Chapter 2, 2.3 (i).

18. See *E* § 407 ff.
19. See *E* § 424 ff.
20. See *E* § 481 ff.
21. *GW* 21, 106/Miller 118.
22. Hegel singles out Aristotle's comprehension of the soul–body relation as a speculative leap in comparison to Plato's treatment of the subject. For an outstanding treatment of Hegel's solution to the so-called mind–body problem and its debt to Aristotelian psychology see M. Wolff (1992).
23. See *W* 7 § 21 Remark.
24. 'etwas Handgreifliches' (*GW* 21, 34/Miller 50).
25. 'Solche Handgreiflichkeit wird zum Beispiel selbst noch in die Platonischen Ideen . . . hineingetragen, als ob sie gleichsam existierende Dinge, aber in einer anderen Welt oder Region seien' (*GW* 21, 34/Miller 50).
26. 'Die Platonische Idee ist nichts anderes als das Allgemeine oder bestimmter der Begriff des Gegenstandes; nur in seinem Begriff hat etwas Wirklichkeit; insofern es von seinem Begriff verschieden ist, hoert es auf, wirklich zu sein, und ist ein Nichtiges; die Seite der Handgreiflichkeit und des sinnlichen Aussersichseins gehoert dieser nichtigen Seite an.'
27. 'eine Ansicht, die in der Sokratischen Dialektik gegen die sophistische vorkommt, und ein Zorn, der umgekehrt wieder selbst den Sokrates das Leben gekostet hat' (*GW* 12, 243 /Miller 832).
28. I translate *sich bewegend* with the non-reflexive 'moving'. In this case, German does not imply the reflexive meaning suggested by the grammatical use of *sich*. Zeno's paradoxes, whose discussion is introduced by the remark quoted, are not about self-motion *versus* motion. This distinction is not a topic in the Zenonian arguments at all. In common German use, the reflexive form *sich bewegen* is attributed to non-living as much as to living things: a car '*bewegt sich*.'
29. On the difference in meaning between Hegel's *an sich* (in itself) and *an ihm* (in it), and thus on the necessity of translating them differently, see M. Inwood (1992) p. 78.
30. 'Dass die Dialektik zuerst auf die Bewegung gefallen, ist eben dies der Grund, dass die Dialektik selbst diese Bewegung oder die Bewegung selbst die Dialektik alles Seienden ist. Das Ding hat, als sich bewegend, seine Dialektik selbst an ihm, und die Bewegung ist: sich anders werden, sich aufheben' (*W* 18, 305).
31. 'das Hinausgehen der philosophischen Idee in ihrer Entwicklung [ist] . . . ebenso ein In-sich-hineingehen' (*GW* 18, 47). This general law has been discussed above in Chapter 1.
32. For a concise account of the formulations and their attributions see G. Vlastos, 'A Note on Zeno's Arrow', *Phronesis*, XI:I (1966) 3–18, especially notes 1, 2 and 3. A detailed account is in M. Untersteiner, *Zenone. Testimonianze e frammenti* (Firenze: Nuova Italia, 1963).
33. For ease of reference, I use the customary 'place' rather than 'position' for the implicit *topos* in Aristotle's reconstruction of the Arrow (at *Physics* 239 b 5 quoted below). However, while a body's place must indeed be always identical to the body's dimensions (it is *kata to ison*, as Aristotle reports Zeno to be saying), the spatial-temporal position of that place or body does not have any dimensions (it can be identified by a pair of numbers) and may

be different at different times. Still, Zeno's question remains: how does the body (or even its place) get to a different position?

34. See Diogenes Laertius, *Leben und Meinungen beruehmter Philosophen*, book four, chapter 2. K. Reich, ed (Hamburg: Meiner, 1967), p. 313.
35. 'Die poebelhafte Widerlegung . . . muss man sich selbst ueberlassen' (*GW* 12, 243/Miller 832).
36. 'Zenons Dialektik der Materie ist bis auf den heutigen Tag unwiderlegt': *W* 18, 304.
37. *Physics* 239 b 5. In the following I use the translation by R.P. Hardie and R.K. Gaye in J. Barnes ed. (1984). On occasion, comparison with the Greek text prompts me to prefer the translation by P.H. Wicksteed and F.M. Cornford, *Aristotle. The Physics* (Cambridge: Harvard University Press, 1968) vols I and II.
38. 239 b 30.
39. 231 a 21.
40. 231 b 5.
41. 231 b 10.
42. I follow Wicksteed/Cornford (1968) instead of Hardie/Gaye (1984) in translating *ei* with 'if' rather than 'since.' It is far from clear, at this advanced stage of Aristotle's discussion, that the *tertium non datur* between rest and motion is still a thesis he embraces. Much in this text indicates rather that he does not.
43. *Physics* 232 a 10.
44. See 232 a 15.
45. See 233 a 25.
46. See 233 a 31 ff.
47. For the Greek *e en chrono e en mekei* I adopt the more accurate 'in a time or in a length' of Wicksteed/Cornford (1968) rather than 'of time or of distance' in Hardie/Gaye (1984).
48. Both Wicksteed/Cornford (1968) and Hardie/Gaye (1984) translate *symbebekos* with 'in an accidental sense' (as in Aristotle, *Metaphysics* 1052 a 18). It seems, however, that a different sense of *symbebekos*, also used in *Metaphysics* (at 1025 a 31) is more plausible in this context, namely 'as a result of the concept' in question. If 'continuous motion' has to have any meaning at all, it implies necessarily that something has moved through the infinite potential parts of a *continuum*.
49. *Physics* 222 a 10.
50. In a dynamic conception of the infinitesimal, 'connecting' and 'dividing' become undistinguishable functions. Aristotle's appreciation of this can be gauged, I believe, from the fact that in order to characterize the instantaneous present *vis-à-vis* past and future he uses indifferently derivatives of *synechein* (to hold together, as in *to de nun estin synecheia chronou, Physics* 222 a 10) and derivatives of its opposite, *diairein* (to divide, as in *to diairoun semeion to proteron kai hysteron, Physics* 263 b 10).
51. *Physics* 234 a.
52. Contemporary mathematics of course does make use of similar notions by defining sets of intervals as behaving differently than sets of points. G. Priest (in 'Contradictions in Motion', *American Philosophical Quarterly* 22:4

(1985), 339–46) makes use of the mathematical notion of 'time-interval' vs. 'instant' to strengthen Hegel's account of the Arrow. According to this approach, the length of a line (a finite set of points with zero extension) traversed in one instant will be zero (as Zeno is said to have assumed) but the length of a line traversed in one interval will be greater than zero, allowing the arrow to move (as Aristotle now maintains). This supports indeed Hegel's re-evaluation of the Arrow. For other highly original contributions in defense of the rational intelligibility of contradiction by the same author see Chapter 1, n. 23.

53. See also *Physics* 234 a 25–30.
54. *CPR* B 432 ff.
55. All references to this work are to I. Kant, *Metaphysische Anfangsgruende der Naturwissenschaft* (1786), *Akademieausgabe* vol. IV (cited in the following as *AA* IV followed by page number). The translations are mine, but I have consulted J.W. Ellington, ed. and trans., *Immanuel Kant: Philosophy of Material Nature* (Indianapolis: Hackett, 1985). My treatment of this work is confined to Chapter 1, Explanations 1, 2 and 3 and the corresponding Observations.
56. *AA* IV, 480.
57. *AA* IV, 481.
58. 'das Bewegliche im Raume' (*AA* IV, 480).
59. 'Ein beweglicher Raum . . . setzt wiederum einen anderen erweiterten materiellen Raum voraus . . . und so forthin ins Unendliche' (*AA* IV, 481).
60. J. Ellington translates *Geschwindigkeit* with 'velocity.' This may give rise to misunderstandings, since in modern physics 'velocity' refers to a vector including speed and direction. Kant's *Geschwindigkeit* does not include direction (a separate parameter of motion). On the other hand, Kant does distinguish the quantity of speed (*Eile*) from speed itself, so I am adopting Ellington's translation of *Geschwindigkeit* (*per se*) with 'velocity' despite its present-day inaccuracy.
61. 'Also ist alle Bewegung, die ein Gegenstand der Erfahrung ist, bloss relativ' (*AA* IV, 481).
62. 'bedeutet nur einen jeden anderen relativen Raum' (*AA* IV, 481).
63. 'die *logische Allgemeinheit* . . . in eine *physische Allgemeinheit* . . . verwechseln, und die Vernunft in ihrer Idee missverstehen' (*AA* IV, 482).
64. *Physics* 232 a 10, quoted above, 6.1 (i).
65. See *AA* IV, 482.
66. Kant's illustration is as memorable as it is uncontroversial: 'Matter, as for example a *barrel of beer*, is moved, means accordingly something else than: the *beer in the barrel* is in motion [Die Materie, als z.B. ein *Fass Bier*, ist bewegt, bedeutet also etwas anderes, als das *Bier im Fasse* ist in Bewegung]' (*AA* IV, 483).
67. '*Veraenderung* der *aeusseren Verhaeltnisse* desselben zu einem gegebenen Raum' (*AA* IV, 482).
68. Plato, *Politeia* 436d–437.
69. In his interpretation of the *Politeia*, A. Bloom points out that this passage is 'the earliest known explicit statement of the principle of contradiction' (A. Bloom, *The Republic of Plato* (New York: Basic Books, 1968) p. 457, n. 25.)

70. 'Ruhe ist die beharrliche Gegenwart (*presaentia perdurabilis*) an demselben Orte; beharrlich aber ist das, was eine Zeit hindurch existiert d.i. dauret' (*AA* IV, 485).
71. For Aristotle's example of oscillatory motion and his use of it to prove that the body in the point of return is at rest (the opposite of Kant's conclusion) see *Physics*, book eight, chapter 8, 264 a 15.
72. 'Ein Koerper, der in Bewegung ist, ist in jedem Punkte der Linie, die er durchlaeuft, einen Augenblick. Es fragt sich nun, ob er darin ruhe, oder sich bewege. Ohne Zweifel wird man das letztere sagen; denn er ist in diesem Puncte nur so fern, als er sich bewegt, gegenwaertig' (*AA* IV, 485).
73. 'so frage ich, ob der Koerper in B als bewegt, oder als ruhig angesehen werden koenne. Ohne Zweifel wird man sagen, als ruhig' (*AA* IV, 485).
74. 'bis zu einem Grad, der kleiner ist als jede nur anzugebende Geschwindigkeit' (*AA* IV, 486).
75. 'einen Raum, der kleiner ist als jeder anzugebende Raum' (*AA* IV, 486).
76. 'In einem *beharrlichen Zustande* seyn und *darin beharren* . . . sind zwey verschiedene Begriffe' (*AA* IV, 486).
77. Not the least of these problems is Kant's swift and repeated switch from descriptions of merely ideal bodies (points) to descriptions of material bodies (that is, those that are both extended and subject to gravity). Perhaps the dis-analogy that makes the comparison between the oscillating body and the vertically moved one so difficult could be eliminated by comparing a swinging material body (subject to gravity, thus to acceleration) with the oscillating ideal body of the first example. But other difficulties remain that cannot be discussed here.
78. M. Wolff, *Der Begriff des Widerspruchs. Eine Studie zur Dialektik Kants und Hegels* (Koenigstein: Hain-Athenaeum,1981) gives the elegant mathematical explanation of the difference between 'rest' and 'lack of movement' (an explanation already used in Vlastos 1966) that lies at the core of the Kantian passages discussed. Both Vlastos and Wolff point out that if velocity is a ratio between space and time ($v = s/t$), then a body can only be at rest ($v = 0$) if it does not traverse any space ($s = 0$) during a positive period of time ($t > 0$). If the time parameter were null as well, the mathematical ratio would become an irrational number ($v = 0/0 = i$), which does not describe a body at rest (but rather perhaps, as anticipated by Aristotle in *Physics* 239 b, the non-existence of the body altogether).
79. The accuracy of Kant's reading of Plato is not my concern here. His paraphrases may refer to the *Parmenides*, 127 d ff. and again 137 c ff., as well as to the *Phaedrus*, 261 d.
80. 'Der *eleatische Zeno*, ein subtiler Dialektiker, ist schon vom Plato als ein mutwilliger Sophist darueber sehr getadelt worden, dass er, um seine Kunst zu zeigen, einerlei Satz durch scheinbare Argumente zu beweisen und bald darauf durch andere ebenso starke wieder umstuerzen suchte' (*CPR* B 530).
81. '[W]enn er unter dem Worte: *Gott*, das Universum verstand, so musste er allerdings sagen: dass dieses weder in seinem Orte beharrlich gegenwaertig (in Ruhe) sei, noch denselben veraendere (sich bewege), weil alle Oerter nur im Univers, *dieses* selbst also in *keinem Orte* ist' (*CPR* B 530).
82. 'Man erlaube mir, dass ich dergleichen Entgegensetzung die *dialektische*, die des Widerspruchs aber die *analytische Opposition* nennen darf' (*CPR* B 532).

I have modified the translation by Guyer/Wood. *Entgegensetzung* and *Gegensatz* being different terms, if we reserve 'opposition' for *Gegensatz* we will need a different term (e.g. antithesis) for *Entgegesetzung*. This all the more as Kant here uses the German *Opposition* as a technical term that includes 'dialectical' and 'analytical' antitheses.

83. *CPR* B 532.
84. For an in-depth treatment of the contrary character of the mathematical antinomies (first: finitude vs. infinity and second: simplicity vs. composition of the world) and the subcontrary character of the dynamic antinomies (third: natural vs. free causation and fourth: existence vs. non existence of a necessary being) see M. Wolff (1981) pp. 48–61.
85. Aristotle, *Physics* 263 b 5 (quoted above, 6.1 (i).
86. *'Insoferns, Seiten und Ruecksichten'* (*GW* 11, 268–9/Miller 420).
87. 'Die gewoehnliche Zaertlichkeit fuer die Dinge aber, die nur dafuer sorgt, dass diese sich nicht widersprechen vergisst hier wie sonst, dass damit der Widerspruch nicht aufgeloest, sondern nur anderswohin, in die subjektive oder aeussere Reflexion ueberhaupt geschoben wird' (*GW* 11, 272/Miller 423).
88. I borrow this subtitle from Priest (1985).
89. 'der Anfaenger der Dialektik' (*W* 18, 295). This commendation appears to stem from Aristotle: see Diogenes Laertius, (ed. K. Reich 1967) book ten, chapter 5, p. 172–3: 'Aristotle calls him [Zeno] the inventor of dialectic, like Empedocles of rethoric.'
90. See above, 6.1.
91. I. Duering (*Aristoteles. Darstellung und Interpretation seines Denkens*, Heidelberg 1966, p. 326) shares Hegel's interpretation: 'Of course it was not Zeno's intention to prove that Achilles would never overtake the turtle. Contemporary mathematics allowed him certainly to calculate exactly when this would take place. What he did want to demonstrate was merely that in his view the concept of motion is full of contradictions.'
92. 'sprach und wandte sich gegen die Bewegung als solche oder die reine Bewegung' (*W* 18, 295).
93. 'Begriffe und . . . Gedanken' (*W* 18, 297).
94. See Aristotle, *Physics* 263 b 5 (the full context is quoted above, 6.1 ii): 'though it is accidental to the line to be an infinite number of half-distances [thus making it seemingly impossible for anything to move], essence is other than being.'
95. 'Aristoteles fuehrt dies an, Zenon habe die Bewegung geleugnet, weil sie inneren Widerspruch habe. Es ist dies nicht so zu fassen, dass die Bewegung garnicht sei. . . . Dass es Bewegung gibt, dass diese Erscheinung ist, davon ist garnicht die Rede; sinnliche Gewissheit hat die Bewegung, wie es Elefanten gibt. In diesem Sinne ist es dem Zenon gar nicht eingefallen, die Bewegung zu leugnen. Die Frage ist vielmehr nach ihrer Wahrheit; die Bewegung ist aber unwahr, denn sie ist Widerspruch. Damit hat er sagen wollen, dass ihr kein wahrhaftes Sein zukomme.'
96. 'man [hat] sich nicht mit der sinnlichen Gewissheit zu begnuegen, sondern zu begreifen' (*W* 18, 306).
97. Compare with Kant, *CPR* B 350: 'Truth or illusion are not in the object, insofar as it is intuited, but in the judgment about it, insofar as it is thought.

[Wahrheit oder Schein sind nicht im Gegenstande, sofern er angeschaut wird, sondern im Urteile ueber denselben, sofern er gedacht wird.]'

98. 'Fuer uns hat in der Vorstellung es keinen Widerspruch, dass der Punkt . . . oder das Jetzt als eine Kontinuitaet, Laenge (Tag, Jahr) gesetzt ist; aber ihr Begriff ist sich widersprechend. Die Sichselbstgleichheit, Kontinuitaet ist absoluter Zusammenhang, Vertilgtsein alles Unterschiedes, alles Negativen, des Fuersichseins; der Punkt ist hingegen das reine Fuersichsein, das absolute Sichunterscheiden und Aufheben aller Gleichheit und Zusammenhangs mit anderem.' On the dialectical identity of absolute connection and absolute separation see above, n. 51.
99. See *GW* 21, 127/Miller 139: 'the *spurious infinite*, the infinite of the *understanding* [das *Schlecht-Unendliche*, das Unendliche des *Verstandes*]'.
100. 'der Widerspruch . . . , wie er in der Sphaere des Seins sich zeigt' (*GW* 11, 287/Miller 440).
101. 'die Quantitaet [ist] nichts anderes als die aufgehobene Qualitaet' (*E* § 98, Addition 2).
102. 'die *reale Moeglichkeit* des Eins' (*GW* 21, 177).
103. It must be stressed, however, that Aristotle develops his arguments further, as indicated in 6.1 (ii). He actually states that continuity contains infinite divisibility—an insight that could have prompted him (but did not) into revising his criticism of Zeno.
104. 'Der begrifflosen *Vorstellung* wird die Kontinuitaet leicht zur *Zusammensetzung*. . . . Es hat sich aber am Eins gezeigt, dass . . . die Kontinuitaet ihm nicht aeusserlich ist, sondern ihm selbst angehoert und in seinem Wesen gegruendet ist. Diese *Aeusserlichkeit* der Kontinuitaet fuer die Eins ist es ueberhaupt, an der die Atomistik haengenbleibt und die zu verlassen die Schwierigkeit fuer das Vorstellen macht.'
105. Hegel is quoting from Spinoza, *Ethica, Pars* I, *Propositio* XV, *Scholion.*
106. Hegel is quoting from Leibniz's dissertation of 1663: *Propositiones ex disputatione metaphysica de principio individui.*
107. 'ein perennierendes *Selbstproduzieren* ihrer Einheit' (*GW* 21, 178/Miller 189).
108. 'unvermeidliche, obzwar nicht unaufloesliche, Illusion' (*CPR* B 399).
109. 'der *daseiende* Widerspruch selbst' (*GW* 11, 287/Miller 440).
110. 'Die aeusserliche sinnliche Bewegung selbst ist sein [des Widerspruchs] unmittelbares Dasein. Es bewegt sich etwas nur, nicht indem es in diesem Itzt hier ist und in einem anderen Itzt dort, sondern indem es in einem und demselben Itzt hier und nicht hier, indem es in diesem Hier zugleich ist und nicht ist' (*GW* 11, 287/Miller 440).
111. '[Zenon] sagt, 'der fliegende Pfeil ruht,' und zwar deswegen, weil 'das sich Bewegende immer in dem sich gleichen Jetzt' und dem sich gleichen Hier, im 'Ununterscheidbaren ist' (*en to nun, kata to ison*); er ist hier, und hier, und hier . . . das nennen wir aber nicht Bewegung, sondern Ruhe . . . Im Hier, Jetzt als solchem liegt kein Unterschied . . . Nicht in diesen sinnlichen Verhaeltnissen, sondern erst im Geistigen kommt wahrhafter, objektiver Unterschied vor.'
112. For a contemporary logical treatment of the limitations of *reductio* as method of rejection of theses deemed rationally untenable see G. Priest,

'Reductio ad Absurdum et Modus Tollendo Ponens' in Priest, Routley, and Norman eds (1989).

113. 'Das Falsche muss nicht darum als falsch dargetan werden, weil das Entgegengesetzte wahr ist, sondern an ihm selbst. Diese vernuenftige Einsicht sehen wir in Zenon erwachen' (*W* 18, 302).
114. 'den Krieg in Feindes Land' (*W* 18, 303).
115. 'Man muss den alten Dialektikern die Widersprueche zugeben, die sie in der Bewegung aufzeigen, aber daraus folgt nicht, dass darum die Bewegung nicht ist, sondern vielmehr dass die Bewegung der *daseiende* Widerspruch selbst ist' (*GW* 11, 287/Miller 440).
116. 'Die Ausrede, durch welche *das Vorstellen den Widerspruch des selbstaendigen* Bestehens der *mehreren* Materien *in Einem* oder die *Gleichgueltigkeit* derselben gegeneinander in ihrer *Durchdringung* abhaelt, pflegt bekanntlich die *Kleinheit* der Teile und der Poren zu sein. Wo der Unterschied-an-sich, der Widerspruch und die Negation der Negation eintritt, ueberhapt wo *begriffen* werden soll, laesst das Vorstellen sich in den aeusserlichen, den *quantitativen* Unterschied herunterfallen. . . . Aber . . . [der] Begriff des Dinges ist, dass im *Diesen* die eine Materie sich befindet, wo die andere, und das Durchdringende in demselben Punkte auch durchdrungen ist. . . . Dies ist widersprechend; aber das Ding ist nichts anderes als dieser Widerspruch selbst; darum ist es Erscheinung.'
117. 'nicht eine Bewegung nur unserer Einsicht, sondern aus dem Wesen der Sache selbst, d.h. dem reinen Begriffe des Inhalts bewiesen' (*W* 18, 303).
118. 'immanente Betrachtung' (*W* 18, 303).
119. See *W* 18, 304: 'The Eleatics . . . came to a standstill with the thought that the object, due to its contradiction, is a nullity [Die Eleaten . . . sind dabei stehengeblieben, dass durch den Widerspruch der Gegenstand ein Nichtiges ist].'
120. 'Bei Leukipp und Demokrit ist die Bestimmtheit . . . physikalisch geblieben; es kommt aber auch im Geistigen vor. In der Sphaere des Willens kann die Ansicht gemacht werden, dass im Staate der einzelne Wille, als Atom, das Absolute sei. Das sind die neueren Theorien ueber den Staat, die sich auch praktisch geltend machen' (*W* 18, 358).
121. 'Noch wichtiger als im Physischen ist in neueren Zeiten die atomistische Ansicht im *Politischen* geworden. Nach derselben ist der Wille der *Einzelnen* als solcher das Prinzip des Staates; das Attrahierende ist die Partikularitaet der Beduerfnisse, Neigungen, und das Allgemeine, der Staat selbst, ist das aeusserliche Verhaeltnis des Vertrags.'
122. See Aristotle, *De generatione et corruptione* 325 a 30. H.H. Joachim trans., J. Barnes (1984).
123. 'das Eins kann man nicht sehen, es ist ein Abstraktum des Gedankens' (*W* 18, 358).
124. See *W* 18, 317: 'Kant's antinomies are nothing else than what Zeno did here already [Kants Antinomien sind nichts weiter, als was Zenon hier schon getan hat].'
125. 'Kant [hat] die Antinomie nicht in den Begriffen selbst, sondern in der schon *konkreten* Form kosmologischer Bestimmungen aufgefasst. Um die Antinomie rein zu haben . . . mussten die Denkbestimmungen nicht in

ihrer Anwendung . . . genommen, sondern . . . rein fuer sich betrachtet werden.'

126. 'Es ist im Ganzen dasselbe Prinzip: 'Der Inhalt des Bewusstseins ist nur eine Erscheinung, nichts Wahrhaftes'' *W* 18, 318.

Works Cited

I. Primary sources

Aristotle. *Aristotelis Opera*, ex rec. I. Bekkeri. Berlin 1831–70. Reprint, Berlin: De Gruyter 1960–63.

Hegel, Georg Wilhelm Friedrich. *Gesammelte Werke*. Edited by the Nordrhein-Westphaelische Akademie der Wissenschaften. 22 vols. Hamburg: Felix Meiner Verlag, 1968–.

——. *Werke in zwanzig Baenden*. Edited by Eva Moldenhauer and Karl Markus Michel. 20 vols. Frankfurt: Suhrkamp, 1969–79.

Kant, Immanuel. *Kants gesammelte Schriften*. Koeniglich Preussische Akademie der Wissenschaften. Berlin: G. Reimer (now De Gruyter), 1902–.

Leibniz, Georg Wilhelm. *Principes de la nature et de la grace fondés en raison*. Edited by André Robinet. Paris: Presses Universitaires, 1954.

Plato. *Platonis Opera*. Edited by John Burnet. 5 vols. Oxford: Clarendon Press, 1900–7.

Rousseau, Jean-Jacques. *Du contrat social; ou principes du droit politique* (1762). In: *Oeuvres complètes* (5 vols) vol. 3. Edited by Bernard Gagnebin and Marcel Raymond. Dijon: Gallimard, 1959–.

II. Translations of individual works and editions containing translations

Aristotle. *The Complete Works of Aristotle*. Edited by Jonathan Barnes. Princeton University Press: Princeton, 1984.

——. *De anima*. Translated by Robert D. Hicks. Cambridge: Cambridge University Press, 1907.

——. *Physics*. Translated by Philip H. Wicksteed and Francis M. Cornford. 2 vols. Cambridge, MA: Harvard University Press, [1934] 1968.

Hegel, Georg Wilhelm Friedrich. *Elements of the Philosophy of Right*. Edited by Allen W. Wood and translated by Hugh B. Nisbet. Cambridge: Cambridge University Press, 1991.

——. *The Encyclopaedia Logic (with the Zusaetze)*. Edited and translated by Theodore F. Geraets, Henry S. Harris, and Wallis A. Suchting. Indianapolis: Hackett, 1991.

——. *Faith & Knowledge*. Translated by Walter Cerf and Henry S. Harris. Albany: SUNY Press, 1977.

——. *Introduction to the Lectures on the History of Philosophy*. Thomas M. Knox and Arnold V. Miller. Oxford: Clarendon Press, 1985.

——. *Lectures on the History of Philosophy*. Translated by Elizabeth S. Haldane and Francis H. Simson. New York: The Humanities Press, 1974.

——. *Phenomenology of Spirit*. Translated by Arnold V. Miller. Oxford: Oxford University Press, 1977.

——. *Philosophy of Right*. Edited and translated by Thomas M. Knox. Oxford: Oxford University Press, 1952.
——. *Philosophy of Subjective Spirit*. Edited and translated by Michael J. Petry. 3 vols. Boston: Reidel, 1978.
——. *Science of Logic*. Translated by Arnold V. Miller. New York: Humanities Press, 1969.
Kant, Immanuel. *Critique of Pure Reason*. Translated by Paul Guyer and Allen W. Wood. Cambridge: Cambridge University Press, 1998.
——. *Philosophy of Material Nature*. Edited and translated by James W. Ellington. Indianapolis: Hackett Publishing Company, 1985.
Leibniz, Georg Wilhelm. *New Essays on Human Understanding*. Translated by Peter Remnant and edited by Jonathan Bennett. Cambridge: Cambridge University Press, 1982.
Marx, Karl. *Early Political Writings*. Translated and edited by Joseph O'Malley with Richard A. Davis. Cambridge: Cambridge University Press, 1994.
Plato. *Complete Works*. Edited by John M. Cooper. Indianapolis: Hackett, 1997.
——. *Plato: Dialogues*. Edited and translated by Benjamin Jowett. 4 vols. Oxford: Clarendon Press, 1953 (first edition 1871).
——. *Platon: Oeuvres complètes*. 14 vols. (Editors vary.) Paris: Les Belles Lettres, 1956–70 (first edition 1920).
——. *Platone: Tutte le Opere*. Edited by Enrico V. Maltese. 5 vols. Roma: Newton & Compton, 1997.
——. *Platonis opera omnia*, 1491. Translated by Marsilius Ficinus.
——. *Platonis philosophi quae extant graece ad editionem Henrici Stephani accurate expressa*, 11 vols, Biponti, ex typographia societatis, 1781–87.
——. *Platons Werke*. Translated by Friederich Schleiermacher. 6 vols. Berlin: G. Reimer, 1855–62 (first edition 1804–7).
Rousseau, Jean-Jacques. *The Basic Political Writings*. Translated by Donald A. Cress. Indianapolis: Hackett, 1987.

III. Secondary literature

Bloom, Allan (trans.). *The Republic of Plato*. New York: Basic Books, 1968.
Brandom, Robert B. 'Some Pragmatist Themes in Hegel's Idealism'. *European Journal of Philosophy* 7 (1999), pp. 164–89.
——. *Tales of the Mighty Dead. Historical Essays in the Metaphysics of Intentionality*. Cambridge: Harvard University Press, 2002.
Cairns, Douglas L. *Aidos: The Psychology and Ethics of Honour and Shame in Ancient Greek Literature*. Oxford: Clarendon Press, 1993.
Campbell, John K., "The Greek Hero." In: *Honor and Grace in Anthropology*. Edited by John G. Peristiany and Julian Pitt-Rivers. Cambridge: Cambridge University Press, 1992, pp. 129–49.
Cherniss, Harold. 'Parmenides and the "Parmenides" of Plato.' *American Journal of Philology* 53 (1932), 122–58.
Cornford, Francis M. *Plato and Parmenides: Parmenides' 'Way of Truth' and Plato's 'Parmenides'*. New York: Humanities Press, 1939.
Dennett, Daniel C. *Consciousness Explained*. New York: Little, Brown, 1991.
——. *The Intentional Stance*. Cambridge: MIT Press, 1997.

Dennett, Daniel C. and Hofstadter, Douglas R. *The Mind's I*. New York: Bantam, 1982.

Diels, Hermann and Kranz, Walther. *Die Fragmente der Vorsokratiker*. Dublin/Zuerich: Weidmann, 1966.

Diogenes Laertius. *Leben und Meinungen beruehmter Philosophen*. Edited by Klaus Reich, translated by Otto Apelt. Hamburg: Felix Meiner Verlag, 1967.

Dover, Kenneth J. *Greek Popular Morality in the Time of Plato and Aristotle*. Indianapolis: Hackett [1974] 1994.

Duering, Ingemar. *Aristoteles: Darstellung und Interpretation seines Denkens*. Heidelberg: Winter, 1966.

Duesing, Klaus. *Das Problem der Subjektivitaet in Hegels Logik*. Bonn: Bouvier, 1976.

——. *Hegel und die Geschichte der Philosophie. Ontologie und Dialektik in Antike und Neuzeit*. Darmstadt: Wissenschaftliche Buchgesellschaft, 1983.

——. *Hegel e l'antichità classica*. Edited by Salvatore Giammusso. Napoli: La Città del Sole, 2001.

Egermann, Franz. *Vom attischen Menschenbild*. Muenchen-Pasing: Filser, 1952.

Ehrenberg, Victor. *The People of Aristophanes. A Sociology of Old Attic Comedy*. New York: Barnes & Noble, 1974.

Erffa, Carl Eduard von. *Aidos und verwandte Begriffe in ihrer Entwicklung von Homer bis Demokrit. Philologus*, Supplementband 30/2. Leipzig, Dieterich'sche Verlagsbuchhandlung, 1937.

Friedlaender, P. *Platon*. 3 vols. Berlin: De Gruyter, 1954.

Fuks, Alexander. 'Plato and the Social Question: The Problem of Poverty and Riches in the *Republic*'. *Ancient Society* 8 (1977), 49–83.

Hankins, James. 'Some Remarks on the History and Character of Ficino's Translation of Plato'. *Marsilio Ficino e il ritorno di Platone* vol. 1. Edited by Gian Carlo Garfagnini. 2 vols. Firenze: Leo Olschki Editore, 1986.

Haegler, Rudolf-Peter. *Platons 'Parmenides'*. Berlin: De Gruyter, 1983.

Harris, Henry S. *Hegel's Ladder*. 2 vols. Indianapolis: Hackett, 1997.

Inwood, Michael. *A Hegel Dictionary*. Oxford: Blackwell Publishing, 1992.

Jacobi, Friedrich Heinrich. *Ueber die Lehre des Spinoza* (1785). In: *Werke*. Edited by Klaus Hammacher, Walter Jaeschke, Irmgard-Maria Piske. Vol. 1,1. Hamburg: Meiner, 1998.

Jameson, Michael H. 'Agriculture and Slavery in Classical Athens.' In: *Classical Journal* 73 (1977–78), 122–45.

Kutschera, Franz von. *Platons 'Parmenides'*. Berlin: De Gruyter, 1995.

Liddell, Henry G. / Robert Scott. *Greek-English Lexicon*. Oxford: Clarendon Press, 1996.

McDowell, John. *Mind and World*. Cambridge: Harvard University Press, 1996.

Nagel, Thomas. *Other Minds*. New York: Oxford University Press, 1995.

Nuzzo, Angelica. 'Thinking and Recollecting. Logic and Psychology in Hegel's Philosophy.' In: *La memoria*. Edited by Gianna Gigliotti. Napoli: Bibliopolis/Vrin, forthcoming 2005.

Peperzak, Adriaan. *Selbsterkenntnis des Absoluten: Grundlinien der Hegelschen Philosophie des Geistes*. Stuttgart: Fromman-Holzboog, 1987.

Perinetti, Dario. 'Philosophical Reflection on History.' In: *The Cambridge History of Eighteenth-Century Philosophy*. Edited by Knud Haakonssen. Cambridge: Cambridge University Press, forthcoming 2006.

Peristiany, John G. (ed.). *Honour and Shame. The Values of Mediterranean Society.* Chicago: Chicago University Press, 1966.

Pinkard, Terry. 'Hegel's *Phenomenology* and *Logic*: an Overview.' In: *The Cambridge Companion to German Idealism.* Edited by Karl Ameriks. Cambridge: Cambridge University Press, 2000, pp. 161–79.

Priest, Graham. *In Contradiction: a Study of the Transconsistent.* Dordrecht: Martinus Nijhof, 1987.

——. 'Contradictions in Motion.' *American Philosophical Quarterly*, 22 (1985), 339–46.

Priest, Graham, Routley, Richard, and Norman, Jean. *Paraconsistent Logic. Essays on the Inconsistent.* München: Philosophia Verlag, 1989.

——. 'What's so bad about contradictions?' In: *The Journal of Philosophy* 95 (1998): 410–26.

Searle, John R., Daniel C. Dennett, David J. Chalmers. *The Mystery of Consciousness.* New York: New York Review of Books Collection Series, 1997.

Schleiermacher, F.D.E. *Platons Werke.* Berlin: G. Reimer, 1855–62.

Spinoza, Benedictus (Baruch) de. *Ethica ordine geometrico demonstrata.* In: *Opera*, im Auftrag der Heidelberger Akademie der Wissenschaften. Edited by C. Gebhardt. Vol. 2. Heidelberg: Carl Winters, 1926.

Ste Croix, Geoffrey E. M. de. *The Class Struggle in the Ancient Greek World. From the Archaic Age to the Arab Conquests.* Ithaca: Cornell University Press, 1981.

Taylor, Alfred E. *Plato: The Man and His Work.* New York: Meridian, 1956.

Tuschling, Burkhard. 'Die Idee in Hegel's Philosophie des Subjektiven Geistes.' In: *Psychologie und Anthropologie oder Philosophie des Geistes.* Edited by Franz Hespe and Burkhard Tuschling. Stuttgart: Fromman-Holzboog, 1991.

Untersteiner, Mario. *Zenone: Testimonianze e frammenti.* Firenze: Nuova Italia, 1963.

Vieillard-Baron, Jean-Louis. *Platon et l'idealisme allemand 1770–1830.* Paris: Beauchesnes, 1979.

Vlastos, Gregory. 'A Note on Zeno's Arrow.' In: *Phronesis* 11 (1966), 3–18.

Westphal, Kenneth R. *Hegel, Hume und die Identitaet wahrnehmbarer Dinge.* Frankfurt: Vittorio Klostermann, 1998.

——. 'Is Hegel's *Phenomenology* Relevant to Contemporary Epistemology?' In: *The Bulletin of the Hegel Society of Great Britain* 41/42 (2000): 43–85.

Williams, Bernard. *Shame and Necessity.* Berkeley: University of California Press, 1993.

Williams, Robert R. *Hegel's Ethics of Recognition.* Berkeley: University of California Press, 1997.

Wolff, Michael. *Der Begriff des Widerspruchs: Eine Studie zur Dialektik Kants und Hegels.* Koenigstein: Hain-Athenaeum, 1981.

——. *Das Koerper-Seele Problem. Kommentar zu Hegel, Enzyklopaedie (1830) §389.* Frankfurt: Klostermann, 1992.

Wood, Allen W. *Hegel's Ethical Thought.* Cambridge: Cambridge University Press, 1990.

Index